AMERICA: NATION OF THE GODDESS

"America: Nation of the Goddess brings to light some of the hidden gems of Freemasonry, including the origins of the Grange and what is the true heart and soul of the Craft. The amazing shadow play of the Washington Monument will forever change the National Mall experience for all who read this book."

SCOTT F. WOLTER, HOST OF H2'S *AMERICA UNEARTHED*
AND AUTHOR OF *THE HOOKED X*

"From the deepest shadows of the medieval Knights Templar to the shining light of the National Grange and Freemasonry, Alan Butler and Janet Wolter lift the many veils of the Venus Families and reveal their central involvement in the founding of America. Gently unwinding the double helix of the Holy Bloodline, they display the eternal Goddess in all of her glorious splendor. Within the pages of *America: Nation of the Goddess,* the mark of the Goddess is not only shown to be on the very foundations of Washington, D.C., and New York City but also on the entire free nation of America!"

WILLIAM F. MANN, AUTHOR OF
THE KNIGHTS TEMPLAR IN THE NEW WORLD,
THE TEMPLAR MERIDIANS, AND
TEMPLAR SANCTUARIES IN AMERICA

AMERICA: NATION OF THE GODDESS

The Venus Families
and the
Founding of the United States

ALAN BUTLER AND **JANET WOLTER**

11-19-22

To Kim,

Warmest Regards,

Janet Wolter

DESTINY BOOKS

Destiny Books
Rochester, Vermont • Toronto, Canada

Destiny Books
One Park Street
Rochester, Vermont 05767
www.DestinyBooks.com

Text stock is SFI certified

Destiny Books is a division of Inner Traditions International

Library of Congress Cataloging-in-Publication Data
Names: Butler, Alan, 1951- author. | Wolter, Janet, author.
Title: America : nation of the goddess : the Venus families and the founding
  of the United States / Alan Butler and Janet Wolter.
Description: Rochester : Destiny Books, 2015. | Includes bibliographical
  references and index.
Identifiers: LCCN 2015012180| ISBN 9781620553978 (pbk.) | ISBN
  9781620553985   (e-book)
Subjects: LCSH: Templars--History. | Freemasonry--United States--History. |
  Freemasonry—Religious aspects. | Goddess religion. | United
  States—History.
Classification: LCC HS517 .B88 2015 | DDC 366.0973/0933—dc23
LC record available at http://lccn.loc.gov/2015012180

Printed and bound in the United States by Lake Book Manufacturing, Inc.
The text stock is SFI certified. The Sustainable Forestry Initiative® program
promotes sustainable forest management.

10 9 8 7 6 5 4 3 2 1

Text design and layout by Debbie Glogover
This book was typeset in Garamond Premier Pro with Gill Sans, Trajan Pro 3, and
Shannon used as display typefaces

All images are provided by the authors unless otherwise noted

To send correspondence to the author of this book, mail a first-class letter to the
author c/o Inner Traditions • Bear & Company, One Park Street, Rochester, VT
05767, and we will forward the communication, or contact the authors directly at
www.nationofthegoddess.com.

This book is dedicated to Scott Wolter,
Janet's husband and Alan's great friend.
Without his advice, inspiration, practical help,
and his camera, this book could not have been written.
Thanks, Pal!

CONTENTS

FOREWORD

Throughout the middle months of 2014 while Janet and Alan were writing this book, I was mostly on the road creating new episodes for Season 3 of H2's *America Unearthed*. I would check on their progress and provide limited input when I was home between shoots, but I was mostly forced to take in their creative efforts from afar. I simply couldn't fully digest the incredible discoveries that they were rapidly making. It was in June when Janet and Alan asked me to read the manuscript and see if I would write the foreword. I was thrilled to be asked and dove into the manuscript thinking I wouldn't be too surprised by its contents. This turned out not to be the case.

My best friend, Rob Wolff, first introduced me to Janet while she was working at a local restaurant where Rob was the assistant manager. I was instantly smitten, and while she was cautious at first—a trait I would come to admire and one I rarely exhibit—I eventually wore her down. After twenty-six years of marriage and raising two beautiful, now adult children, Grant and Amanda, we are excited to spend our empty-nest years pursuing our passions, which largely include the Venus Families, a group you will be learning about here, and historical research. While it is my name and face that have been out there on the books I've written and television programs I've appeared in, Janet, for all these years, has been the guiding light that has tempered my excitement by providing the necessary skepticism and balance when evaluating a new research discovery.

One of the major early discoveries we made about the Hooked X

symbol on the Kensington Rune Stone and four other medieval artifacts discovered in North America is that besides representing the *a*
sound within the messages, it was also a symbol representing the ideology of the Venus Family members (Cistercians and Knights Templar at
the time) who created the messages. The Hooked X ideology is nothing
more than monotheistic dualism, which is the concept of opposites that
keep things in balance such as male/female, heaven/Earth, good/bad,
light/dark, and so forth. If you keep this in mind as you read this book
and realize the mind-set at work by the Venus Families throughout the
past two millennia, it will help you understand and enjoy this amazing
book all the more. Only a decade ago did I come to fully realize and
understand that for all these years Janet and I have literally been practicing dualism, and that has led to so much of the success in my writing
and, indeed, my entire life. Janet, of course, knew this all along.

I first met one the most intelligent and warmest individuals I've ever
known at arguably the most beautiful Cistercian ruin, Rievaulx Abbey,
in his home country of England in 2006. Shortly after realizing the
authors who carved the North American rune stones with the Hooked
X symbol were the Cistercians and Knights Templar, I immersed myself
in books to learn as much as I could. The books that most resonated
with me were written by a man named Alan Butler. I was captivated
by his engaging and fluid writing style, which is as enjoyable as it is
educational, and I hoped that someday I would have the opportunity to
meet the man. Alan and his wife, Kate, and I hit it off that sunny day
at Rievaulx, and when Janet and Alan eventually met, a new formidable
research force was born.

What Janet, Alan, and I came to realize is that the Venus Families
instigated the greatest coup d'état in history, which the world has yet to
realize. The reader will come to learn the details of how and why these
incredibly patient and brilliant strategists stayed true to the long-range
goals of restoring their ancient beliefs systems, which the Romans and
their church suppressed two thousand years ago. Janet and Alan present a
plethora of evidence of the Venus Families' long-range plan, which began

in Jerusalem, and is just now successfully coming to fruition as the New Jerusalem of the United States of America. As I write this on America's Independence Day, I am thankful for the freedoms afforded me today by the countless generations who successfully implemented their plan. Over the past several years the three of us have been contacted by and certainly have personally met some members of Venus Families, but we would never reveal their identities. What has been patently obvious and most important about these meetings is that it is clear they support the research we have presented and will no doubt approve of the startling new discoveries presented in the pages of this book.

The truly incredible new discoveries described in this book are examples of what happens when knowledgeable people work together, collectively piecing together evidence that could never happen if working alone. The unique backgrounds of Janet and Alan provided a collection of experience and knowledge, which has been a synergistic dynamo, that was a joy to watch rapidly unfold. This manuscript is like a flowing river of facts that eventually come together in a satisfying and convincing sea of conclusions. This epic work could only have been done by two of the most truly selfless individuals I have ever known. Not only have Janet and Alan brought together their collective knowledge from their unique lifetimes of experience, but we can't forget their discoveries presented in *America: Nation of the Goddess,* could never have happened without the combination of their male and female perspectives. If nothing else, we should all learn from this book that the most valuable things in life can never be realized without that balanced perspective.

SCOTT F. WOLTER

Scott F. Wolter, husband of author Janet, is a forensic geologist in St. Paul, Minnesota, and the host of H2's *America Unearthed* and cohost of History's *Pirate Treasure of the Knights Templar.* He is the author of *The Hooked X: Key to the Secret History of North America* and *Akhenaten to the Founding Fathers: The Mysteries of the Hooked X.*

INTRODUCTION

A SINGLE WORD

Only very few times in their careers will historical writers and researchers discover something so absolutely odd, so utterly incongruous, that they begin to wonder whether the whole thing is some peculiar sort of dream. Such rare happenings are a time of wrinkled brows and frantic searches of the bookshelves and Internet to verify that there are rational answers to be had. Generally, patience and persistence win out—but not always. When subsequent research only complicates the issue and makes the fog thicker, there is nothing to be done but to feel the thrill of excitement that attends the start of any adventure and to say, as did the fictional character Sherlock Holmes, "The game's afoot!"

What began this particular adventure for us was a single word. It was a word that was of importance to both of us, but for what seemed at first to be totally different reasons. That word was *grange,* and it began a quest that had more twists and turns than a medieval maze and that shows no sign of finishing any time soon.

But first you, the reader, should learn some things about us and how we made these discoveries.

Janet Wolter is a citizen of the United States. She lives and works in Minnesota, where she is occupied in researching some of the oddest and least expected chapters of North American history. Alan Butler lives four thousand miles away in Great Britain, where he writes books examining equally strange mysteries from around the globe. Janet and

Alan were introduced by Janet's husband, Scott Wolter—who is also a writer, and in addition a documentary television series host and a forensic geologist.

The word *grange* first took on a mutual fascination when Alan met Scott at Newgrange in Ireland, an ancient passage tomb that figured as part of an episode of Scott's television show, *America Unearthed*. All that was certain at that time was that to Alan a "grange" was the outlying farm of a medieval Cistercian monastery, while to Janet it was the name of what is probably the most peculiar and unlikely organization ever to spring up in the United States of America in the nineteenth century.

Alan had previously shown that although most people have never heard of it, the monastic grange was a supremely important factor in the rise of the modern Western world. Its existence led to the Cistercian order of monks becoming the most powerful and richest Christian monastic institution that has ever existed. The grange system, especially in Great Britain, led to a revolution in farming that ultimately drove many thousands of people from the land and into towns and cities. In effect, this revolution in the way farms operated—and especially in the rearing of sheep—resulted in another kind of revolution: this one based on industry. As Alan pointed out in his book *Sheep,* published by O Books in 2010, it is quite likely that without the invention of the Cistercian grange the world in which we live would be radically different from what it is today.

Janet had become fascinated by a very different sort of grange, in part because much of the research she undertook had a close association with Freemasonry, an institution that played a very important part in the creation and development of the United States republic: probably the greatest political and economic experiment humanity has ever known.

In the American sense "the Grange" was and is a sort of self-help group for farmers. It developed in the years after the American Civil War as a way for subsistence farmers to join together. This cooperation was not only to fight against growing industrial monopolies—especially those of the railroad companies that controlled the transportation network used by the farmers to get their wheat to market—but also to inspire better and more productive methods of producing greater yields.

Janet recalled that as a child she had loved the Little House book series written by Laura Ingalls Wilder, which ultimately became a very popular television show. The stories were about the life of Laura and her pioneer family struggling to survive in Minnesota in the late 1800s. Janet remembered the story of Laura's father—a farmer—being a member of the Grange in the television series and how, as a united front, small farmers like the Ingalls made progress against the restrictive practices of the powerful United States railroad barons.

Fig. I.1. The emblem of the Grange, Order of the Patrons of Husbandry, on the exterior of the Grange National Headquarters Building in Washington, D.C.

When Janet began to look at the way the Grange had been organized—and in particular at its very peculiar rituals and practices—it occurred to her immediately that it had a great deal in common with Freemasonry. This puzzled her, because many of the farming communities consisted of very conservative and often deeply religious people who, by upbringing and inclination, would definitely not be the sort of individuals who would ever be drawn to Freemasonry. In reality, many early members of the Grange had religious beliefs that would have held the esoteric aspects of Freemasonry to be sacrilegious.

It might seem at first sight as if the monastic medieval meaning of the word and the way it was used in nineteenth-century America had little or nothing in common except that they originate from the

Fig. I.2. A typical, original Grange hall in Minnesota
Photo courtesy of Scott F. Wolter

Latin word *gran,* meaning "grain." As a result the word *grange* was closely associated with the word *granary,* a place where grain is stored. However, in the way the Cistercians used it, *grange* meant an outlying farm, separate from but yet directly owned and run by a particular abbey. In the case of the Grange in the United States, more properly known as the National Grange of the Order of Patrons of Husbandry, it meant a gathering together of many thousands of independent farms all across the country but associated by mutual interest and common problems. In this way it served as the farmers' "union." This was similar to the organizations that were developing in the northern U.S. states at around the same time factory workers formed labor unions to demand better working conditions and fair wages.

As is often the case in life, our recognition that there was a very tangible link between the two types of granges stemmed from information we had both previously researched. In one sense it was inspired by Alan's understanding of the Cistercian order of monks, an organization that represented a significant departure from anything that had existed before it came into being in the twelfth century.

At its height the Cistercian order was composed of many hundreds of abbeys spread across large parts of Europe and even into the Middle East. The organization's headquarters was at Cîteaux in central France, where the order began in 1098. The early Cistercians were seeking a simple and austere form of Christianity. In each abbey the monks worked for the common good of the abbey and ultimately for the whole Cistercian family. When funds allowed, groups of monks would set out from any particular monastery in order to found a new house elsewhere. Any secondary abbey created in this way became a "daughter house" of the original abbey. Thanks to this constant search for new land and new abbeys the order spread exponentially. Each newly formed abbey owed allegiance to its mother house, and all abbeys were ultimately subservient to the original mother house in Cîteaux.

Other monastic orders had similar ways of spreading, but it was the grange that set Cistercianism apart, together with the fact that it had not one but two types of monks. First there were the choir monks, who sang the services and attended masses on many occasions each day. And then there were the lay brothers, who were not ordained priests and whose duties were mainly of a manual nature. Lay brothers were allowed to live at a significant distance from their abbey, which is how it was possible for them to run the granges, the produce from which ultimately came back to the abbey.

Granges were often on quite distant land, usually given to the abbey by willing patrons. It was often marginal or very poor land, but the Cistercian monks became expert at making any land fertile and useful. Once a series of granges were formed in relation to a particular abbey the Cistercians would start to negotiate with, and sometimes even bully, the owners of land between their abbey, and the granges to exchange or donate such land. In this way some of the Cistercian abbeys, especially those in Great Britain, acquired massive estates.

We will have much more to say about the Cistercians in the pages that follow, but suffice it to say that except for the fact that they were farmers, the medieval monks appeared to have little in common with the American nineteenth-century Grange members. However, there was a connection that occurred to us both, though at first it seemed somewhat tenuous.

We were both aware that the Cistercian monks had sponsored a military order of monks as its sister order. This order became known as the Knights Templar, and it was officially sanctioned by the Catholic Church in 1129. With the same zeal as its Cistercian counterpart, the Knights Templar soon became both rich and extremely powerful. Its brothers were fighting monks who originally existed to help in the Christian struggle against the Muslim forces in the Near and Middle East. The institution lasted just under two centuries, and, such was its influence in all manner of ways that, just as with the Cistercians, Europe and ultimately the world would never be the same as a result of its presence and exploits.

Like the Cistercians the Templars were great farmers who also kept monasteries (which they called *preceptories*) with outlying granges. In fact the whole structure of the Knights Templar was simply a modified version of the order or rule of the Cistercians.

Because of our respective past researches we also knew that tradition had it that, sometime after its destruction in 1307, the order of the Knights Templar had been at least partly responsible for the commencement of the more modern institution of Freemasonry. We also very soon learned that of the eight people responsible for starting the Grange in the United States, at least five were known to be practicing Freemasons. So Freemasonry may connect the United States Grange to the Knights Templar, and if so the use of the word *Grange* for the organization just might not be such a coincidence as it had first appeared. This seemed all the more likely as we uncovered more and more about the way the Grange conducted its business and in particular the symbolism it used and the rituals it undertook during its weekly meetings in hundreds of locations across the United States.

As our mutual research began Alan was spending more and more time in the United States, both working on television documentaries and also researching for his book *Washington DC: City of the Goddess.* Alan believed and still believes that Washington, D.C., capital of the United States, is probably the most extraordinary deliberately planned city anywhere in the world.

One of the observations that had caused him to look in great detail at the founding of Washington, D.C., was the tremendous proliferation of goddess statues to be found within its civic heart and also throughout its parks and intersections. He had also shown in his own work, and in cooperation with fellow English writer Christopher Knight, that the whole of Washington, D.C., had been planned and built using a form of geometry and a measuring system that were ultimately at least five thousand years old.

The conclusion had been that underpinning the avowed secular stance of the founding government of the free United States had been a particular reverence for a strong feminine component within the spiritual beliefs of at least a fair proportion of the Washington, D.C., designers.

Fig. I.3. One of the many goddesses of Washington, D.C., this unnamed goddess is on the Merchant Seaman's monument close to the Capitol.

Because many of those who created Washington, D.C., were Freemasons, and also because to those in the know there is a secret "goddess slant" to Freemasonry, it was not too difficult to see why all the goddess statues were present.

However, this bias toward the feminine does not present itself openly to either aspiring or even most practicing Freemasons. It is deeply enmeshed in the symbols, rituals, and practices of the organization. It has been carefully hidden to such an extent that countless thousands of Freemasons must have followed the Craft* through many decades of their lives without ever appreciating the secret that lay at its heart. It is a secret hidden in plain sight. Janet's own research had led her to exactly the same conclusion, which was why both of us were astounded when we discovered what thousands of Grange members had been doing on a weekly basis ever since the nineteenth century.

Like Freemasonry, the Grange consists of a series of stages of initiation that are known as degrees. Those who wish to become members of the Grange have to proceed, stage by stage, through the degrees in order to reach the top of the Grange ladder of initiation. Accompanying the degrees are specific costumes, role-playing, and carefully memorized dialogue.

Because members of the public are not generally admitted to the ceremonies that accompany the degrees—especially the highest ones— even the Grange itself would have to admit that there is a secret aspect to the way it functions. Nevertheless, in these days of mass communication details of the first five of the seven possible degrees available to Grange members can be viewed online. The moment we saw them we were both astonished. We will deal with the subject matter of the Grange degrees in detail as our story unfolds, but what we encountered was, for us, a genuine Eureka moment. It not only confirmed a great deal we already suspected, but it also opened doors to discoveries regarding the United States that had been beyond our wildest imaginings.

---

*Freemasonry is often referred to as "the Craft" because it developed from one of the old trade associations, or "crafts," that were common in medieval Europe. Although Freemasonry today is not concerned with the cutting and dressing of stone, it used to be.

It is the nature of the degrees of Grange membership—together with the fact that right from the start they were all available to both men and women—that set the Grange apart from its Masonic origins. What is more, many of the presiding officers present during the conferring of Grange degrees are not only women, which in itself is surprising for the period the Grange developed, but moreover women who take on the names of different goddesses, all of whom were known in the ancient world to be goddesses of nature and agriculture.

To the majority of those taking part across so many decades, all of the costumes, the play-acting, and the carefully learned lines must have been a fascinating departure from the humdrum lives of the subsistence farmer and his family. Grange meetings not only cemented communities together, probably for the first time in many isolated townships, but the Grange ultimately gave small farmers a *national* voice. The Grange brought people together on a regular basis and must have been a social godsend—especially to hard-pressed and generally isolated women. The feeling of warmth, inclusion, and the quite inexplicable sense of calm that we both felt when we visited the oldest of the surviving Grange halls is difficult to describe. It was as if the companionship, the joy of sharing something very special, and the mystical nature of the ceremonies that had taken place there for so long had seeped into the very wooden walls of the simple building.

All the same, no matter how significant and important the Grange has been to its many members, in our estimation it remains one of the greatest enigmas of developing society in the United States. This is primarily because throughout the whole of the degree rituals we have been able to study in detail, neither the name Jesus nor the title Christ is ever mentioned, despite the fact that the Grange has always considered itself to be a Christian institution. In the United States, farming communities have tended to be very conservative in their outlook, and they have often consisted of people from a strong and quite fundamentalist Christian background. It is almost incomprehensible that such people would have taken part in ceremonies that have an unabashed pagan feel to them.

We think and we hope to show that the reason the Grange has survived with its truly astounding role-play and rituals is because it speaks to a deeply subconscious part of humanity that is so ancient and so instinctive it simply "feels" right. There appears to us to be no other rational explanation. What is most astounding of all is that in the United States, not just recently but almost since its appearance, Freemasonry has been the object of unbridled criticism from a wealth of different religious, political, and social groups, whereas this definitely has not been the case for the Grange.

It turns out that the use of the word *Grange* for this unique experiment in agricultural cooperation was no coincidence at all. It was quite deliberately chosen by a group of people who have been doing everything they can to steer the ship of humanity for a very long time. We call these people the Venus Families, but they have appeared in many forms and guises. It was they who took control of western Europe in the eleventh century and who were responsible for both the Cistercians and the Knights Templar. Moving forward in time, they set the scene for European settlement of North America from the twelfth century on, and they left ample evidence of their presence and of the alliances they formed with the indigenous peoples.

The dream of the Venus Families was always the same. They believed in self-determination, equality, and fairness—a foundation they laid with the cornerstone that was placed with great Masonic ceremony at the northeast corner of the Capitol in Washington, D.C. They also believed vehemently in religious freedom, despite holding fast to personal beliefs that are older by far than any organized religion in the world today.

As it turned out, our growing awareness of the extraordinary Grange movement merely represented a launch platform for a wealth of other discoveries regarding the development of the United States. It caused us to look at the nation as a whole but at the same time focused our attention back on its capital, where we began to detect veritable wonders that we had never suspected previously.

From the moment we compared notes about that simple word,

grange, we have shared an adventure of discovery that has led us to a vision of the United States that surrounds everyone living across this vast country but which hardly anybody has been trained to really *see.*

For more than three centuries people have traveled from across the planet to try to gain a share in the American Dream, and yet very few of them have any real understanding of what the dream is and how far back in time it goes. They have no idea of the political, spiritual, or even the physical treasures that exist right before them, or of the tremendous journey and the number of generations that led to the Declaration of Independence. What follows is a fascinating story, and we hope that when you have accompanied us on its many twists and turns and have learned about the truly ancient motivations that have funded the American journey, you will never look at the United States in the same way again.

At the forefront of the whole story is the Goddess, who has been worshipped by humanity since at least the time of the Stone Age hunters. A mere millennium and a half ago, after maybe a hundred thousand years of adoration, an effort was made to extinguish the Great Goddess from the Abrahamic faiths, but it was an attempt doomed to failure. In the United States at least she is seen everywhere. Her ancient festivals have been made synonymous with the celebrations of the Republic so they will never be forgotten, and they are spelled out on a massive scale in the capital during the passing year in sun and shadow. Nearby, the remains of the Goddess's most recent earthly representation, Mary Magdalene, rest in a secret chamber in the most prominent place in the entire United States. The Goddess is to be seen in gigantic form, looking out over New York Harbor and on top of the Washington, D.C., Capitol, and though very few people realize the fact, her enduring symbol is written large on the ground of every village, town, and city of the United States—we guarantee it!

The fact that almost nobody realizes any of this only goes to prove that for so much of our lives we walk around with our eyes tightly closed.

Prepare to be very, very surprised!

Part One

FREEMASONS,
GODDESSES,
AND
GRANGE HALLS

THE PATRONS OF HUSBANDRY

On the north side of the National Mall in Washington, D.C., close to Fourth and Madison, if a visitor looks carefully down on the grass he or she will see a wholly unremarkable stone slab that carries a weathered, green copper plate. This tiny monument may be just about the smallest example anywhere in Washington, D.C., and the truth is that in the early gloom of a very rainy spring evening it took us quite awhile to find it.

All the same, we were delighted to see and photograph what is said to be the only private monument of any sort on the National Mall, because it already represented something truly important to us. Here is what is written on the plaque:

> Near this site the National Grange of the Patrons of Husbandry was organized on December 4, 1867, in the office of the Superintendent of the Propagating Gardens Department of Agriculture. The founders of the Grange were: Oliver H. Kelley, John Trimble, Francis McDowell, William Saunders, John H. Thomson, William M. Ireland, Aaron B. Grosh—assisted by Caroline A. Hall. This tablet erected by the National Grange, 1951.

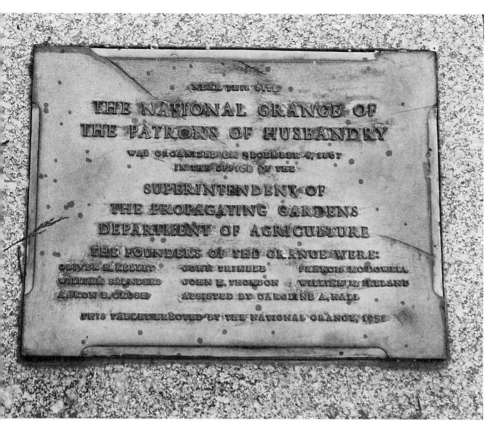

Fig. 1.1. This marker stone commemorating the founding of the
National Grange of the Patrons of Husbandry in 1867,
located on the National Mall in Washington, D.C.,
is the Mall's only private monument.

In truth the National Grange of the Patrons of Husbandry is represented in a grander way in Washington, D.C., than by this fairly insignificant marker. Just over a mile away to the northwest, close to the
White House and Lafayette Square, is the Washington, D.C., headquarters of the Grange. Standing in a prestigious part of the city, the headquarters of the Grange is significant if not exactly startling. However,
neither the little monument nor the Grange headquarters reflects the
true significance of an organization that had a profound effect on the
development of the United States.

Fig. 1.2. Headquarters of the National Grange in Washington, D.C.,
located just northwest of Lafayette Square

If the opinions of some of the Founding Fathers of the United States
had been followed to the letter, the country would never have developed into the unparalleled superpower it is today. Thomas Jefferson in
particular, third president of a free United States and an author of the
Declaration of Independence, wanted to see his country become an agricultural idyll. His wish was for a nation of small farms, all participating
in North American self-sufficiency. To a great extent, in the early years
he got his way. By the time of the Civil War, which began in 1861, the
vast majority of farms in the United States were small-scale operations.
In many areas life was tough, and by far the majority of settlers who
tilled the soil lived a hand-to-mouth existence.

Most jobs on the farm were performed by manpower, with only the aid of a few animals for plowing and transport. Even though farming technology did exist it was prohibitively expensive and equally costly to get to remote areas. Any profits made by subsistence farmers were barely enough to feed and clothe a family; weather conditions were often a problem, and transport of any surplus was not only extremely expensive but also too long for perishable crops to survive.

What should have given a boost to small-scale farmers in previously remote places was the arrival of the railroads. Trains were starting to push their way into the heart of the continent as early as the 1830s, but from the outset most of them represented a local monopoly for the railroad owners. These were men who had made huge financial investments, and they were not about to see their profits diminish in order to be a charitable institution for the sake of small-scale farmers. In short, the farmers were robbed blind by the railroad companies in all manner of ways, so that rather than benefiting from the availability of transport to get technology in and produce out, most subsistence farmers found the presence of the railroads more likely to bankrupt them than to support their efforts.

The situation was always particularly bad in the South, but it was made much worse by the Civil War. Even rich plantation owners with vast acres of land and many slaves were brought down by the blockades, the lack of labor, and the constant fighting on so many fronts that accompanied the years between 1861 and 1865. For the subsistence farmer it was even worse. He had few savings to tide him over during these dreadful years and often lost his sons to military service. Even if he had produce to sell, the local populace gradually became poorer as the war progressed, and few people were better off than he was.

The result was destitution on a massive scale all over the South and the West. In any age, to any nation, civil war is a truly terrible event, but the American Civil War was one of the bloodiest conflicts that had ever taken place up to that time. The Confederacy suffered about 250,000 deaths, more of whom died from hunger and disease than from enemy action. Together with the mutilated, this meant that more than

25 percent of those fighting for the Confederacy would never again work to support their families and their communities. The cost to the North was even greater, but the Union states did at least have the manpower, the money, and the infrastructure to absorb their losses more successfully.

Once the war was over the federal government worked hard to get the nation back on its feet, but this wasn't easy for many reasons. Not the least of these reasons was the deep resentment and distrust for the federal government felt by those who had fought for Southern independence and who had lost everything as a result. Since much of the wealth of the South had come from farming rather than industry, something had to be done to get things moving again.

At the same time, even farmers from the Union states were not necessarily prospering. They too were at the mercy of the weather and the railroad monopolies; they also struggled to farm what was often inferior soil, using methods little different from those used by their medieval forebears in Europe. By their very nature, small-scale farmers across the whole of the United States were independent-minded men who believed in self-help and stoicism. However, there were a few farsighted types who knew that if farmers in the United States were ever to get a fair deal and to secure enough income to gain better education and move forward technologically, they would have to come together and gain economic strength by sheer force of numbers. One such man was Oliver Kelley.

Oliver Kelley was born in Boston, Massachusetts, in 1826. He was the son of a tailor by the name of William Kelley. Oliver clearly had some education and from the outset showed no inclination to follow his father's trade. By the time he was twenty-one Kelley was in Chicago and already a newspaper reporter. Writing would be important to Oliver for his entire life. Clearly he also had a restless streak, because he traveled from Chicago to Peoria and then on to Burlington, Iowa. In 1849, Oliver married his wife, Lucy, and two months later they set off to the virgin territory of Minnesota, settling for a while in the then tiny settlement of St. Paul.

Fig. 1.3. The restored working 1860s farm of
Oliver Kelley, Grange founder, near Elk River, Minnesota.
Photo courtesy of Scott F. Wolter

In one of those strange coincidences, which seems to attend the efforts of historical researchers, Janet reports that the farm Oliver and Lucy created by the Mississippi in then Itasca, near Elk River, was only a stone's throw from where she and Scott live. Moreover, she already knew that Oliver Kelley's farm—instead of eventually becoming prime real estate or being incorporated into some massive, modern factory farm—still existed more or less in its original state. It is now a working 1860s farm designated a National Historic Landmark and run by the Minnesota Historical Society.

❧❧

Throughout much of his life Oliver Kelley was not always a very successful entrepreneur. He originally staked a claim on the Itasca land
because there were rumors that the district would become the new state
capital. As a result, he estimated that he would make a healthy profit
if he already owned land in the vicinity. The plan never happened, but
Oliver was an optimistic man who always showed a talent for making
the best of any situation. When it became obvious his land would never
be worth a fortune, the tailor's son turned himself into a farmer.

Kelley became what was known at the time as a "book farmer."*
He didn't have generations of experience to call on, so he studied the
subject of farming in detail. Throughout his years as a farmer he always
sought to innovate and to use what resources he had in the best and
most modern way possible. Sometimes his plans worked; often they did
not, but he remained undeterred throughout.

One thing Kelley did learn very quickly was that small-scale farmers were at the mercy of just about everyone else in the growing nation.
They did not have the clout of the emerging corporations—especially
the railroad companies—and they never seemed to be able to raise
enough capital to modernize their farms to an extent that would allow
them to make decent profits. In Oliver Kelley's mind there was only one
alternative: farmers had to group together in order to have more political and economic influence. In this respect he was the right man in the
right place. He had been brought up in New England where labor was
already beginning to organize itself. This had been a tortuous process,
but it was much easier in the industrializing states where many workers
lived and worked in close proximity. Kelley must have seen what was
taking place in the industrial East and considered the same collective
efforts could also apply to farming.

By 1858 the farmers of Minnesota were doing better than average,

---

*Rhoda Gilman and Patricia Smith. "Oliver Hudson Kelley, Minnesota Pioneer, 1849–
1868" December 1967: 333.

and many of them did have produce to spare, but what could they do with it? Distribution systems were improving dramatically, but the transport companies, in particular the railroads, were charging farmers so much that the profits that might have been made were lost before the produce reached its ultimate market.

In an attempt to assist himself and his fellow farmers, in 1852 Oliver Kelley instigated the Benton County Agricultural Society, and it was in the education, joint enterprise, and collective voice of this organization that the seeds of the later National Grange developed.

Kelley always kept detailed records and wrote for the Agricultural Society and for newspapers. In truth, he made a lot of noise—so much so that his voice was ultimately heard as far away as the nation's capital. Kelley spoke out personally and in his many columns against merchant speculators, restrictive practices of all kinds, and in particular against the railroad owners. His life in the following years encountered many twists and turns as, in addition to his farming, he became a real estate agent, sometimes called himself a notary or a lawyer, and found himself on the brink of ruin several times. Through it all he formed or encouraged farmers' unions and agricultural associations until at last, by 1864, he was offered a job as a clerk for the United States Bureau of Agriculture. It was at this time that he moved with his family to the capital.

By 1864 the Civil War was beginning to draw to its close. It was no longer a case as to *whether* the Union would win but merely *when*. Kelley was doubtless building up contacts and influence during 1864, but he rose to prominence after the assassination of President Abraham Lincoln, which took place only a few days after the Confederate forces surrendered in April 1865. Kelley's greater prominence and influence at this time was due to two factors. Andrew Johnson, Lincoln's vice president, who was sworn in as president on the day Lincoln died, had his own origins in a tiny log cabin in North Carolina. And, like Oliver Kelley, the new president was a Freemason.

It is impossible to say whether the president approached Kelley or if Kelley knocked on the door of the White House. What is certain is that

President Johnson thought Oliver Kelley was just the man he needed to help him get farming moving again in the South. This was possible for Kelley, partly because he was a farmer himself, but mostly because he was a Freemason. Federal government representatives were not very welcome in the Confederate heartland just after the Civil War and could not be expected to achieve the degree of cooperation necessary to kick-start the economy of the South. However, Freemasonry was popular in the Confederate states, and to all brothers of the Craft it represented an allegiance that stood above any political, economic, or regional boundary.

At the president's request Oliver Kelley began to undertake a series of extended journeys to the Southern states. There he visited Masonic lodges and developed the trust of men who would have barely spoken to him had he arrived as a representative of the Department of Agriculture. Reading between the lines, it is obvious that he came to the conclusion that the embittered Southerners would never be persuaded to throw in their lot with Washington—but they might be convinced to help themselves by cooperating with other farmers across the United States.

Kelley's experience with the Benton County Agricultural Society and other similar organizations he had instigated now came into its own. However, just as surely as his own farming enterprises had been dogged by a lack of available capital, so his efforts at bringing farmers together had always been restricted by an absence of funds. Now the situation was very different. He had the backing of the president, as well as something he had often lacked: like-minded people who enjoyed his own level of intelligence and who could lift some of the immense burden from his shoulders.

In the end it wasn't Oliver Kelley who created the National Grange, no matter what popular history might say. It was an able and strong committee composed of individuals whose various skills and specialties could be brought together to a common end. The members of this committee were Kelley himself, John Trimble, Francis McDowell, William Saunders, John H. Thomson, William M. Ireland, Aaron B. Grosh, and the one woman on the committee to whom much of the credit for the

Fig. 1.4. Monument to Grange founder Oliver H. Kelley and his farm near present-day Elk River, Minnesota (then Itasca, Minnesota), on the Mississippi River. The site is now a working 1860s-era farm owned and operated by the Minnesota Historical Society and is designated a National Historic Landmark. Photo courtesy of Scott F. Wolter

ultimate success of the Grange must be given, Caroline A. Hall.

Plans were ready by December 1867, and the National Grange of the Patrons of Husbandry was created with its headquarters in an office in Washington, D.C., close to the Mall. The whole structure had been very carefully designed, and its working practices were virtually synonymous with the structure and procedures of Freemasonry.

Using Masonic principles and even its practices was a masterstroke. It was important from the start that the Grange should offer its members a sense of exclusivity. Theirs was an independent and even a secret society, which shielded them from any consideration that they were being manipulated by the federal authorities or indeed any other organization beyond their own control. From the word go the Grange was planned to be scrupulously democratic in the way it functioned. It was, without any pun intended, designed to be a "grass roots" organization.

The Grange was and remains probably the most astonishing departure in terms of a popular organization with self-help intentions that we have encountered in the modern world. At least four of the founders of the Grange were practicing Freemasons, and one of them, Francis McDowell, may have been more responsible than the others for the extraordinary way the meetings of the Grange were organized.

McDowell was a very successful banker and had traveled extensively. During his journeys in Europe he had shown an interest in Freemasonry and its offshoots; while in Paris, France, he had been initiated into a little-known religion called the Eleusinian Mysteries by its supposed high priest, the Duke of Ascoli.

Freemasonry in France was developing rapidly in the nineteenth century, though it had already enjoyed significant popularity before and during the French Revolution, which took place between 1787 and 1789. Beyond the original three degrees, which made a new member into what is referred to as a Master Mason, many side degrees and quasi-Masonic groups had developed in Paris and beyond. Influential and charismatic characters such as Antoine Court de Gébelin (1719–1784) had introduced ancient Egyptian elements and had helped to create the Nine Sisters Lodge in Paris, of which the American Founding Father Benjamin Franklin became Master of the Lodge in 1779.

As for the Eleusinian Mysteries, as a Masonic institution little is known about it. According to the information the Duke of Ascoli offered to Francis McDowell, it had come from southern Italy, where the town of Ascoli is situated.

In the ancient world the Eleusinian Mysteries were extremely well known. They took place annually in the small settlement of Eleusis, not far from Athens in Greece, and were dedicated to the extremely popular goddess Demeter, who had a special significance in terms of vegetation and who was also closely associated with death and rebirth. Both men and women could be initiated into the Mysteries of Demeter, and even slaves were not precluded. For more than 1,500 years the rites were practiced, with sometimes thousands of people taking the route from Athens to Eleusis in the third week of September.

Once arriving, the initiates underwent a complex ceremony about which little is known. Aspirants were warned that to divulge even the smallest part of the Mystery they undertook meant certain death. Judging by the comments of some very elevated individuals from antiquity, whatever did take place was extremely impressive and emotionally charged. All that is known for sure is that after a ritual meal and drink, initiates took part in a drama related to death and rebirth that was so convincing it changed the lives of countless thousands forever.

The Mysteries of Demeter were finally stamped out in 370 CE, thanks to the growing influence of the Christian Church. However, the Duke of Ascoli told Francis McDowell that the Mysteries had not ceased. Rather, he suggested, their celebration had been transferred secretly to southern Italy, where goddess worship—both in the form of Demeter and also her Egyptian counterpart, Isis—had always been strong. There, close to Ascoli, the yearly celebrations had continued in secret for twelve centuries or more and had later been brought to Paris by the duke, who claimed he was the most recent High Priest of the Mysteries.

There is no doubt that McDowell believed the Italian duke, and he was thrilled to be initiated into what was termed "the degree of Demeter." He was given documents and an ancient and very beautiful hat to bring back to the United States when he left Paris, and his return coincided with the final plans for the creation of the Grange of the Order of Patrons of Husbandry. He was cordially received by the other members of the committee who also showed every sign of believing that both the duke and the surviving rites of Demeter were genuine. McDowell's influence and his encounter in Paris would have a profound bearing on the rituals and ceremony of the Grange, and in particular its 7th degree (which was that of Demeter). He became the first High Priest of Demeter in the organization. But before we begin to

Fig. 1.5. Copy of a bas-relief depiction of
Demeter, Persephone, and Dionysus
Photo courtesy of Scott F. Wolter

Fig. 1.6. An early poster relating to the Grange of Patrons of Husbandry
Photo courtesy of Scott F. Wolter

learn what took place at Grange meetings it would be sensible to look at how the Grange was organized, and to see if it had any similarities with those other "Grangers": the Cistercians.

HOW THE GRANGE IS ORGANIZED

It was initially stated that anyone who was old enough to manage a plow and who came from a farming background was eligible to join the Grange, whether they were male or female.

Each farming community was encouraged to set up a local chapter of the Grange, known as a Subordinate branch. This might begin at any convenient location, though in reality Subordinate branches usually created their own halls—invariably simple wooden structures—which quite often came to serve as village halls for all manner of local functions. This is the place where the first four degrees of the Grange are conferred. Officers of the Subordinate branch were and are elected by all members in a free vote. Whoever is chosen as Master is eligible to pass to the regional level, which is known as Pomona.

Pomona level takes place at a district or county gathering where Subordinate branches come together. Once again, officers are elected by vote, and it is within Pomona that the 5th degree of initiation is conferred to new Pomona representatives. The presiding officer of the Pomona level represents all of the district's Subordinate branches at State level.

The State-level procedure is identical in that those present choose their own officers by vote. Those attending State level are initiated into the 6th degree of the Grange: they represent all the Pomona branches in their state, and the elected leaders of the State level travel to Washington, D.C., to become part of the National level.

Masters of State branches gather in Washington, D.C., where officers of the National Grange are chosen by free vote. Here, the 7th and final degree of the Grange is conferred. Each member present represents her state, together with all its Pomona-level and Subordinate-level branches. What this means is that every single member of the Grange has an equal voice in the way the entire organization is run. Any member can climb the ladder to National level if they are sufficiently interested and committed, and all are genuine representatives of their peers. It was this structure that made us view the Grange as being virtually identical in principle to something far older and at least at first sight quite different.

THE CISTERCIAN ORDER

According to most historians, like many reformed monastic institutions the order of the Cistercians grew out of a desire in the early twelfth century for monks following the Benedictine rule to get back to the nuts and bolts of the monastic life as it had been espoused by St. Benedict of Nursia in the sixth century. These reformers, mostly in France, believed that many Benedictine monasteries had become too prosperous and that those running the very rich abbeys had forgotten the values that their calling was meant to represent.

We will have much more to say about the Cistercians, and especially its most famous leader, St. Bernard of Clairvaux, but for the moment we want to restrict ourselves to a description of the way the Cistercian "empire" was run.

All Cistercian monasteries (often referred to as "houses") were managed in the same way. The first Cistercian monastery was established at Cîteaux in Burgundy, France, in 1098, where the various mechanisms by which Cistercianism functioned were quickly adopted. All Cistercian monasteries were comprised of two types of monk. The ordained monks, known as choir monks, lived and worked in the monastery and its immediate environs. They were not allowed to journey from the monastery except under very specific circumstances. The second tier of monks consisted of lay brothers. The lay brothers were not ordained priests, though they did take vows when entering the order. Their function was to work for the abbey, and most lay brothers were drawn from the laboring classes—people who were unlikely to be educated but who sought a monastic life.

Unlike the choir monks, the lay brothers were allowed to live and work away from the monastery to which they belonged. They had been specifically trained to run the outlying granges that belonged to each monastery, together with workshops, brew houses, or whatever was necessary to the successful running of the house.

Although Cistercianism was built upon a form of grass-roots democracy, this did not include the lay brothers. It was probably thought that, though they were valuable to the order, the lay brothers were not sufficiently worldly wise or spiritually trained to take significant decisions that would have a bearing on the Cistercian order as a whole (though particularly bright and committed lay brothers could and did become choir monks).

Choir monks met each day in a form of meeting known as "chapter." All decisions relating to the officers of the monastery and regarding its general running were discussed and voted on at chapter. Each choir monk had an equal vote.

MOTHER AND DAUGHTER HOUSES

When Cîteaux became successful and prosperous enough to have more monks than it needed, groups of choir monks set out to create new monasteries in other locations. Each of these in turn became a daughter house of Cîteaux. In time many of the original daughter houses also became successful and sent out brothers to create second-tier daughter houses. In this way the Cistercian order grew rapidly, eventually possessing hundreds of monasteries, many of which were exceptionally successful and wealthy.

The procedure for running the Cistercian organization was extremely simple but very effective. Each monastery had an abbot, a prior, and other officers. These were chosen from among the choir monks at chapter. If the abbot or any of the other monks holding positions of responsibility were considered to be failing in their duties they could also be removed by way of chapter and therefore the democratic votes of their peers.

Abbots of mother houses were expected to visit their monastery's daughter houses on a regular basis and abbots of daughter houses had to attend gatherings at their mother house, some of which had many daughter monasteries. All abbots of mother houses were expected to attend a gathering every year at Cîteaux, unless extreme distance, illness, war, or some other eventuality prevented them from doing so.

What this effectively meant was that genuinely elected representatives of choir monks ran the institution at every level. Even the abbot of Cîteaux, the Cistercian headquarters and mother abbey of the whole order, could be removed by a chapter of his fellow abbots if it was felt he was not doing his job properly. Only the lay brothers were excluded from this democratic process for the reasons mentioned above.

THE ECONOMIC BENEFITS

The creation of the Cistercian order was a masterstroke, and the success of the organization outstripped that of any other Christian monastic institution that ever existed, and yet its principles could not have been simpler.

When a group of usually twelve monks set out to found a new monastery they looked around a particular district for tracts of marginal land that were of no real use to their owners. Using a little spiritual blackmail, they encouraged the landowners to donate such land to the order. In most cases the owners were glad to do so, because they lived in an age when it was generally believed that to give to the church afforded one a better chance of one day getting into heaven.

The Cistercians were excellent farmers, practicing the latest techniques available in their day. Invariably with the use of large flocks of sheep the monks would gradually turn the marginal land into good pasture or land that would bear crops. Sheep can survive on just about any sort of land and could be guaranteed to clear it of weeds and to fertilize it with their dung—as well as provide an annual cash crop in the form of wool.

Land between a monastery and its outlying granges was eventually procured in one way or another, resulting in sometimes massive holdings. Nearly all the wool and a large percentage of the crops grown by Cistercian monasteries could be sold into the market, adding more and more funds to the order as a whole. What the Cistercians also eventually gained was a great deal of economic and even political power. Cistercians could get the best rates possible from suppliers of any commodity they could not procure for themselves, and when working together they were able to practice economy of scale. Eventually few people, not even kings, argued with the Cistercians. They gradually created for themselves an enviable position built upon vast islands of democracy in the midst of feudal states.

THE SIMILARITIES

It should be obvious why we were extremely surprised when we learned how the Grange in the United States was organized. The way the Grange was run was, in many respects, virtually identical to the Cistercian model of organization. There was also another common factor in that both depended upon and ultimately drew strength from farming.

For these and other reasons that will become obvious as our story unfolds, we are certain that those who created the Grange based it squarely on the Cistercian model. Despite their ingenuity, Kelley and his colleagues must have realized immediately that the common glue that held the Cistercian empire together was faith. All Cistercian monks were zealots; they received no material compensation for their lives of dedication except the clothes they wore, the food that sustained them, and rudimentary care if they became ill.

Since the outset the Grange had to be nondenominational. To account for the variety of beliefs across the United States the Grange would lack that all-important component that fired up the Cistercians. If those organizing the Grange wanted it to work they had to place something at its heart that all Grangers could hold in common, preferably something that people outside the Grange did not possess. This was commonality of belief allied to commonality of purpose.

At least four members of the committee knew how powerful a Masonic tie could be because they were already committed wholeheartedly to the Craft. Obviously Freemasonry as it already existed could not be used in the case of the Grange. Some Christian denominations believed that Freemasonry contradicted their beliefs; also it was a male-only preserve at that time, and it dealt with subject matter that would have meant little or nothing to the vast majority of United States farmers or their families. Nevertheless, although the actual rituals and practices of Freemasonry could not be used, its basic principles and operating mechanisms could be.

History shows that for a significant period of time the methodology worked well. Interest in the Grange soon went through the roof, and to the people for whom it was created it fulfilled a number of needs. The Grange gave farmers a voice and a very powerful voice at that. It offered men, women, and even children an alternative to the humdrum nature of their life on the land. The Grange inspired confidence and even education to people who for decades simply did not count; it gave women a real stake in society, and it assisted in great measure in healing the sores of the Civil War and in lifting the United States into the realms of massive agricultural production.

Is this the whole explanation for that first Grange committee, virtually copying the democratic practices of the Cistercian order so faithfully? Were the rituals and the degrees of the Grange simply a mechanism to give common cause to Grange members in the form of exclusive, shared secrets? The truth is that we are totally confident that all of this is only a small part of the story. We can find our next important clues in the nature of the Grange degrees and the ritual and symbolism they contained.

2

THE NEED FOR
DIVERSION AND THEATER

The Play's the Thing

Anyone who has read that excellent book by Mark Twain, *The Adventures of Huckleberry Finn,* will already have some idea about the nature of the isolated communities in the United States in the last quarter of the nineteenth century and especially those in the South. Much of the book is taken up with a journey undertaken by Huck with the slave Jim down the mighty Mississippi River. The pair travel many miles on an abandoned raft they found, and through many chapters of rib-tickling adventure they visit a wealth of farming communities that clung to the river's banks.

One of the facts that comes across in the book is that everyone in the remote settlements of the area was extremely fond of entertainment. It is not hard to see why. Farms were often remote, so that even visiting a local town probably would have been a treat. Life would have been dull beyond belief—following the rolling of the seasons, year in and year out—with little to divert the minds of farmers and their families. If Mark Twain is to be believed, there is nothing these people enjoyed half so much as a traveling show. Small productions—probably consisting of only a handful of players—traveled all around, stopping for a few days at each little town, putting on plays and variety shows. Along with the quacks, the charlatans, and the peripatetic con men these little shows represented just about the only diversion people in remote communities could expect.

Part of the genius of those who thought up the practices of the Grange was that they recognized this love of diversion and theater and employed it to their own advantage. It might not be possible for the farmers, their wives, and their children, as well as local townspeople, to see theatrical productions on a regular basis, but there was nothing to prevent them from dressing up and creating performances of their own. Perhaps in larger towns this was already taking place, and certainly in the cities there would have been amateur theatrical and operatic companies. But smaller communities with farms spread over a wide area lacked the cohesion or the knowledge to promote such societies for themselves.

In particular, we have to look at the daily grind for women who lived in farming communities. Farmers' wives, especially in more remote communities, must have lived lives that were tedious in the extreme. Families tended to be large, so there was no shortage of work for a farmer's wife to do, but in many cases any sort of social life would have been out of the question. Another American novel reflecting this period is *Little Women* by Louisa May Alcott. This book was published in 1868 and is set in a Northern community; its story illustrates the growing need of women in the 1860s to join together with their peers and simply have a good time.

The March family daughters, the heroines of the book, are forced in on themselves for a wealth of reasons—not least of all relative poverty; yet they manage to create a sort of "other world" filled with fictional characters and played out through costume dramas and improvised tableaus. By this means they learn to realize their own potentials, to better educate each other, and to simply enjoy lives that otherwise could have been insufferably boring. In a way this was easier for the March girls than it would have been for many farmers' wives or daughters. Not only were they reasonably well educated, there were enough of them to represent a workable community from which characters for the plays could be drawn. Nevertheless the book does demonstrate how much young women of the period loved to get together, to dress up in costumes, and to share common adventures.

Herein lies the first strength of the Grange movement. It had at its organizational heart a woman whose background was very similar to that of the March girls in *Little Women.* Caroline Arabella Hall was born in 1838 in Boston. She was from an educated family and became a schoolteacher in rural communities. Caroline Hall was distantly related to Oliver H. Kelley; she was no radical, but she was clever and astute. Hall had seen the plight of rural women firsthand and was a staunch advocate of the right of women to receive an education and to participate in society. From the outset she argued that if the Grange was to succeed it needed the cohesion and interest that women could bring to it. We can be absolutely certain that the role-play and use of costume, as well as the nature of many of the characters involved in Grange ritual, are due to the influence of Caroline Hall. It is surely a mark of respect to the male members of the committee that, despite the social norms in America at the start of the movement, they recognized Hall's abilities and also her reasonable point of view.

Any young woman attending a Grange meeting for the first time back in the nineteenth century most likely would have been instantly enchanted and intellectually stirred by what she encountered there. She may have been initially surprised to discover that much of what took place at the Grange was run by women, and when it came to voting, women members had the same rights as men.

In order to understand why this was important we have to look at women's suffrage in the United States. Despite a constant battle from as early as 1848, full female suffrage took a long time to become a reality. It was not until the presidential elections of 1920 that women across every state were eligible to vote for the candidate of their choice. However, Grange meetings were held from the 1870s, and women had the right to vote at all levels from the moment the organization began, a half-century before women could have a hand in deciding the destiny of their country. To half of society in the farming communities such a state of affairs was not simply novel, it was positively revolutionary.

Equally surprising would have been the realization that Grange meetings and even Grange rituals relied absolutely on female participation. In the meetings and rituals each woman was important in her own right. Once again, this might not seem at all unusual now, but we have to remember that these were people who were used to being controlled by their menfolk at every stage of their lives, from cradle to grave. A daughter was in every real sense the property of her father, and a wife was entirely subordinate to the wishes and even the caprices of her husband. If this was true in the educated North and East it was certainly the case in the more conservative farming communities of the South and West.

All of this had a profound bearing on the nature of the Grange. From the outset it was a temperance society in which liquor of any sort played no part. Abstinence would have been very unlikely if Grange business had been entirely the prerogative of the farmers themselves, some of whom may already have been committed to the ideas of temperance but by no means all. Grange meetings and particularly Grange ceremonies were conducive to gentility and amicable cooperation. Nonalcoholic fruit punch replaced rotgut whiskey, and considered opinions superseded barroom brawls.

The more we looked at the Grange and the way it had been created from the very start, the greater became our admiration for the committee that had sat together in Washington, D.C., and collectively dreamed it up. The National Grange of the Patrons of Husbandry was much more than a simple self-help group for impoverished and struggling farmers, although of course it did serve that function extremely well. The Grange was a social club, which would have been especially important to adolescents of both genders. It was also a platform for education, a nucleus of local organization that gave people confidence to take part in their own communities. The Grange promised a greater voice to women than they had hitherto known in any mixed-gender organization, and it taught everyone the true importance of discussion and democracy.

Ultimately, from such simple but truly important beginnings, the Grange became one of the most powerful bodies in the United States. It lobbied politicians at all levels, from county to federal, and forced rural issues to the surface that otherwise would have been swamped in the rush toward industrialization and capital. The presence and power of the Grange would not allow farmers, and especially small-time farmers, to be either sidelined or ignored, and for a few very crucial decades it was an island of moral certainty in a sea of conflicting interests as the huge landmass of the growing United States was colonized and exploited.

A major reason the Grange became possible was because it removed the obstacle of "diverse beliefs" from its members and replaced these with a common spirituality that was quite different from anything that existed elsewhere in the society of the time—except perhaps within Freemasonry.

People had entered and were entering the United States from all points of the compass. Although the vast majority of those living and arriving in the country during the nineteenth century were from Christian backgrounds, the nature of their beliefs and practices varied tremendously. As we shall see, an acknowledgment of Christianity was never far from Grange meetings and ritual, but this was a form of Christianity from which all dogma and historical conflict had been utterly removed. In truth, what remained was hardly Christianity at all, because it was supplemented by something radically different. Despite its protestations of inclusiveness, nineteenth-century Christianity of just about every sort was fiercely paternalistic. In many of the denominations that were present in the United States, God was genuinely meant to be *feared* as much as loved. Anyone who looks carefully at the words used in Grange ceremonies will notice that this aspect of the Christian God, derived in part from the Hebrew scriptures, is absent. Passages seem to have been carefully chosen to highlight a nurturing, caring deity.

We would go so far as to suggest that in the strictest sense of the word the nature of the spirituality espoused within the Grange halls was an enlightened paganism, overlaid with fairly generalized Judaic and Christian trappings. While this would send a shiver of horror down the spine of many evangelical Christians even today, it cannot be denied that it worked extremely well and allowed the Grange to develop at a meteoric rate. By 1875 the Grange had 858,000 members, spread throughout hundreds of communities that spanned almost every part of the United States. This was out of a population of around 38 million, which meant that one person in every forty-four in the United States was a member of the Grange movement. Individually this would have meant little, but as a cohesive pressure group the movement would have been ignored by all politicians at their peril.

As had been the case all those centuries earlier in the Cistercian empire, officers of the Grange at every level—from Subordinate to National—were selected by their peers. Those who would eventually find themselves running the Grange in Washington, D.C., had achieved their positions because at every level they had been trusted and were liked by other Grange members. Nobody could represent the Grange's interest anywhere or even take part in its deliberations unless they had undertaken at least one of the seven degrees that lifted members from Subordinate to National level. So what did the elevated souls espousing Grange ideas and proposals in Washington have to go through before they could be trusted to represent the organization among the highest echelons of power?

THE FIRST FOUR DEGREES

The first four degrees of the Grange are named after the seasons of the year, during which farming communities go through all processes from the sowing of seed through the harvest and then back to sowing again. Grange membership began young, at the time a boy could follow a plow or a girl could glean in the fields. Those young men and women wishing to undergo the 1st degree of the Grange would notify the Subordinate Grange in their locality and would be invited to take part.

Upon arriving at the 1st degree ritual, candidates would be hoodwinked—in other words, bags would have been placed over their heads so that they could not witness what was taking place around them until the appropriate time. The candidate would place her hand on the shoulder of an assistant and would be led into the Grange hall. The lesson of the 1st degree is Faith, and the tableau scene re-created for the ritual is that of a farm in spring.

As was the case well over a century ago, a number of Grange officers are present in the room when the candidates enter. A series of questions and commands follows, which are very similar to those used in Masonic ritual. After answering the requisite questions asked by a number of the officers in different parts of the hall, the candidates have their hoods removed so that they can fully see the spectacle that has been prepared for them. However, they must first take a solemn oath not to reveal any of the secrets of the Grange and declare themselves to be desirous of sharing in its mysteries.

All the officers wear regalia, as do the attendants and helpers. If the season permits, the hall may be decked with spring flowers, and an open Bible rests on a stand together with other tokens related to farming.

After having received instruction as to the aims and objectives of the Grange, as well as being introduced to some of its symbolism, the candidates are finally introduced to characters who are referred to as the Three Graces. The names of these characters, who are played by female Grange members, are Ceres, Pomona, and Flora. One after the other these characters offer the candidates both gifts and advice, after which the candidates confront the Worshipful Master, who infers on them the honor and privilege of the 1st degree.

Although not as convoluted as degree ceremonies in Freemasonry, the rituals of the Grange are still fairly complex. They contain passages from the Bible and also metaphors appropriate to a life in farming that speak about moral standing, love, and responsibility. The candidates themselves wear green cloaks and find themselves confronted with a host of characters who are also attired in symbolic and colorful clothes.

Most striking to us when we first read about the Grange's ceremony for the 1st degree was the presence of Ceres, Pomona, and Flora. These are not simply arbitrary characters plucked from fiction. All

Fig. 2.1. A typical Grange hall interior showing the three seats reserved for those taking the part of the goddesses Ceres, Pomona, and Flora
Photo courtesy of Scott F. Wolter

three of these names relate to goddesses of fertility and nature. Ceres, for example, is the Roman counterpart of the Greek goddess Demeter, about whom we will have a great deal to say in due course. On one level the presence of these characters was tolerated or even encouraged in the nineteenth century because they represented an ancient idyll and a reference to the classical period that had been much in vogue since the eighteenth century. Their presence would have added to the historical and romantic feel of the ceremony, though as we will see, we should not assume their inclusion to be nothing more than a poetic whim. When *all* the Grange degrees are studied it becomes obvious that representations of the Earth Goddess are present all the way through, and it is clear that her position is even more significant in the higher degrees.

The 2nd, 3rd, and 4th degrees of the Grange follow the same basic pattern as the 1st. However, step by careful step, candidates are led on a journey through the seasons, while at the same time learning how moral lessons can be drawn from the natural cycles of nature. Through each degree the candidates are reintroduced to the three goddesses—Pomona, Flora, and Ceres—who offer words of wisdom and further lessons in understanding the symbolism that lies behind even simple things. As they advance, candidates are expected to learn about the aims and objectives as well as the rules of the Grange; they are tested at each stage on what they have learned before they are allowed to progress. There are constant reminders about death and rebirth and frequent allusions both to God and the Bible, but any dogma associated with scripture is scrupulously avoided—leaving only those parts of the Faith with which any nominal Christian, or indeed a person from some other faith, would find no fault.

Having undergone the first four degrees of the Grange, members become full members of the organization. However, this is certainly not the end of the line for those who wish to take matters further. As we have seen, Subordinate branches send chosen members to the next level of the Grange, which is a regional one, most often associated with a county. This second stage is known as Pomona, and the 5th degree of the Grange, also called Pomona, belongs to this gathering. The 5th degree, like the previous four degrees, has been in the hands of the National Grange itself since 1874. The 6th and 7th degrees are responsive to another body known as the Assembly of Demeter. The nature of the 5th degree is broadly similar to the previous four. It carries its own symbolism and role-play and is attended by a significant number of participants. At the conferring of the 5th degree the woman taking the part of Pomona is surrounded by ten or twelve attendants, and everyone involved in the initiation wears beautiful costumes. Pomona and her attendants reside in what is described as a fairy bower. Candidates gain admission to Pomona's fairy bower by the use of passwords, and secret hand gestures form part of the ceremony.

Probably because the first five degrees are administered by the National Grange, and it is possible to obtain copies of the ceremonies with all the instructions necessary to stage them. This is not true of the 6th and 7th degrees, which are conferred at State level and National level, respectively. Despite a diligent search, we have been quite unable to gain access to any specific details regarding the 6th and 7th Grange degrees, though it is clear from the testimonies that do exist that these are both directly related to the Mysteries of Demeter, mentioned in chapter 1. We can therefore assume that they include some symbolic death and rebirth ceremony of the sort that took place for so many centuries in Eleusis.

In these days of the Internet, when full details relating to just about all possible Masonic degrees can be accessed easily, and when even many previous State secrets are accessible as a result of spies and whistle-blowers, it seems almost incredible that no account of the 6th and 7th degrees of the Grange have surfaced. This surely demonstrates how well they are protected and likewise indicates that the degree of secrecy that attended the original rites of the Mysteries in Greece is still being maintained by those who have been initiated.

Of course members of the Grange across the years have had far more to do than to simply take part in seemingly archaic rituals. At every level there is a striving to increase the knowledge of Grange members and to pass this knowledge on to others. The organization has been paramount in education and has been incredibly influential when it came to legislating for the good of farming. The Grange has run cooperatives through which farmers could benefit from the economy of scale when it came to making necessary farming purchases, and the Grange even spawned an insurance arm to better protect its members, similar to that of Freemasonry.

Grange halls were used and in some places are still being used for all manner of meetings and activities beyond the scope of the Grange itself. There must be many thousands of people in the United States who spent significant parts of their formative years attending events in Grange halls, which of course would never have existed without the Grange movement.

Perhaps sadly, the Grange does not retain the influence or the member base it once had and is now a shadow of its glory days. Nevertheless, it still has a part to play in local communities, and Grange gatherings are held each year all over the United States. As far as the lower levels of initiation are concerned, the Grange is now much less secretive than it once was, though, as we have seen, this is not the case at the National level.

No doubt there will be some people who will claim that the Grange was a bad thing, although after looking at it very closely we would find it difficult to see how this could be the case. Such criticisms are rare despite the fact that the Grange has so much in common with Freemasonry.*

The real challenge for us, as researchers, is whether it is possible to see the Grange in isolation. All things considered, we find this to be impossible. The Grange is most certainly a child of Freemasonry, but its true paradox is that it reveals more about the secret and unknown heart of Freemasonry than the Craft itself does. In other words, aspects of the Grange—particularly its tableaus, symbols, and rituals—contain clues regarding the "true" nature of Freemasonry that are difficult or impossible to find anywhere else.

---

*On the Internet there are many thousands of websites that are critical of Freemasonry but hardly any that point an accusing finger at the Grange.

3

NOT A SECRET SOCIETY BUT A SOCIETY WITH SECRETS

A Brief History of the Craft

It is not our intention to offer an exhaustive history of Freemasonry in this book. Such information can be found in other places for those wishing to study the Craft in greater detail. However, we do want to give those readers not familiar with Freemasonry at least a rudimentary understanding of where it came from and what it represents.

Those who know nothing about Freemasonry, save for what they might casually read on the Internet or in newspapers, probably assume that the Craft is a secret society. This is not the way Freemasonry describes itself. Rather it seeks to be known as a society *with* secrets. Many people, having embarked on a sojourn with Freemasonry in the hope of discovering what these secrets might be, have ended up being very disappointed. Alan's coauthor on several previous books, Christopher Knight, began his writing career in the hope of better understanding what Freemasonry was really all about, because so much of the ritual had seemed to him to be little more that pseudohistorical nonsense. It takes years of research, or presumably years of membership, to tease out of Freemasonry what it "really" represents, but a casual acquaintance with the Craft shows it to be a mostly fraternal society, offering its members a good, moral foundation on which to build their future lives, and a commitment to raising money for good causes.

There are many different forms of Freemasonry, but they ultimately appear to have sprung from a single source. The name "Freemasonry" derives from the profession of cutting and carving stone, though members of the Craft—unless they happen by chance to be stonemasons—never get involved in the dusty side of the profession. Instead, the symbols of Freemasonry, together with a moral foundation based on its precepts, are used by the Craft to pass on its timeless truths, mainly by way of rituals known as degrees.

Despite the many differences of emphasis and the level to which Freemasons can be elevated in different forms of the Craft, all Freemasons must undergo three distinct degrees in order to become what is known as a Master Mason. The three degrees are known as Entered Apprentice, Fellow Craft, and Master Mason. As with the Grange degrees, each degree of Freemasonry is attended by costume, oaths, stories, and symbols, all of which assist in remembering the learned rituals. The degrees involve oaths of secrecy and horrible threats of the sort of retribution that will be meted out to anyone who betrays the Craft's secrets to non-Freemasons, though these are strictly symbolic in this day and age. It is likely that the rituals themselves were a way of recording information in allegory form that was meant to be preserved for some later time when it would be understood.

Masonic ritual relies heavily on the origins it suggests for itself, which begin in ancient Jerusalem when the first temple was being created there by King Solomon. Very little of what is supposed to constitute history in the Masonic lessons and rituals is anything of the sort. It is comprised mostly of fables with supposed connections to passages from the Hebrew scriptures, along with the inclusion of names and characters who owe nothing to either history or the Bible but which may be allegories for something else. Stories are told of the original designer of the temple, a man by the name of Hiram Abiff, who was said to have been murdered in the temple because he refused to offer uninitiated workers an explanation of the temple's secrets or other secrets related to Freemasonry itself.

The story of Hiram Abiff's murder, the hiding of his body, and its ultimate rediscovery are central to the first three degrees of the Craft. The 3rd degree sees those taking part as symbolically dying and being reborn into the rights and privileges of Freemasonry. It has to be said that when one trawls through all the ritual involved in the three degrees, it is not surprising that Christopher Knight was left wondering what the whole business was really about. Of course there are compensations. It's good to get together for social gatherings with friends, which is something Freemasons do frequently, and there can be no denying that many good and inspirational moral lessons are learned on the way to the achievement of the 3rd degree.

It has been suggested that Freemasonry was always intended to be a self-help group. In other words critics have frequently asserted that Freemasons have used their membership to rise through certain professions, to obtain preferential treatment, and to generally scratch each other's backs. In our opinion, though undoubtedly true, this has been no more the case than it might be in any other sort of society where people become close and learn to trust each other.

Once the 3rd degree has been achieved, Freemasons in some forms of the Craft can go on to further studies, and further degrees, though it is always emphasized that these stand apart from the necessary qualification of the three degrees that make a person into a full-fledged Freemason.

According to those who run the Craft, Freemasonry is most definitely not a religion, though anyone who wishes to become a Freemason does have to admit to a belief in a supreme deity. The nature of the deity is not specified, but technically speaking it would not be possible to be both an atheist and a Freemason. Some branches of Freemasonry beyond the three degrees do mention Christianity and Christian themes, and even the initial three degrees make great reference to events associated with the Hebrew scriptures, but Freemasonry would be as open to a Jew, a Hindu, a Buddhist, or indeed a member of any religious creed as it would to a Christian.

Every Freemason is a member of what is known as a Blue Lodge and each Blue Lodge elects its own officers from within its own ranks. Rituals are carried out in a room called a Temple, though several lodges could and do use the same Temple at different times during any given week. Generally speaking, each nation has its own Grand Lodge from which Freemasonry is run and organized. Representatives of lodges, especially Past Masters, often visit other lodges at a local, regional, or a national level. In the United States in the Blue Lodge, or Craft Lodge, each state has its own Grand Lodge, and there is no national-level governing body. However, a Master Mason can elect to pursue further degrees in appendant bodies such as the York Rite and/or Scottish Rite organizations that both have a national-level governing body.

THE ORIGINS

There are so many puzzles associated with Freemasonry that it might help if we could pin down where the organization truly began, but even this search is fraught with difficulty. This is because within the Craft itself there are many different claims and counterclaims regarding Freemasonry's origins. English Freemasonry, run from London, deliberately absents itself from any speculation by simply stating that Freemasonry began in the eighteenth century when a group of lodges in London came together to form Grand Lodge, which now stands at the heart of almost all English Freemasonry. Of course this explanation is really no explanation at all, if only because the lodges that came together to create Grand Lodge had obviously existed prior to their cooperation.

Hardly anyone suggests that the ancient Hebrew origins, espoused in the degree rituals and lessons, represent anything other than a series of fairy tales. Many of the characters involved appear to have no genuine historical authenticity, and in light of modern historical knowledge these stories are not merely implausible—some of them are downright impossible.

Because many years of careful research into Freemasonry underpin this book, we will explain to our readers where we assume Freemasonry originated. There will most certainly be people who disagree with us, but what follows seems to us to be the true genesis of the Craft.

There was a time when those working at cutting, dressing, and erecting stone formed the same sort of self-help groups that existed for all trades and mercantile professions. They were members of a Masonic guild. A guild was part trade association and part trade union. People who had spent many years of apprenticeship learning a particular trade obviously would not wish their skills to be undermined by people who had not gone through the proper instructions and practical experience. Trades and professions were often referred to as "mysteries," and that is the way that most of those involved wished them to stay. Trades often remained within families, and even marriages were frequently arranged to ensure the continuity of a trade.

Guild members would meet regularly to discuss the business of their particular guild and also to instruct new members and to ensure that everything within the trade or profession was being run according to established rules and procedures. Guilds were not only common from the Middle Ages onward but in some cases were extremely powerful institutions. In cities all over Europe there were guilds for almost every profession, and this certainly included stonemason's guilds. It is toward these guilds that some historians point in order to identify the Freemasonry of today. The important difference between a working mason and a member of a Masonic lodge is that the working mason is known as *operative,* while the Masonic brother is referred to as being *speculative.*

If Freemasonry did ultimately spring from the need of medieval stonemasons to regulate their profession, why are there not also many other fraternal organizations based, for example, on speculative wood-carving, wool dying, millinery, or metalworking? The only real answer that seems to be forthcoming is that there was something special about one particular group of freemasons that allowed at least some of their knowledge and much of their inner mysteries to be passed to people who had never been directly involved in cutting or shaping stone.

In our opinion, this unique group did exist, and it came into being in the twelfth century in France. In subsequent chapters the reader will learn about the Cistercian order of monks, who have a profound part to play in our unfolding story. But the Cistercians were far from being the only reformed Benedictine order that sprang up from the eleventh century on. There was another that was almost as successful as the Cistercians, at least initially, and it is toward this group of religious zealots that it seems we have to look in order to find the origins of Freemasonry.

The monks in question were called Tironensians, a name that came from their original abbey, which was at Tiron (sometimes known as Thiron), not far from Chartres in France. The order was the idea of a man who is variously known as Bernard of Ponthieu, Bernard d'Abbeville, or indeed Bernard of Tiron. This monastic reformer was born near Abbeville in 1046. At around twelve years of age Bernard moved to the monastery of St. Cyprien, near Poitiers, in order to become a novice. Later he became the abbot of another abbey, Saint-Savin-sur-Gartempe, but he soon fell out with those in control of the most powerful of the French Benedictine monasteries, which was Cluny. Bernard wanted to get the Benedictine order back to the simplicity and austerity it had once enjoyed, and this proved to be impossible within the established French Benedictine order, which was heavily influenced by the abbey of Cluny. After many adventures and periods spent as a hermit, Bernard of Abbeville created his own abbey and his own monastic order at Tiron.

From the very start of the Tironensian order a strict emphasis was placed upon hard manual labor. To the Tironensians this predominantly meant building in stone. The monks soon became proficient in their chosen occupation and were as keen to help out in the local communities where they lived as they were in enlarging and beautifying their own abbeys. From their base at Tiron the Tironensians spread out across France and beyond. Within five years—an incredibly short period of time—there were 117 Tironensian abbeys and priories in France and across the British Isles. The Tironensian order was so successful in the twelfth century it is almost incomprehensible that in the present day it has been all but forgotten.

In addition to attending to their own order, the Tironensians also ran an establishment akin to a school of stonemasonry and building in Chartres. It is likely that they were instrumental in creating the new cathedral there, which was built in the astonishingly short period between 1194 and 1250. Chartres Cathedral encapsulated the very latest techniques in what became known as the Gothic style of architecture, which was brand new and quite revolutionary at the time. Gothic architecture was radically different from the Romanesque style it replaced because of its use of high, sweeping arches, huge windows, and its ingenious methods for keeping walls relatively thin, allowing much higher and more grandiose structures to be created.

The Tironensians rubbed shoulders with all the new monastic orders that were springing up throughout France during the twelfth century. This included the phenomenally successful Cistercians and the fighting brotherhood of the Knights Templar. Undoubtedly both the Cistercians and the Templars learned a great deal of their own building acumen from the Tironensians, and, as we will see, the relationship among the three orders probably went much deeper.

The kingdom of Scotland always had good relations with France, so it is not too surprising that some of the first Tironensian abbeys outside of the French region were founded in Scotland. The first of these was Selkirk in 1113, followed by Kelso in 1128. Slightly later were Kilwinning in 1140 and finally Arbroath in 1178. In our opinion it is toward the Tironensian monastery in Kilwinning, in North Ayrshire, south of Glasgow, that we must look if we wish to find the true origins of Freemasonry.

There is a tradition among Freemasons in Kilwinning that theirs is the oldest Masonic lodge of all. They claim that the lodge began in the Chapter House at Kilwinning abbey almost as soon as building began there in 1140. This may not be as fanciful as it seems. The Tironensians were somewhat hampered by their own success. Their order was spreading rapidly, not simply in Scotland but all across the British Isles and France. No matter how skillful they may have been, it is highly unlikely that the Tironensians could ever have personally completed the building that was required by the order. For this reason they would have taken on local men in whatever district they found themselves and trained them in the art of stonemasonry. This is what seems to have happened at Kilwinning, and it is suggested that this early school of stonemasonry eventually became the first Masonic lodge.*

During the twelfth century there was an explosion in architecture and building. New structures, especially religious ones, were being created all over Europe. To the Tironensians, architecture, building, and the ornamentation of stone were much more than simple, manual tasks: they were a form of *worship*. Those responsible for the building of some of the most magnificent structures ever created required knowledge of mathematics and especially geometry, as well as the practical skills of quarrying and shaping stone. The new Gothic style that was emerging was much more demanding than the solid, squat Romanesque. There was nothing archaic about what the Tironensians were doing; they were right at the cutting edge of the technology of their day.

All the same, every task the Tironensians undertook was an expression of their devotion. It was filled with mystique and a deep spiritual significance. As a result, the instruction they gave to the locals who would assist in the building of Kilwinning and other Tironensian projects would have been far more than simple lessons in handling chisels and cranes. They would have been taking part in what was genuinely considered to be a mystery. This knowledge would have been considered sacred with a very special connection to the deity.

---

*The importance of the Tironensian order cannot be overstated. Readers interested in looking further into their possible connections with developing Freemasonry may want to look at the electronic book *The Great Architects of Tiron* by Francine Bernier. Available at www.themasonictrowel.com/ebooks/fm_freemasonry/Bernier_-_The_Great_Architects_of_Tiron.pdf (accessed April 21, 2015).

As a result it is certain that the lay workers involved considered themselves to be privileged. They would have retained a strong sense of identity and willingly guarded the secrets that had been given to them. Although Freemasonry as we know it today still had a very long way to go, it is probably in the Chapter House of Kilwinning that it found its first expression. In the Chapter House there would be religious instruction as well as practical training, and this would invariably concern itself with the Hebrew scriptures because that is where the biggest and the most important building project in history had been described. It was the building of the first Jerusalem temple by King Solomon.

People in western Europe at the time were obsessed with Jerusalem and its temple. Jerusalem was as much an ideal as a real place. It was nothing less than the city of God. Known as the navel of the world, Jerusalem had been wrested from the forces of Islam during the First Crusade only a few decades earlier and was held, albeit somewhat shakily, by the Christian forces of the crusaders. It is hard if not impossible for the modern mind to understand the motivations of people living in the eleventh century. There are scant records relating to the Tironensian commitment to architecture and building, but it is highly likely that they viewed everything they created as being a pale reflection of Jerusalem and its original temple. They were fired with a religious zeal to re-create the city of God wherever and whenever they could, and this belief and desire would surely have been passed on in the lessons they gave to their lay workers.

It is most likely for this reason that Freemasonry took on its obsession with Jerusalem and the temple, a fascination that still stands at the heart of the Craft, even if very few present-day Freemasons understand why.

To follow the developing path of Freemasonry we must now travel east from Kilwinning to Midlothian, not far from Edinburgh. A large amount of land in this area once belonged to a family by the name of St. Clair, a name that eventually became Sinclair. The St. Clair family had originally come from the same part of France where Bernard of Abbeville had been born. They had come to England with William the Conqueror in 1066, when the Normans invaded England, but later moved to Scotland to become vassals of the Scottish kings.

The Sinclairs prospered, and thanks to judicious marriage alliances they eventually became the earls of Orkney, an area that is a large series of islands just north of the Scottish mainland. Nevertheless, the Sinclairs kept a strong presence in Midlothian, and one of their family members, William Sinclair, embarked on the project of building a very special church on his land at Roslin, which he commenced in September of 1456. William Sinclair had recently renounced his right to the earldom of Orkney in favor of an alternative one in Caithness, and this brought a large cash settlement from the Scottish crown. This meant William had money, and he spent a considerable sum on his plans for Rosslyn Chapel, which is undoubtedly one of the gems of Scottish architecture.

Rosslyn Chapel, made famous by Dan Brown's novel *The DaVinci Code,* is not large, and it has been suggested that this is because it was never finished. It was supposed to have been merely the Lady Chapel of a much larger structure. This may have been the impression William Sinclair wanted to give when he embarked on the project, but there are a number of reasons for believing that this was never the case. What stands on the site now is something that looks like a giant version of one of the most ornamental of the Renaissance reliquaries, fabulous ornamented boxes in the shape of chapels that were created to hold the relics of saints.

Both inside and outside, Rosslyn Chapel positively drips with stone carvings. Riots of foliage, strange apparitions, musicians, mythical buildings, and innumerable other creations make the place seem like something from a bizarre medieval dream. The front of the chapel interior has three highly ornamental pillars and the roof is a riot of stars. At one time the whole interior of the chapel was painted in bright, vivid colors, and the effect must have been spectacular. It seems as if hardly a square foot of available space was ignored by the carvers; no wonder that as small as it is the chapel took forty years to finish.

Some of the ornamentation within the chapel defies logic. For example, there are representations of leaves that could only realistically

Fig. 3.1. Victorian photograph of Rosslyn Chapel from the north

be meant to represent the aloe plant, which is native to Central and South America and was supposed to be unknown in Europe at this stage of the fifteenth century. In addition there are examples of maize, so accurately portrayed that they simply could not be anything else. Once again, maize was unknown in Europe at this time.

A possible explanation is that the Sinclairs had Viking blood flowing in their veins, thanks to their Orkney connections. There is a story that William's grandfather Henry Sinclair organized a voyage to the New World, and this is certainly not out of the question because now nobody doubts that the Vikings, those incredible Scandinavian warriors and sailors, had visited America on a number of occasions, centuries before Columbus.

Rosslyn Chapel is closely associated with both the Knights Templar and Freemasonry. It has often been suggested that strong Knights Templar influence in Scotland was partly responsible for Freemasonry's origins, and the Craft certainly features the Templars in many of its subsidiary degrees. We will come across the Knights Templar again and again in the pages that follow, but suffice it to say for the moment that they were an order of fighting monks who were an offshoot of the Cistercian order. The Scottish crown failed to persecute the Knights Templar when they were shamed and dissolved after 1307, and it has been suggested that a significant number of Templars escaped from France and settled in the west of Scotland. It is therefore entirely possible that the descendants of Templars were present when Rosslyn Chapel was created and that they were among those who knew its innermost secrets.

What makes this even more likely is the fact that Rosslyn Chapel was always intended to represent the Jerusalem temple. Those who doubt this persistent assertion, which has been circulating for centuries, point out that the chapel is tiny in comparison with the Jerusalem temple and of a different architectural form. This is true, but what the critics fail to realize is that it was not the shape and size of the Jerusalem temple that was built at Rosslyn but rather its creators were attempting to re-create the soul of the temple.

In short, Rosslyn Chapel represents a mélange of historical possibilities and holds the position of being one of the most mysterious buildings in Britain. There are, however, some things we can say about the chapel that are self-evident. First, it was built by people who really knew what they were doing. The chapel is a positive workbook of Gothic architectural techniques and contains more examples of different styles of Gothic arches than perhaps any other building in the world. At the time it was created, Scotland was something of a backwater country, so much so that stories were invented to suggest that William Sinclair had to bring artists and sculptors from Italy, though there is no evidence that this was the case. In reality he did not need to search abroad for people with the skill to create and ornament the chapel; they existed on his own doorstep.

In addition to their Caithness holdings the Sinclairs had extensive lands elsewhere in Scotland, including areas around Kilwinning. William Sinclair would have been more than familiar with the Tironensian monks there and in their other abbeys in southern Scotland. The order was still flourishing at this time in the fifteenth century. The most likely explanation for the glory that is Rosslyn Chapel is that it was created by the Tironensians themselves, ably assisted by later generations of the secular stonemasons who had been tutored at Kilwinning for three centuries or more. Gothic architecture, of which Rosslyn Chapel is a textbook example, was probably created by the Tironensians. And even if they did not build Rosslyn Chapel, it is a perfect representation of their knowledge and skills.

Alan has researched and coauthored two books about Rosslyn Chapel, *Rosslyn Chapel Decoded* and *Rosslyn Revealed,* with writer, broadcaster, historian, and film cameraman the late John Ritchie. John was born and raised in the village adjacent to Rosslyn Chapel and probably knew more about the place than anyone else. Over a period of several years Alan and John delved deeply into the chapel's known history, its folklore, and the many legends that surround it. They came to many conclusions, all of which can be studied by interested readers in *Rosslyn Revealed* and *Rosslyn Chapel Decoded.* The following is a synthesis of some of the findings.

- Rosslyn Chapel was always intended to be something very special and to be very different from any conventional Catholic church of the time.
- In addition to its supposed ecclesiastical role, Rosslyn Chapel is also a cunningly and cleverly created naked-eye observatory, allowing an unparalleled view of the entire eastern horizon, from north to south.
- The designers of Rosslyn Chapel incorporated a series of underground chambers and passages, some of which joined the chapel to the nearby Rosslyn Castle. These chambers were difficult and costly to create, and it stands to reason that they were designed to safeguard something of great importance and probably inestimable value.
- The connections between Rosslyn Chapel and the Knights

Templar are not easy to prove, but because of the Sinclair family connections and also on account of the historical nature of the legends, Alan and John both believed that the connection did indeed exist. There is absolutely no doubt about the chapel's association with Freemasonry, which goes back a very long time.

- Rosslyn Chapel once contained relics of the disciple and gospel writer St. Matthew, after whom the chapel was named and other relics such as supposed parts of the True Cross. It is also almost certain that a proportion of the treasures found by the Knights Templar in and around Jerusalem found their way, via Champagne and ultimately Kilwinning Abbey, to be hidden at Rosslyn Chapel.

- There is ample evidence to suggest that most, if not all, of these treasures were removed from Rosslyn Chapel, most likely in the 1860s, and were taken to the United States, where they remain to this day.

For all these reasons there was much about Rosslyn Chapel that William Sinclair would not have wished the Roman Catholic authorities to know. The Knights Templar had been disbanded and made illegal at the beginning of the fourteenth century. They were considered to be heretics, and any association with them or their memory would still have attracted the most severe penalties in the fifteenth century. Templar treasures from Jerusalem would have been of great interest to the church as well as the English who were constantly at war with their neighbors in Scotland. It was therefore absolutely essential to the earl that any knowledge of the *real* reasons for the building of Rosslyn Chapel were safeguarded absolutely.

This presented him with a great problem because he needed skilled workers to create the chapel, complete with its secret tunnels and chambers. He simply had to find some way to keep them quiet, not only while construction was taking place, but into perpetuity. He did, however, have one great advantage. Because the monks and the lay workers from Kilwinning already represented a tight and secretive brotherhood, and had done so since Kilwinning was founded, there was a strong base upon which Earl William could build his own plans for absolute secrecy.

It would appear that in return for excellent treatment of his workers, and the promise of continuing work once Rosslyn Chapel was complete, William was able to tighten up the Masonic status of the workers even more, obtaining from those involved a sacred promise, on pain of death, that no word of the true nature of the chapel would ever be revealed. Herein is the truth behind the commencement of Freemasonry. Of course, not everyone involved on the project was a worker in stone, so it was necessary for the earl to make his Masonic brotherhood open to those who were not masons. These people were the first speculative Freemasons, who were made party to the mysteries and rites of the brotherhood and as a result were sworn to absolute secrecy.

As time went by the Masonic brotherhood flourished around Roslin and soon found its way to the nearby Scottish capital of Edinburgh. Speculative Freemasonry had existed since Rosslyn Chapel was being built, but its popularity grew, and long after the chapel was little more than a ruin lodges were formed and Freemasons met on a regular basis in many parts of Scotland. Ultimately Freemasonry spread even farther. It found its way into England, and probably as early as the seventeenth century there were lodges of Freemasons meeting regularly in London.

Freemasonry also traveled to France, most probably thanks to the Garde Écossaise, a company of Scottish bodyguards who traditionally defended the French kings. Scotland had long enjoyed a special relationship with France. This was not only for reasons of trade but also born out of the adage "my enemy's enemy is my friend." There were constant wars between England and Scotland, just as surely as England was often at odds with France. Siding with the French gave the Scots a level of security from their larger southern cousins than they might otherwise have enjoyed. In addition, soldiers have always been a good conduit for Freemasonry. Many regiments had their own field lodges, and the Garde Écossaise would have been no exception.

Present in two distinctly different environments outside of Scotland,

Freemasonry began to change subtly. The rise of Protestantism in England led to one version of Freemasonry, while France remained Catholic and therefore probably retained more of the original flavor of Freemasonry as it had been practiced in Scotland. Ultimately, both forms of Freemasonry became represented in the American Colonies, and both are still present.

Many new Masonic institutions and degrees developed in France, and a number of these found favor in the American colonies, especially during the period when the Revolutionary War took place against the British. The French were great supporters of American independence, and a significant number of French citizens fought alongside the colonists during the war.

Still more degrees were added in the free United States, and by the end of the American Civil War, Freemasonry across the country was in something of a mess. After the end of the Civil War, American Freemasonry began to take on a more cohesive form. There are now thirty-three degrees of Scottish Rite Freemasonry available to brothers of the Craft in the United States, and, though diminished somewhat in recent years, Freemasonry still flourishes on the western side of the Atlantic. Freemasonry's somewhat more conservative branch is still much in evidence in England. English Freemasonry has sometimes been referred to as a "Gentleman's Club," though a more closed and traditional form survives elsewhere in Europe.

This then is a brief description of Freemasonry and its origins. We recognize that our explanation is somewhat oversimplified, not least of all because modern Freemasonry and especially Scottish Rite Freemasonry contain significant components that were incorporated into Freemasonry from other directions. Nevertheless, the core of the Craft is still in place, as it must have been in the years when Rosslyn Chapel was being constructed. There is also a secret but ever-present core that lies at the heart of Freemasonry, generally unseen, even by most of its members. We would suggest that this has been present right from the start and that it came to be at the center of the Craft as a result of the influence brought to bear by the Tironensians and especially the

Knights Templar. Because to a great extent the Templars were simply Cistercians in battle armor, the overall influence of Cistercianism on Freemasonry cannot be dismissed. And although Freemasonry appeared as a peculiarly Scottish institution that began well over a thousand years ago, the true motivation that lay behind it can only be found in the region of France, still called Champagne.

4

THE CHAMPAGNE FAIRS AND INTERNATIONALISM

If we want to truly know why the United States is indeed the Nation of the Goddess we have to look far back into the mists of time. This is a complex story, and attempting to find a single way into it is quite impossible. There was a whole plethora of happenings across several thousand years that resulted in this brave and most extraordinary experiment in democracy and government. However, there is one series of events that was more responsible for the emergence of a free United States than any other. To understand it we have to travel east across the Atlantic to western Europe to a place that to most Americans will be synonymous with sparkling wine rather than with the origins of their own history.

Some eighty-eight miles southeast of Paris (141 kilometers) is the city of Troyes. Although now simply another town in France, Troyes has an illustrious past, and, together with the region of which it was the capital, it once enjoyed a high degree of autonomy. At the end of the eleventh century Champagne, with Troyes at its heart, owed fealty to France. So it wasn't exactly independent, but most of those living there viewed it to be.

Champagne was ruled by counts who were as powerful in their own domains as the king of France was in his. At the time France was not nearly as large as it is today. France proper extended north from Paris toward what we now know as Belgium, but much of its former western territory had been captured and annexed centuries before by the Vikings. This area became Normandy, and it would be a long time before the large area the Normans controlled would once again be part of France. So, in effect, the kingdom of France was actually fairly small.

Despite the nominal duties and responsibilities it owed to the French crown, Champagne regularly had spats with Paris, some of which might even be considered short but vicious wars. There were always considerable differences of opinion between French kings and the Champagne counts, and in the years leading up to the end of the eleventh century these were very much in evidence. Just as much culture and learning were present in Troyes and the other cities of Champagne as existed in Paris. Champagne was an area rich with historical diversity, a mixture of the old Celtic traditions and those of the Franks who had occupied the region from the fifth century. What was definitely present as the eleventh century advanced toward its close was a desire on the part of the rulers of Champagne to eclipse France and therefore to slip out from under her skirts. This desire for freedom led to a series of events—stage-managed in Troyes—that were to forever change the face of western Europe and ultimately the world.

Any one of the decisions and actions taken by the rulers of Champagne between the last decade of the eleventh century and up until the second half of the twelfth century might not appear especially significant when taken in isolation. It is only when *everything* emanating from Champagne during this period is seen collectively that it becomes obvious that the rulers of the region were working on a carefully considered, multipronged plan that was both secretive and subversive.

To understand Champagne at this time we have to take a look at those who were in charge. Beginning in 1094 this was Hugh, a son of Theobald III, Count of Blois. Theobald had regularly crossed swords with the kings of France, which had led to him losing a part of his lands in 1044. He was later able to consolidate his position, bringing a number of his possessions together that would result in the large region of Champagne. Theobald never styled himself as Count of Champagne. This title was taken by his son Hugh in 1093, when an older brother died, and a final consolidation of the family's holdings became possible.

Hugh seems to have had very definite ideas regarding what he wanted Champagne to be. In addition, although nominally a Roman Catholic, almost from the start he showed himself to have rather strange religious beliefs. He was always a staunch supporter and benefactor of renegade monastic orders, especially those that showed a strong allegiance to the feminine aspect of Christianity in the guise of the Virgin Mary and Mary Magdalene. It is entirely possible that the rulers of Blois, Chartres, and Champagne had secretly supported a heretical form of Christianity for many generations. Well into Christian times a pagan deity by the name of Rosemerth had been popular in this part of France. She was a version of the Great Goddess who had been significant across western Europe since the New Stone Age. It would have been easy for supporters of this goddess to worship Rosemerth in the guise of the Virgin Mary, who as the mother of Jesus held a unique place in the Catholic faith. In this way they could have continued their age-old beliefs under the pretense of being perfectly ordinary Roman Catholics.

For countless generations in significant parts of what is now France there had been a mistrust of the Catholic Church on account of the murder of Dagobert II in the forest of Stennay in 679 CE. Dagobert II was the last of the Merovingian kings, a long dynasty of Frankish rulers who from the time of King Clovis (466–511) had enjoyed a special relationship with the Roman Catholic Church. Clovis had promised to support this branch of Christianity just as long as the church in Rome held his family as undisputed kings in what today is France.

It has been suggested that Dagobert II had been assassinated with the explicit approval of the Catholic Church, thus breaking a promise between the church and the Merovingian kings that went back to the baptism of Clovis I in 496. Clovis had been baptized in Reims, another city in Champagne, and Merovingian support remained strong in the area long after a new dynasty, the Carolingians, had taken and kept the

French throne. Most of the aristocracy of Champagne could trace its origins back to the Merovingians.

It seemed for centuries that the Merovingians held some trump card in its dealings with the Roman Catholic Church. As recently as the twentieth century documents appeared in Paris that claimed the true secret shared between the Catholic Church and the Merovingian monarchs was that the church knew very well that Jesus had been married to Mary Magdalene, that he had fathered children, and that his family's blood still flowed through the veins of the Merovingian kings.

The Merovingian monarchs were certainly a strange bunch. They stood aloof from almost any practical decision that involved their domains and left most of the decisions to underlings—especially the "Mayors of the Palace." Merovingian kings were treated more like gods than mortals and appear to have had an almost mystical hold over their leading subjects—and for a long time over successive popes in Rome.

Of course if the Merovingian kings were descendants of Jesus, they held a virtual sword of Damocles over the heads of those who led the Catholic Church. There was no mention of a married Jesus in the Christian scriptures or any reference to children he may have had. Such a situation, if generally known, would radically change the whole Christian story. As a result it made sense, when Dagobert II became the only remaining claimant to the Frankish throne, to get him out of the way and to install a new dynasty who was prepared to follow Catholic dogma to the letter.

The Carolingian kings became not only the rulers of France, but also they ultimately took possession of Catholicism, which became a more brutal, authoritarian, and jealous institution. Any continuing knowledge of the truth behind the Christian story was driven underground and held only in the hearts of the families who had descended from Merovingian times. Centuries later the old knowledge would still be known to the upper aristocracy of the region, most probably including Hugh of Champagne, who himself had Merovingian forebears. It is also clear that Hugh of Champagne was obsessed with Jerusalem, the Holy City in the Hebrew and Christian scriptures. As we have seen, it was in Jerusalem that Solomon had built the famed temple, probably around 1000 BCE. There are very detailed descriptions of the temple in the Hebrew scriptures, together with its specific dimensions. These were of great interest to medieval people and were drawn into sharper focus by what is probably the most peculiar book of the Christian scriptures: the Book of Revelation.

The Book of Revelation is supposed to have been written by John the Apostle. John was one of the original disciples of Jesus, and he is credited with having written the Gospel of St. John, which is also part of the Christian scriptures. There is some doubt as to whether both these works were actually written by the same individual, but until modern scholarship looked at these matters it was accepted that this was the case.

What makes the Book of Revelation so strange is that much of it is composed of a series of prophetic visions that the writer states he has undergone. Many of these deal with the city of Jerusalem and in particular the "New Jerusalem," which, the writer prophecies, will arise in the future. At the core of the material included in Revelation is a skein of knowledge extending way back into the past of the Hebrews, probably as far back as 2000 BCE or substantially earlier. Parts of the Book of Revelation are very reminiscent of another, almost lost work of the Hebrew scriptures, the Book of Enoch. This Book of Enoch was known about for a very long time, but no example of it was forthcoming in the relatively modern era until 1774. Nobody reading both the Book of Enoch and the Book of Revelation could doubt the two works are connected, even though their authorship may be divided by more than a thousand years.

These are complicated matters—and it would be quite easy to write an entire book about both the Book of Enoch and the Book of Revelation—but the relevant point as far as our present research is concerned is that the rulers of Champagne almost certainly had a special reverence for both works. This fascination was never actually mentioned by the counts of Champagne but is pointed to regularly when their decisions and actions during the pivotal period in question are analyzed.

If he was indeed a real character, Enoch appears to have lived in the Bronze Age or perhaps even in the New Stone Age. Although adopted into early Hebrew religion, Enoch is far older than the Hebrews. He is said to be the great-grandfather of Noah, and since Noah was a character drawn from Babylonian and ultimately Sumerian mythology, Enoch's origins lay so far back in time it is difficult to know exactly what his era may have been.

The Book of Enoch is long and convoluted. It concerns itself quite freely with matters that are not specifically related to religion. For example, it has a long section describing how calendars work and astronomy. In addition, throughout the book Enoch, the firsthand narrator, is taken on lengthy journeys by a mysterious group of people known as the Watchers, who were clearly very knowledgeable. In their book *Uriel's Machine*, Christopher Knight and Robert Lomas theorize that Enoch was living at the time the earliest megalithic structures were being created in the British Isles. Knight and Lomas suggest that from a detailed description in the Book of Enoch one of the sites to which the Watchers brought Enoch could only have been the passage grave of Newgrange, in Ireland.

During their investigations into the story of Enoch, Knight and Lomas came across a very early Masonic ritual that dates back to 1740. The ritual contained information that could only have been gleaned from the Book of Enoch, even though it is known that the ritual was committed to the written word twenty-four years before the Book of Enoch came to light in the modern era. Knight and Lomas, who are experts in Freemasonry, suggested that the ritual in question was already old before it was ever written down, and, bearing in mind that the Book of Enoch had been lost for many centuries, there is every chance that this was indeed the case. The conclusion must surely be that the first Freemasons possessed the lost Book of Enoch themselves, or at least had significant knowledge of its contents.

In addition to the parts of the Masonic ritual that relate directly to the lost Book of Enoch, Freemasonry also tells a story of how Enoch was the first person to be taken to Mount Moriah, where the Temple of

Solomon would one day stand. The ritual tells of how Enoch had dug a series of deep chambers on the mountain and that within them he had hidden secret knowledge given to him by the Watchers. In addition, he had placed there a strange, triangular device known as the Delta of Enoch, which contained the secret name of God. According to Masonic sources, these treasures had been found again when Solomon began to dig the foundations for the first Jerusalem temple, but they were reburied beneath the temple with great veneration. This is a story to which we will return, but for the moment it is safe to say that reverence for Enoch and the site of Jerusalem was particularly strong at the end of the eleventh century in Champagne. As we shall see, it is very likely that Count Hugh of Champagne and his trusted vassals were aware of the same legend that is played out in the Masonic ritual that surfaced centuries later.

John's Book of Revelation, although much more recent in composition, was clearly intentionally linked to the days of the Hebrew patriarchs and especially to Enoch. One of the main themes of Revelation is the destruction of the old Jerusalem and its replacement by the New Jerusalem, which John described in detail. The New Jerusalem was to be a place of fairness and sound laws. John declared that the New Jerusalem would need no temple, because the Deity would be at its heart. There is no suggestion that the New Jerusalem would be physically associated with the old version, and in fact the text leads the reader to believe that it will be somewhere else.

At the period when Hugh of Champagne lived, Jerusalem was in the hands of the Seljuk Turks, who had captured it from the more amenable Egyptians in 1070. To Western Christians the Turks, and indeed all Muslims, were the infidel. The fact that access to the sacred sites in the Holy Land was being restricted to Christians and that the Turks were also threatening Eastern Christianity in Byzantium had led to a great desire on the part of the West to capture the Holy Land for Christianity, while at the same time defeating the feared Seljuk Turks.

It would appear at first sight that Hugh of Champagne agreed wholeheartedly with the idea of a Crusade to free the Holy Land and to make it a Roman Catholic region, the more so because in the end his family and their nobles arranged for it to happen. However, what Hugh's *real* motives may have been will only become evident when the whole story of Champagne is told. We hope to demonstrate that the Champagne nobles, together with their kin in other regions around the French heartland, had only a passing interest in the old Jerusalem and hardly any in the established Roman Catholic Church. What they actually sought was to create the New Jerusalem as described in the Book of Revelation. To them, the biblical Jerusalem was effectively a lost cause, though there were sacred objects buried there that would be crucial to the creation of its replacement, so it would be necessary for them to have unrestricted access to the Old City in the first instance.

There was certainly no lack of enthusiasm for a Crusade to free the Holy Land from Islam—it was something that was discussed in the West throughout the second half of the eleventh century. What was lacking was not the desire but the necessary cohesion to make such a venture possible. Kings all across Europe at the time were more likely to wage war against each other than to cooperate about anything, so it would take someone of real influence to bring them together in a common cause.

Arranging for this was the first part of the plans that were carefully laid in Troyes, not by Hugh himself but by his father, Theobald III. What was clearly needed was a pope who would stand up and tell all Christians that it was their duty to wage a Crusade in the Holy Land. Previous pontiffs had not been keen to try, for all manner of local political reasons but also because the leaders of Western Christianity in Rome did not get on well with their counterparts in the Eastern church.

Things soon changed when Pope Urban II came to power in the Vatican in 1088. The pope's birth name was Odo (or Otho) of Lagery, and he was the son of an aristocratic family from Champagne. It is difficult to say whether Odo was a blood relative of Hugh of Champagne or his father, but bearing in mind the high degree of intermarriage that took place among aristocratic families at this time it is extremely likely he was.

Odo had been raised in Rheims, where Hugh's father, Theobald, spent a great deal of his time, and it is certain that they knew each other and were most likely on good terms. When the previous pope (Victor III) died, the rulers of Champagne would have lobbied furiously to get one of their own into the Vatican, the more so because once they did, their plans could begin to be put into action. Theobald would have had some influence over the election of Odo to the papacy, because he wielded great power not only in Champagne but also within France itself.

Odo took the papal name of Urban II. He was a strong and charismatic man who showed great deference for his ancestral homelands but scant regard for the king of France, with whom he was invariably at odds. In November of 1095, Pope Urban II held a great gathering at Clermont, a city right in the center of modern France. There he called for all Christians to wage war on the infidel and for the kings and princes of Europe to unite to drive the Turks from the Holy Land. In truth, Urban had a multitude of reasons for thinking that a Crusade would be a good thing. These are itemized in detail in Alan's book *The Goddess, the Grail & the Lodge*. What matters to our present research is that it suited Champagne and its rulers.

Initially the Crusade was very successful. The rulers of Europe did indeed cooperate, and the Holy City of Jerusalem was captured for Christianity on July 15, 1099. Included in the ranks of those who first stormed the walls of the city were many of the nobles from Champagne, together with their blood relatives from other regions of France.

There was never any chance that Christians, most of whom came from far away in western Europe, would ever be able to control the Holy Land indefinitely, and the wisest among the Crusaders must have realized this from the start. The Christian kingdom staggered on for a while, but Jerusalem fell back into Muslim hands in 1187. However, as far as Hugh of Champagne and his descendants were concerned, access to the city and its holy sites had been available for long enough.

Count Hugh's next move was to start an economic revolution in western Europe. Champagne lay at an important crossroads, and Hugh set out to exploit the fact. At almost the same time as Jerusalem was being captured by the Crusaders, Hugh began to create a series of markets in various cities within Champagne. These were far from being small local gatherings. Hugh invited merchants and traders from all points of the compass. The Champagne Fairs were international gatherings, allowing merchants to bring goods from their respective homelands to trade with their counterparts from elsewhere. Hugh guaranteed them safe passage and employed a significant police force to supervise the events. At one site or another, the Champagne Fairs extended across most of the year. Accommodation was provided for participants, as well as credit facilities so that people did not have to travel with large amounts of gold.

All manner of goods were traded at the Champagne Fairs, but by far the most important commodity was wool. The British had always been great breeders of sheep, and the English economy was especially reliant on its exports of wool. Much of this wool eventually found its way to the Champagne Fairs where it was sold for processing in Flanders or even much farther south in Italy. Wool was phenomenally important to everyone during this period, but as reliant as England was, especially on its production of raw wool, there wasn't enough being traded to please the rulers of Champagne, which in part led to the next phase of their plans. In the meantime the existence of the Champagne Fairs began to have a very definite effect on the countries of western Europe.

At this period in history all of Europe depended on a form of government that is known as the feudal system. This relied on a model that can be seen as being like a pyramid. At the top point of the pyramid was the king. Immediately below him were the great earls and barons who owed fealty to the king but who controlled vast areas of land. The lesser nobility came below the great lords. These middle aristocrats looked to the greater lords for support and also offered their own assistance as vassals. They would supply soldiers in times of war and paid dues to those above them in the pyramid. Toward the bottom of the pecking order came very minor aristocrats who once again passed money and assistance back up the pyramid in return for support and protection. Finally, at the very bottom came the freemen and the serfs, many of whom were tied to a particular manor and a specific lord. They gave tribute in terms of both money and labor and held some land of their own that they could use to feed themselves and their families.

Adventures such as the Champagne Fairs began to break down the feudal system because they created new classes of individuals—such as merchants and artisans. These people were not tied to the system in the way serfs were, and what was more they were beginning to trade across international borders—something that feudal kings tended to frown upon. The success of the Champagne Fairs and what followed them in other parts of western Europe did more to erode the forces of feudalism than any other factor. Open and unrestricted trade among people who were free to make their own decisions and who embraced the concept of democracy and capitalism would eventually become the hallmarks of a free United States—an experiment that truly began in Champagne.

In 1098 a man named Robert of Molesmes, together with a group of enthusiastic followers, established a brand-new monastic order just south of Champagne in northern Burgundy. Robert was from the same sort of aristocratic Champagne family as was Pope Urban II. His new order would become known as the Cistercians, and the part it played in European and world history was colossal. As we mentioned earlier, the Cistercians were great breeders of sheep. This was especially the case in the many great abbeys they founded in the British Isles. Most of the wool from the Cistercian sheep ultimately found its way to the Champagne Fairs, which benefitted not only the monks but also Champagne.

Robert of Molesmes was soon obliged to quit his new abbey at Cîteaux and return to his former abbey of Molesme. As a result, there was a chance that Count Hugh would lose control of the new order. To make certain that this would not be the case, a young Burgundian by the name of Bernard, whose own family ties were from Champagne, was dispatched to Cîteaux in 1113, with no less than thirty enthusiastic relatives and retainers. They collectively joined Cîteaux as novice monks and effectively represented a coup to the new order, which at the time was still very small. Within three short years Bernard had been brought north from Cîteaux to found his own Cistercian monastery on land given to him by Hugh of Champagne. The new abbey was called Clairvaux and was situated just a few short miles from Hugh's capital of Troyes.

Bernard of Clairvaux, as he became known, quickly went on to become one of the most powerful voices in Western Christendom. During his life he exercised enough power to "make" popes, and he regularly advised kings and emperors. Although he never became the actual head of the Cistercian order, this could only be because his interests and influence lay elsewhere. Bernard of Clairvaux easily could have become pope himself, but this was another position he simply did not want; his influence from Clairvaux was that of a "king-maker," which made him infinitely more powerful than any single king or even a pope could be.

Once Bernard's position had become solid enough at Clairvaux, the next part of Hugh's plan could be put into action. In 1119 a group of eight knights from Champagne and the surrounding area was gathered together by Hugues de Payens, who was a relative and a vassal of Hugh of Champagne. This little group set out for Jerusalem. Their avowed intent was to guard the roads from the Mediterranean coast to the Holy City so that pilgrims would be safe on their journeys. The whole notion was plainly preposterous for a number of reasons. In fact Hugues de Payens and his men completely disappeared from history for nine years. What they were doing during that time remains a mystery—at least as far as the historical record is concerned. What is known is that Hugues de Payens and his knights returned to Troyes in 1129, where a great church gathering had been stage-managed by the new count, Theobald II, in order to have the knights recognized as a fighting monastic order and to introduce them to the world. Hugh of Champagne had not died during the intervening period, but in 1125 he had abdicated his position in Champagne in favor of his nephew

Theobald. Upon doing so, Hugh immediately joined the original knights in Jerusalem and became a member of the order.

The new order was to be called the Poor Knights of Christ and the Temple of Solomon. They had been welcomed with open arms by Baldwin II, who was the Christian king of Jerusalem and had been given accommodation on the Temple Mount close to where the temple had once stood.

The rule of the Templars was almost exactly the same as the one adopted by the Cistercians. It had been specifically modified by Bernard of Clairvaux to better suit the needs of a fighting brotherhood. So popular was the idea of a Christian army fighting in and for the Holy Land that the Templars began to grow at a phenomenal rate. Under the feudal system sons who were not the oldest surviving of the family could not inherit land. Joining the Templars gave them an exciting alternative to merely being a vassal to their eldest brother. Soon the Templars had properties in just about every part of western Europe and beyond. There was no doubt about their acumen as fighters, and they could be found in many different parts of the Holy Land supporting the limited number of crusaders still there. At the same time the Templars were growing in wealth. They helped to police the Champagne Fairs and ran massive farming enterprises of their own. Creating a huge fleet of ships, they also began to be a significant maritime force, and they eventually became powerful bankers. Even long after Christianity lost its final hold on the Holy Land, the Knights Templar remained as a private army, supposedly dedicated to the pope but in fact plowing their own furrow.

For more than 150 years Champagne remained the commercial powerhouse of the West, in no small part thanks to the impetus that had been offered by both the Cistercian order and that of the Templars. However, it was all destined to come to an end eventually. Very early in the fourteenth century, thanks to a judicious marriage by the French monarch and some bad luck on the part of the rulers of Champagne, the region fell back into the hands of the French crown. The dream was over. Almost immediately the French king arranged for the Templars to be accused of every form of heinous crime, and the Templar order was pronounced heretical and was officially disbanded. No sooner did the French have their hands on Champagne than the famous fairs quite mysteriously began to decline rapidly. Trade went elsewhere, and the whole region disappeared into relative obscurity.

If it had ever been the dream of the rulers of Champagne to locate the New Jerusalem anywhere in their own region, that dream was over. In all probability this was never their intention. These were very patient people who were quite willing to look to successive generations to fulfill the dreams that began at the end of the eleventh century.

There is a persistent rumor, which has existed for centuries and refuses to go away, that in those early years in Jerusalem the first Templars had been digging below the Temple Mount and perhaps looking for treasures and items in and around Jerusalem. Whatever the Templars had been sent to Jerusalem to find and bring back to the West had been shipped out of France long before King Philip IV began to plot the downfall of the Templars and getting his hands on Champagne. The treasures would ultimately find their way to the New Jerusalem that would eventually be created. When it was, it would bear a striking resemblance to the visions of St. John in his Revelation. However, it would be about as far from the original Jerusalem as was possible.

5

THE NAMES IN
THE TALPIOT TOMB

Just over three miles south of the Old City of Jerusalem is what was
once an outlying village but is now the suburb of Talpiot. In 1980
construction workers were creating new apartments in the area for the
growing number of Israeli citizens who were keen to live in and around
Jerusalem. The demolition and blasting that took place in March of
1980 revealed the outer court and ultimately the inner chamber of a
rock-cut tomb. This was interesting but not especially unusual. People
had lived in this place for countless centuries, and many other tombs had
been found all over the area; doubtless many still remain undisturbed.

What made the Talpiot tomb of specific interest was what it contained. Building work was stopped on the site, and archaeologists were
brought in to catalogue the tomb and to remove its contents. The tomb
dated back around two thousand years to a time when burial practices
were a little odd when viewed by today's practices. When a relative died
their body was prepared in the outer chamber of a tomb, then it was left
for a year or more to decompose in the inner chamber. After this time
relatives would return to retrieve the bones, which would be placed into
a stone box known as an ossuary. This would then be given a cover and
placed with other ossuaries in the tomb proper.

The Talpiot tomb contained ten ossuaries, some of which bore inscriptions. Once again, there was nothing odd about any of this. Some ossuaries were inscribed and decorated, some were not. What was definitely strange was that under a layer of a meter deep *terra rossa* (red earth) soil, which had been brought into the tomb by natural processes across the centuries, were found three skulls, arranged in a triangular pattern. Ideally, if families were able to complete the burial process, all bones were ultimately placed in ossuaries. To find three skulls arranged in a pattern on the floor of a tomb was distinctly odd.

It is lamentable that more care was not taken to secure the contents of the ossuaries at the time the tomb was first discovered. In a way this is understandable. In and around Jerusalem there are literally thousands of ossuaries from this period and later. They were and are not in the least unusual and back in the 1980s were probably treated with far less scientific scrutiny than would be the case today.

The reason the Talpiot tomb would eventually become so significant and famous was because of the inscriptions on some of its ossuaries. The names were as follows:

- Jesus, son of Joseph
- Maria
- Mariamne Mara
- Jos'e [taken as a shortening of the longer name Joseph]
- Judah, son of Jesus
- Matia [Matthew]

Understandably this list of names eventually raised attention. Speculation as to whether this was in fact the family tomb of the biblical Jesus and members of his family was not great at first, because the names on the ossuaries were in common use at the period they had been placed in the tomb. However, when it was discovered that one of the bodies present had been referred to as "James, son of Joseph," the connections to the Christian scriptures began to become apparent and to attract interest. Skeptics still pointed out that few if any of these names were unusual or uncommon for the period of the tomb, but this was countered by an ingenious statistical analysis published in 2008, "Statistical Analysis of an Archaeological Find," by Andrey Feuerverger, professor of statistics and mathematics at the University of Toronto. Feuerverger pointed out that to simply suggest many of the names on the ossuaries were not unusual was far from addressing the real issue. He went on to conclude that what really mattered was the list of names found *together* in the same tomb. In other words a more rigorous statistical analysis was called for to ascertain how unlikely it would be to find all these names in the same place. Depending on the criteria adopted this varied between 1 in 600 and 1 in 1,000,000.

If this was indeed the tomb of Jesus and his family, it would be necessary to account for the people in it whose ossuaries carried inscriptions. According to the writers and researchers Simcha Jacobovici and Charles R. Pellegrino in their book *The Jesus Family Tomb,* all the names involved could be traced to people either related to Jesus or associated with him.

For example, Jesus, son of Joseph, would be a good description of Jesus himself. Maria would be Mary, his mother. Jos'e (the shortened version of Joseph) was one of Jesus's brothers. Jacobovici and Pellegrino suggested that Mariamne was the Greek version of a name representing the character in the Christian scriptures and known disciple of Jesus usually referred to as Mary Magdalene, while Judah, son of Jesus, would logically be the son of Jesus.

It was suggested that one of the original ossuaries had disappeared from the excavations, almost from the first day of the tomb's discovery, and that this was actually an ossuary that had found its way onto the open market. This ossuary carried the inscription "James, son of Joseph, brother of Jesus." There was great controversy regarding this particular ossuary, which became the subject of intense legal activity. It was owned by Oded Golan, an Israeli engineer and antiques collector who was accused of having added the second part of the inscription himself in order to give the ossuary more significance and value. Although some authorities still state that the James ossuary did not come from the Talpiot tomb, according to Jacobovici and Pellegrino microscopic tests of the chemical composition of the environment of the tomb still found clinging to the ossuary proved that it had.

Ultimately, Oded Golan was acquitted of having forged part of the inscription on the James ossuary. If the inscription on the James ossuary is genuine, and if it did come from the Talpiot tomb, it raises the chance of this tomb belonging to the family of Jesus to an incredible level.

As Jacobovici and Pellegrino point out, other ossuaries from the same period have been universally accepted as being associated with characters from the era of the Christian scriptures. These include that of Caiaphas, the high priest who interrogated Jesus and sent him on to Roman judgment, and also the ossuary of Simon of Cyrene, who is supposed to have been tasked with helping to carry Jesus's cross on the way to his execution. Why, the authors wish to know, is the world willing to accept the existence of people specifically mentioned in the Gospels but yet so reticent to recognize the existence of a Jesus family tomb?

After a long and careful appraisal of the evidence we would have to say that to us the case for a Jesus family tomb at Talpiot is proved beyond all reasonable doubt. Nevertheless, despite what we see as being conclusive proof, it does not particularly surprise us that the Talpiot tomb is still not universally accepted as being that of the biblical Jesus and his family.

Christians generally would not be too happy about a Jesus family tomb that contained Jesus himself. The inference of Mary Magdalene being present, together with a son attributed to Jesus, would suggest that Mary Magdalene was actually the wife of Jesus—a fact that is not mentioned in the Gospels that form part of the Christian scriptures. Since Jesus had an ossuary himself, there is also an inevitable implication that he did not rise physically into heaven, as is suggested in the Christian scriptures, but that he was buried like any normal mortal.

Meanwhile scientists generally fight shy of anything to do with religion. Many scientists are agnostics or atheists who would find it difficult to go so far as to suggest that Jesus and the holy family were genuine historical characters. In addition, the whole business of the

Talpiot tomb became a powder keg of potential controversy, which is something that academics—all too protective of their reputations and careers—avoid like the plague.

In other words, there are actually very few individuals or groups that have a vested interest in supporting the notion of the Jesus family tomb and some very rich and powerful pressure groups that oppose it.

There are a few significant facts regarding the Talpiot tomb that interest us. In particular we would point to the presence of the three skulls on the floor of the tomb—arranged carefully in a triangle. The archaeologists who studied the tomb were also of the opinion that the tomb must have been entered at some time after it was first sealed. Small objects such as oil lamps, which are invariably found in such tombs, were missing. No damage had been done to the ossuaries, and because of the presence of the skulls this would have to be one of the first times in history when rather than ransacking a tomb in a search for valuables robbers actually left more behind than they took.

We are aware that the first Templar knights were residing in Jerusalem for nine years prior to their return to Troyes, at which time they were made into an official order by the pope. It has been suggested since time out of mind that one of the things they were doing during this extended period was searching for treasures and artifacts that they knew to be present in the area. Was it these men who first found their way into the Talpiot tomb? In veneration and praise, did three of them ultimately leave their skulls there when they died—in a symbolic triangle—a calling card, and all of which were found facing the Temple Mount? This is certainly what Scott F. Wolter discusses in his book *Akhenaten to the Founding Fathers: The Mysteries of the Hooked X*.

Further to this, did those first Templar knights remove some of the bones from the ossuaries? Since the Israeli archaeologists made no study regarding what bones belonged to which ossuary, we cannot answer this question with any certainty, but we hope to show that the idea is at least very likely. There is also significant evidence from other directions that the Knights Templar may have shown a very definite interest in the Talpiot tomb and what it contained.

Fig. 5.1. Typical skull and crossbones

Figure 5.1 is a drawing of a skull and crossbones. It is hard these days not to associate this symbol with all that is piratical. Strangely enough, the skull and crossbones never actually featured as a pirate symbol until the publication of *Treasure Island* by Robert Lewis Stevenson in 1883, not that the skull and crossbones was in any way a new symbol at that time. Stevenson lived in Scotland and was born into a family replete with Freemasons. Representations of the skull and crossbones are to be found on gravestones almost anywhere that Freemasons are buried but especially in Scotland.

Before Freemasonry the skull and crossbones was a regular feature of Knights Templar iconography, and it might be interesting to speculate why they adopted it. We need to bear in mind the way people were buried in the Talpiot tomb and countless others in and around Jerusalem. Their bodies were left to decompose before their bones were placed in specifically made ossuaries. The ossuaries in question were significantly smaller than coffins. It would never have been possible to place an articulated skeleton in one—not even that of a child. In reality the only way to contain most skeletons inside an ossuary would have been to cross the thighbones, which are the longest bones in the human body, diagonally across the ossuary. The logical place to put the skull would then be in the gap at the top of the crossed thighbones, as in figure 5.1 above.

Ossuary burials were the norm for a relatively short period in and around Jerusalem, primarily the first century, but they were never a part of burial traditions in the west of Europe. Because the symbol of the skull and crossbones played such an important part in Knights Templar grave iconography, it seems more than logical to suggest that they acquired it from the Middle East—and specifically in the Jordan Valley, close to Jerusalem. Could we assume that the symbol most likely arose from that first group of Templar knights who had been the first people in more than one thousand years to set foot in the tomb of Jesus and his family? It may sound like stretching credibility, but the evidence shows conclusively that the Templars were in Jerusalem to discover *something* and to bring it out of the Middle East. Hugues de Payens and his companions were descendants of the Merovingian bloodline. They may even have been the descendants of a particular form of early Christians known as Ebionites, a sect that was persecuted by Catholics for centuries because of its unorthodox views regarding Jesus as a mortal rather than a divine character. The subject of the Ebionites is dealt with in detail in Butler and Richie's *Rosslyn Revealed*.

If those first Templar knights did enter the Talpiot tomb, they could never have done so by pure chance. They went to the location because they *knew* where it was and also because they were aware what they would find there. To have done this during the time the Seljuk Turks occupied Jerusalem would have been impossible, as indeed would have been the case when the Egyptians were in charge. Only with the whole region secure under Christian rule could excavations of this sort take place. But this was no case of tomb robbery. The Templars in question obviously treated the place with reverential awe—even to the extent of three of their number, when their demise came, wishing their own skulls to be left guarding this holy place.

If acceptance of the validity of the Talpiot tomb is a problem to many Christians in the present era, this is nothing compared to the problems it would have caused nearly a thousand years ago. The first Templars existed at a time when the dogma and doctrine of the Catholic Church was written in stone. To suggest that Jesus did not ascend physically into heaven and that he was married and had at least one child would have represented heresy of the worst sort. The Christian scriptures, together with the writings of the early church fathers, were held as sacrosanct. Anyone deviating from the official line in the slightest way faced torture and death.

The official Christian line on Jesus's ascending bodily into heaven comes of course from the versions of the Christian Gospels that form the generally accepted Christian scriptures. Many people still do not realize that the Gospels in the Christian scriptures, upon which the church relies, are far from being the only documents dealing with the life and ministry of Jesus. It was not until the 1940s that caches of lost Gospels from the period of Jesus began to be discovered and recognized for what they truly were, not least at Nag Hammadi in Upper Egypt, where examples of the Gnostic Gospels were discovered. These are books about Jesus and his mission that were written as early as the second century CE, but the story they tell is often deeply at odds with the Christian scriptures upon which most Christians rely today.

What is particularly interesting about the Gnostic Gospels is that they are very early in composition. Anyone who assumes that what they read today in the authorized version of the Christian scriptures is an untouched version of the Gospels as they were originally written by Matthew, Mark, Luke, or John is laboring under a misapprehension. These Gospels have been pawed over, interpreted, reinterpreted, altered according to changing Christian dogma, and generally refashioned for many centuries. The authorized Gospels reflect much more what we are *expected* to accept than any genuine account of the life and times of Jesus.

While all the changes to the official Gospels were being made, the Gnostic Gospels, safe in a pottery jar in Upper Egypt, slept away the centuries in exactly the same condition as they were when they were created: without a single alteration of any sort. In other words, if we want to get a truthful view of the story of Jesus—as close to his own time as we will ever find— it is likely to be in the Gnostic Gospels and not the much altered and adulterated authorized versions.

One of the most obvious differences regarding the ministry and life of Jesus demonstrated by the Gnostic Gospels is the part played in the story by Mary Magdalene. On her ossuary at Talpiot she is referred to as "Mariamne Mara." The Mariamne component identifies her with the character known in the authorized Gospels as Mary Magdalene, but the word *Mara* is also very telling. It is Greek and means "teacher" or even "master." It shows this woman to have been of significant importance in her own right. Mariamne (or Mary Magdalene) is referred to in the Gnostic Gospels as the disciple Jesus loved the most. There is every reason to believe that she was his wife. In reality the idea that Jesus was celibate is little short of preposterous. No rabbi or teacher at this period would have been taken seriously if he were *not* married. It was the Jewish way and was absolutely expected of people in Jesus's position.

In 2012 a fragment of a papyrus known as the "Gospel of Jesus's Wife" was announced by a Harvard Divinity School historian, Karen L. King, and was immediately hotly contested. In her 2014 article, "Jesus said to them, 'My wife . . .': A New Coptic Papyrus Fragment," King describes how it is the only papyrus currently known in which Jesus is quoted as using the words "my wife." Additionally it says, "She will be able to be my disciple." Very recent tests have revealed that the ink and papyrus are very likely to be ancient. Of course the papyrus does not prove that Jesus was married but certainly leans in that direction. If the scholars can now move past the authenticity arguments, perhaps they can begin to discuss what this may mean to the true historical record.

What is quite obvious when a comparison is made between the Gnostic Gospels and the authorized versions we rely upon today is that a successful hatchet job was undertaken regarding the real ministry of Jesus in order to make sure that all trace of his female disciples as being credible teachers and ministers in their own right was utterly eradicated. There was absolutely no place in early or even later Catholicism for women, except through the heavily sanitized version of the Virgin Mary, who throughout the narrative of the Gospels is portrayed as a lackluster victim of events—with no significant intellect to speak of—and who is a person doomed to perform the role of a bit-part extra whose every move is determined by someone or something else. Meanwhile Christian doctrine, without any support from even the authorized Gospels, suggests that Mary Magdalene was a minor follower of Jesus at best and also a reformed prostitute.

Let us suppose for a moment that those first Templar knights were born from families that had retained knowledge of the true story of Jesus. Like many of the very early Christian sects that were ultimately rooted out and destroyed by developing Catholicism, they may have been fully aware that Jesus never claimed to be divine, except perhaps in a symbolic way. This would not necessarily detract in any way from an understanding and acceptance of the teachings of Jesus and his followers or diminish the reverence of the Templars for his story. Such a reverence would certainly extend to the physical remains of the holy family, but it would have been utterly certain that if they so much as whispered a word about either their knowledge or their discovery beyond their own inner circle, they were doomed.

It is unlikely that the first Templar knights spent nine long years in Jerusalem simply to locate the Talpiot tomb. Persistent rumors especially in terms of Masonic teachings and ritual indicate that they were also digging elsewhere. One fact we do know about Hugues de Payens and his colleagues is that they were given accommodation in the stables of the king's palace, on the Temple Mount in Jerusalem. In other words, they were sitting right on top of the ruins of the original Jerusalem temple.

It is surely not likely that these men simply dug holes indiscriminately in the hope of finding something of either value or religious significance. Having noted that the whole capture of Jerusalem was stage-managed by the Count of Troyes and bearing in mind that Hugues de Payens was a vassal and a relative of the count, it seems far more credible to assume that the first Templars *knew* what they were looking for and had a good idea where to find it. They had traveled to Jerusalem as soon as it was safe to do so in order to carry out specific investigations.

For decades speculation has been rife regarding what this supposed Templar treasure may have been. Some writers have suggested that the Templars were seeking the famed Ark of the Covenant. The ark was a wooden box covered with gold, supposedly containing the Ten Commandments Moses received from God. The Hebrews brought the ark with them out of their slavery in Egypt, and it accompanied them for forty years during their wanderings. Ultimately, the Ark of the Covenant took pride of place in the holy of holies in the Jerusalem temple when it was built by King Solomon. Subsequently the ark was lost to history, and it is fair to say that in one way or another people have been looking for it ever since.

The true significance of the Ark of the Covenant may be something quite different from its role as a holy container for God's laws. Judaism as we know it today is a relatively new thing. The Hebrew tribes that set up their first capital in Jerusalem were not as committed to a single, masculine deity as present circumstances in Judaism and Christianity may suggest. There is evidence from the Hebrew scriptures that King Solomon was not merely committed to the old storm god who was to become Jehovah but also to an extremely important female deity named Astoreth. Astoreth was simply a local name for a powerful goddess who was significant across the whole region, under a number of different names. It is not stretching credibility in the least to suggest that the sacred Ark of the Covenant, behind its veil in the holy of holies, was the place where those early Hebrews believed God and Goddess came together in a holy communion. The very existence of the concept of the Shekinah (something we will deal with presently) undoubtedly reflects this ancient belief. Astoreth may have disappeared as Judaism developed, but her feminine presence in the form of the Shekinah still remains.

The religion established by the patriarch Moses during the time the Hebrews wandered in the desert after their escape from Egypt bears a striking resemblance to a somewhat heretical belief that developed in Egypt itself in the same period. This was led by the pharaoh Akhenaton (also spelled Akhenaten), who briefly tried to create a monotheistic religion to replace the many gods and goddesses who had predominated in Egypt and to modify the Egyptian dependence on Ra, who was synonymous with the sun. In his book *Akhenaten to the Founding Fathers,* Scott Wolter has pointed out the similarities between what is known as Atenism and the religion that developed among the Hebrews. He suggests that Moses, who we know was raised by an Egyptian princess, was an advocate of this new religion. The inference is that both Judaism and ultimately Christianity owe a great deal to Egyptian religion, although Atenism was a short-lived affair and disappeared in Egypt when Akhenaton's reign was over.

This view has strong merits. The Ark of the Covenant, for example, was not a Hebrew invention. On the contrary, very similar arks existed throughout ancient Egyptian history, and some have been found among the grave goods of buried pharaohs. It is also a fact that the Hebrews (or rather the tribes that would become the Hebrews) had lived for generations in Egypt. It is highly unlikely that they would have escaped aspects of Egyptian religion, even though these appear to have been modified out of all recognition once the tribes occupied their new home in Judea.

Those mysterious nine years during which the proto-Templars were left to their own devices in and around Jerusalem are a closed book. Speculation is all that we have in trying to assess what they were doing there and why they remained silent for so long. Because it is certain that aspects of Templar beliefs eventually became enshrined in Freemasonry, many researchers have turned in that direction in order to better understand what the Templars may have been seeking and, indeed, what they probably found in Jerusalem.

We know that the ancient stories of Enoch mentioned in chapter 4 demonstrate that at the instruction of the mysterious Watchers, Enoch buried certain items on Mount Moriah, where the Jerusalem temple would one day stand. Masonic legend suggests that these items were found again by Solomon's workers when the foundations for the temple were being created. These same stories assert that Solomon reburied the treasures of Enoch below his new temple.

The Book of Enoch makes it obvious that knowledge was very

important to the patriarch, whomever he might actually have been. We are told that he created two pillars, carved onto which was the accumulated knowledge of the Watchers. Since so much of the Book of Enoch deals with calendars and astronomy, we can take it that the knowledge he committed to these supposed pillars was probably of a very practical nature. It has always seemed likely to Alan that the "pillars" were probably the distorted and misunderstood name given to scrolls, which may have been placed in cylindrical containers to protect them, as indeed was a regular practice. Was it this information that had the first Templars digging like moles on the Temple Mount, and did they actually find what they were looking for?

Events back in Troyes show that this may indeed have been the case. Troyes contained many schools and what we would today call universities. It was a place of high culture and, because of the Champagne Fairs, was a melting pot of people from across the known world and even beyond. Troyes had scholars and linguists, including a high proportion from the Jewish faith. Jews had been present and successful in the region of Champagne from the seventh century or even earlier. They had their own schools and religious leaders, and it is interesting to note that the Cistercian leader Bernard of Clairvaux on several occasions went to great lengths to protect Jews, not only in his native region but also in other parts of France.

It is likely that documents of any significance found by the first Templars in and around Jerusalem were shipped back to Troyes so that their contents could be translated and carefully examined. Added to the scrolls discovered below the temple could have been a wealth of other documents the Templars sought out in the bazaars and among the scholars of the area.

There were certainly technological breakthroughs taking place during this period and soon after. These might be reasonably explained in terms of the documents the Templars had discovered. The most important of these was probably the development of a new form of architecture, which, in the years after the Templars became an established order, spread across western Europe at a whirlwind pace. This type of architecture became somewhat erroneously known as Gothic, and it represented an absolute seed change, in fact a positive revolution in building techniques.

Prior to the twelfth century in Europe, major buildings such as cathedrals were built in a style known as Romanesque. This style of architecture relied on round arches, massive walls, and small window openings. Romanesque buildings stood the test of time primarily because so much masonry was used in their construction. Then, quite suddenly during the second decade of the twelfth century, something new occurred. Unlike Romanesque architecture the new Gothic style was based almost exclusively on pointed arches for windows, doors, and even for the vaulting. Walls became much thinner, windows were greatly enlarged, and many of the stresses of a given building were transferred outside, where they were dealt with by what were known as flying buttresses. The conspicuous differences between the squat, dark Romanesque structures and the much higher, lighter (and in our view far more elegant) Gothic buildings that replaced them are truly striking. It has been suggested that contact with Muslim architecture in the East was partly responsible for the arrival of Gothic architecture, but surely what had really changed is that designers of cathedrals and castles had begun to understand a great deal more about geometry and stresses. Gothic vaults and window and door shapes, together with flying buttresses, allowed the weight of a building to be more evenly distributed than in the case of the older Romanesque architecture. Gothic architecture is often referred to as sacred architecture. It was taught in the school of building in Chartres and was readily adopted by the Templars themselves, together with their sister order, the Cistercians. It was also adopted early by the Tironensians. We will probably never know whether the sudden arrival of Gothic architecture owed anything to information brought back by the Templars from Jerusalem, but it has to be considered a significant possibility.

Both the Templars and the Cistercians were innovative in all manner of other ways. Both groups were among the first to fully exploit mineral deposits on their lands, to establish mills, and to begin innovations in the smelting of metal. Their achievements in farming techniques and animal husbandry were astounding, while the internal administration of both organizations was revolutionary and ultimately inspirational to other sections of European society. Both the Templars and the Cistercians also rapidly became colossally rich. This was partly due to the clamor of supporters who wished to offer the orders money and land but also sprang out of a series of innovations the like of which had not been seen before.

From the outset the Knights Templar were deeply secretive, which was possible because there was no other organization that could inspect, sanction, or criticize their practices or plans.

Whatever Hugues de Payens and his colleagues did discover in and around Jerusalem was almost certainly brought, initially at least, to France and most likely specifically to Troyes. These finds could be kept safe behind the high, stout walls of any number of Templar commanderies and especially in Troyes, which remained the primary base of the Templars for well over one and a half centuries.

It would be of great interest to uncover what happened to these early Templar discoveries in the centuries that followed. If the intention had always been to create the New Jerusalem of the Book of Revelation, where was this planned to be? Was there actually anywhere in Europe that was safe enough to place the New Jerusalem and to re-create the "heretical" version of the story of Jesus, his wife Mary Magdalene, and his children?

Even more to the point, what did the Knights Templar and the movers and shakers in Champagne actually believe? Whatever it was, they kept extremely quiet about it. There are a few hints related to the accusations made against them in 1307, but the only real legatee of Templarism is Freemasonry. It seems likely that if we can discover what really lies inside the secret fraternity that still exists and that is available for us to examine, we may also come to understand what motivated the counts of Champagne, their followers, the Templars, and even the Cistercians. If a New Jerusalem was the ultimate objective for these people and the Freemasons that followed them, where did they intend it to be? The answers to these questions are breathtaking.

6

THE TEMPLAR-FREEMASON CONNECTION

There is absolutely no doubt that Freemasonry believes itself to be related to the Knights Templar. All over the world and in different branches of Freemasonry it is possible to become involved in degrees—which lie outside of the initial three degrees—that are named for and that deal with the Knights Templar.

Without writing yet another book on the topic, of which there are already many, perhaps the most important factor involved is this belief that Freemasonry and the Templars are related. Why would Freemasons claim to have associations with the Knights Templar if this was indeed not the case? At the time Freemasonry began to appear, the Knights Templar were simply a failed monastic order, destroyed centuries ago at the behest of a rapacious French monarch and his accomplice of a pope. We hear so much about the Knights Templar these days that it might seem as if they have been a source of intense fascination since their demise in the fourteenth century, but this is simply not the case. All the same, even though the Templars were once considered to be of little significance in the great tapestry of history, Freemasons for a considerable period of time have recognized that their own institution owed a great deal to this lost monastic order.

Alan has written and coauthored a number of books dealing specifically with the connections between Templarism and Freemasonry. Those who, for whatever reason, fail to recognize or acknowledge the connections are hardly likely to change their opinions any time soon. On the other hand, if we acknowledge that the association between the Templars and Freemasonry is real, we can probably learn a good deal about the less illuminated recesses of Templarism by looking closely at what genuinely lies at the heart of Freemasonry.

In particular we have shown how after their earliest period in Jerusalem the Templars brought back to Europe not only whatever tangible treasures they had found there but also a seed change in knowledge. The rise of Gothic architecture demonstrates that geometry especially was becoming far more important in western Europe, as was the study of mathematics and also astronomy. Therefore, it is probably not in the least surprising to learn that these topics lie at the very heart of Freemasonry; in fact, it is based solidly upon them.

Beyond this there can be little doubt that not all the charges of heresy brought against the Templars by the French king and his coconspirator of a pope were entirely without foundation. What evidence remains makes it clear that although the authorities charged with destroying the Templars failed to understand *exactly* what was wrong with Templar religious beliefs, they did differ significantly from the normal Catholic faith. It could well be the case that part of the reason the Catholic Church distrusted and perhaps even feared the Templars was because the Templars had been so willing to find commonality with believers from other faiths. The Templars were accused of making alliances with Muslims, and they had also been very tardy when it came to taking part in a later Crusade fought against a branch of Christian heretics known as the Albigensians. The simple fact is that the Knights Templar had good relations with all manner of people and did not make it their prime objective to convert those from different religious backgrounds.

None of this is remotely at odds with Freemasonry, membership of which is not restricted to Christians. It most definitely does not attempt to alter anyone's religious inclinations, and all believers in a deity of some sort are welcomed into its fold. Paradoxically this is not to suggest that Freemasonry fails to have its own religious imperatives. Despite the protestations of many of its members that Freemasonry has no specific religious core, anyone who has looked closely at the Craft must ultimately come to the conclusion that it most definitely does.

The important fact here is that only those Freemasons who decide to learn as much about the Craft as they can will ever encounter what lies at its core. For the vast majority of brothers, Freemasonry remains an interesting and sometimes useful social club based on good, sound, moral imperatives and a strong desire to do good in a wealth of different ways.

In all probability the same was true of Templarism. The Knights Templar eventually represented a huge, multinational institution. By far the majority of those who called themselves Templars were farmers, horse breeders, makers of armor, brewers of beer, shipbuilders, merchants, or civil servants. Only a small core of Templars represented the white-clad, red-cross-bearing warriors of fame and legend, and even many of these would have contented themselves with their lives as good, Christian monks. It is likely that the number of Templars that ever experienced or embraced the heretical beliefs that lay at the institution's heart was always very small. This is one reason why it was very difficult for the French and other European authorities to dig up any genuine evidence for the deviant practices of the Templar order after 1307. Most of those who lived as Templars had no idea what they were!

So, very few Templars had any idea of the secrets that lay at the core of their order, just as surely as only a very few Freemasons ever get to appreciate what all the ritual, allegory, and symbolism of the Craft really mean.

As with Templarism, Freemasonry was, until comparatively recently, only open to men. Despite this fact we have already seen that the very essence of Freemasonry leans in the direction of the sacred feminine. This aspect of Freemasonry is carefully hidden, but with the advent of the Grange movement, mentioned in the first two chapters of this book, it began to take a more prominent place and made itself obvious. We are entitled to ask where this bias originally came from. If we could also find it as an integral part of Templarism, the supposed connection between the two organizations would be appreciably strengthened.

In order to discover this we need look no further than to the region of Champagne at the same time as all the other plans of the Champagne counts were being put into action, immediately before and after the First Crusade.

COURTLY LOVE

Anyone who is interested in the stories that were precursors to those of King Arthur and his round table, and especially the Holy Grail, undoubtedly will have encountered a man by the name of Chrétien de Troyes. We know very little about Chrétien de Troyes except that he was living and working in the city of Troyes between 1160 and 1172. He was a poet and a writer of stories. His most famous work—and the one that started the age-old quest for the Holy Grail—was called *Perceval, the Story of the Grail,* and it remained unfinished at his death around 1172. It was dedicated to Marie of France, Countess of Champagne, who was the wife of Count Henry I of Champagne, who was an ancestor of Count Hugh of Champagne. Hugh was ultimately responsible for the creation of the Knights Templar, and he eventually became a member of the Templars.

What is particularly telling about Chrétien de Troyes' work is that it featured what was a relatively new concept. At the time this concept had no single name, but as recently as the nineteenth century it became known as "courtly love." The whole concept of courtly love seems to have developed in and around Champagne, and it created a veritable revolution in the perceived relationship between men and women. It can hardly be denied that feudal Europe was a heavily masculinized society in which women were not really expected to take any part except that allotted to them by men. There were exceptions, but in general even women of aristocratic birth were useful for the purpose of dynastic marriage and child-bearing and very little else. The concept and practice of courtly love changed this situation dramatically. With hindsight it appears that the introduction of courtly love was every bit as much an intended strategy on the part of the Champagne counts as were the First Crusade and the creation of the Champagne Fairs.

The essence of courtly love was the adoration of a particular woman—often one who was absolutely unobtainable by a man of knightly birth. The woman in question could be the wife of his lord or some other woman at court, but whomever she was, she became the single most important consideration in his life. This was a strange sort of love because it was frequently unrequited, and there were even occasions when the woman in question had no idea she was the target of some young knight's adoration. Courtly love may have been filled with sexual repression, but this rarely, if ever, manifested itself between the parties involved. These same young men would drop everything to go off on some quest at the behest of the lady in question, asking nothing in return and being willing to face any dangers simply because she had made the request—and even sometimes when she had not.

The importance of the appearance of courtly love cannot be overstated. It had a dramatic and tangible effect on the court of Champagne, and it soon spread far and wide to all the other aristocratic courts of Europe. The fact that the woman concerned was almost always unobtainable did nothing to quench the ardor of her suitor, and one gets the impression that what probably lay behind the whole, strange departure was the idolization of the feminine ideal. If that meant facing death, then so be it. This was definitely a form of worship, and the fact that there would never be any tangible, physical reward gave it an even more pseudo-religious flavor. Young men involved called the lady of their desires by the same name as they did those to whom they were vassals: literally, "my Lord."

One of the most interesting facts about courtly love is how much the Catholic Church disliked it. By the thirteenth century it was officially considered to be not merely inadvisable but actually heretical. Some scholars think the church saw in courtly love a form of sexual rebellion, but the whole situation probably went much deeper than this.

The church certainly took the situation very seriously, and any charge of heresy could result in execution.

Alongside courtly love the Champagne counts also helped to institute another form of feminine veneration that definitely did have a religious intent. This was the worship of the Virgin Mary, which also came close to being a heresy on occasions. Christian knights such as the Templars showed the same sort of devotion to the Virgin Mary as aristocratic knights did to their courtly would-be lovers. On many occasions the relationship of an individual to the Virgin Mary and the form his devotions took would probably be considered deeply odd by today's standards. One good example is that of Bernard of Clairvaux, the man who effectively took over the infant Cistercian order and made it his own vehicle. The reader will remember that Bernard was given his own monastery at Clairvaux, very close to Troyes, and that in the fullness of time he became undoubtedly the most powerful man in the Christianity of his day (see chapter 4).

Bernard's adoration of the Virgin Mary knew no bounds, and it all started with a most unusual encounter when he was a young priest. According to his own words, Bernard had been praying before a statue of the Virgin when she lifted her hand to her breast. Drops of milk then fell from her breast into Bernard's open mouth. From that moment on he committed himself exclusively to the Virgin Mary, and it was something he passed on. Although historians often point to the veneration the Knights Templar had for John the Baptist, in reality their patron was always the Virgin Mary. This was something they had inherited from their sister order, the Cistercians. St. Bernard of Clairvaux, the leading light of the Cistercian order at the time and the man who literally "invented" the Knights Templar, had an almost fanatical regard for the Virgin Mary and almost all Cistercian abbeys were named for her, as were many if not most Templar churches. It was the Virgin's name Templar knights shouted as they went into battle. This in itself is interesting because it sounds very similar to the actions of a knight enmeshed in the intricacies of courtly love. He too would cry the name of his amour as he embarked on some battle or quest. With regard to the Knights Templar we have to remember that in terms of their beliefs, practices, and behavior they were conforming to instructions specifically created for them by Bernard of Clairvaux.

The whole situation regarding this elevation of the feminine becomes even stranger when we learn about Bernard of Clairvaux's fascination with a particular book of the Hebrew scriptures: Solomon's Song of Songs. For many years Bernard pored over the Song of Songs, which is the most peculiar work imaginable to be included in the Bible. It is a distinctly poetical, very beautiful but also deeply erotic conversation between two individuals referred to as the Bride and the Bridegroom. According to Bernard's published letters and sermons on Song of Songs, he took it as representing the relationship between Jesus and his church, though we are sure that if our readers take the trouble to read Song of Songs they will be as puzzled as we are by this explanation.

We need to remember that the full name of the Knights Templar was the Poor Knights of Christ and the Temple of Solomon. When we also point out that almost everything associated with Freemasonry is in some way involved with Solomon and his temple, the connections between the Templars and Freemasonry begin to strengthen even more. In addition, so do the connections between Freemasonry and Bernard of Clairvaux, particularly since an open Bible forms a part of the adornments of a Masonic temple when it is being used. In many lodges this Bible lays open at the start of Solomon's Song of Songs.

The pertinent point here is that there was a clear object of worship in the sights of knights under the influence of courtly love and also of Templar knights who threw themselves into battle. In each case we find an unattainable feminine presence who, to those who learn the truth of the situation, is actually the Great Goddess, whose worship predominated among humanity for countless thousands of years.

This was an ingenious strategy because, for at least two centuries in the case of courtly love and a little longer with regard to the Knights Templar, it kept those involved away from accusations of heresy. Safe in the confines of their own communities Templar knights who proved themselves to be trustworthy would gradually achieve a higher status and at the same time would also be slowly introduced into what the Virgin Mary *actually* represented. With no such close-knit community available in the case of secular knights, a different strategy was necessary, which is one of the reasons why the Grail appeared.

The Grail, undeniably created in Champagne by Chrétien de Troyes, was a strange and enigmatic symbol. As its presence was taken up by subsequent writers, such as the German Wolfram von Eschenbach and the French Robert de Boron, the Grail took on different forms. However, no matter what the Grail was conceived as being, it served more or less the same objective in all cases. It represented the start of a quest to achieve spiritual awareness on the part of those who set out to discover it.

Eventually the Grail became universally recognized as the cup from the Christian Last Supper, and even Chrétien de Troyes may have intended the Grail to be a cup or chalice of some sort; we simply do not know. From a linguistic point of view the Grail sounds as though it was indeed intended to represent a vessel of some sort. The word probably derives from the old Catalan *gresal* meaning a pottery cup, but it is almost certainly associated also with the Latin *gradalis,* which itself ultimately derives from the earlier Greek *krater,* which was a vessel for wine.

Alan has believed for some time that at least part of the true intention of the Grail was astronomical in nature. In its form as *krater,* or the Latinized *crater,* the Grail is a small constellation of stars associated with the larger constellation of Virgo. The first-century writer and poet Marcus Manilius, while discussing the original meaning of some of the heavenly constellations, came close to the essence of the Grail as a Eucharist cup. He believed it was representative of the cup drunk at the festivals of the god Bacchus. These ceremonies, which in later times were thought of as being orgies, actually evolved as celebrations of new wine, a drink that was sacred to the god Bacchus. In his book *The Lost Light,* author Alvin Boyd Kuhn goes further and suggests that the bowl used in the celebrations was suggestive of a cluster of stars known as the Crater, which means "bowl," and was also linked with the later Grail.

The proximity of the small constellation Crater to Virgo undoubtedly plays a part in the reasons why it became associated with the blood of a slain harvest god. *Virgo* means "the virgin," and this particular constellation has always been associated with the Great Goddess of ancient times. In a wealth of Mystery religions it was believed that the god of the harvest had been conceived in a union of heaven and Earth (in practice most commonly the sun and the Earth) at the time of the winter solstice. After nine months the Goddess gave birth to the young god, in the form of nature's bounty at harvesttime. To partake of this bounty humanity had to effectively "kill" the god and consume his body in the form of cereal grain and his blood as wine. This transmutation was part of the literal mystery upon which these celebrations were based.

Commensurate with this belief, around harvesttime the constellation Crater can be seen to have inverted as it appears closer and closer to the horizon, symbolically becoming the vessel from which the Goddess pours her bounty onto the Earth. In the weeks that follow the wine of the harvest becomes drinkable, at the same time the sun grows weaker and weaker and the days shorten. By the time of the winter solstice, around December 21, the sun's journey south at dawn halts, and it resumes its journey north again; in effect the sun is reborn at the winter solstice and eventually regains its strength and potency during the spring and summer.

In all the ancient Mystery religions the god is constantly born and dies, while the Goddess is eternal, and in terms of what ancient peoples actually observed in the Northern Hemisphere this is understandable. In the summer and autumn the sun is vigorous; it stays in the sky for a large part of the day. As a result the weather is warm and life is easy. With the winter the sun is only present for a short part of each day. It lacks light and heat, and life becomes less pleasant. Winter was a time of want and of genuine misery, when death was more likely to visit most communities. In every real sense the Sky God was absent during the coldest months.

It seems self-evident that to those in the know the Grail at least partly represented the Goddess herself. Like all deities she was ever-present but unobtainable, something she shared in common with the amour of a knight in courtly love and with the Virgin Mary in the case of the Templars. Time and again in our research we have come across this sort of symbolism, which remains veiled to the uninitiated but reveals itself to those who have undergone the gradual education necessary for spiritual understanding. This constant nudging of society back to a more balanced view of the Godhead is not merely evident in the case of the Templars and Freemasonry. It also lay at the heart of another institution that appeared at the beginning of the seventeenth century and that, for a century or more, had great appeal.

The name of this religious and even social departure was Rosicrucianism. Right from the start there seems to be some association between it and Templarism because the supposed founder of the organization was named Christian Rosenkreuz. *Rosenkreuz* literally means "rosy cross" or "red cross," and of course readers will instantly be drawn to that famous emblem of the red cross that was carried on the tabards and shields of all Templar knights.

According to the legends of the Rosicrucians the doctrine began with its founder, Christian Rosenkreuz, who may or may not have been a real person. It was suggested that he had been born in the fifteenth century and that he was a doctor who had committed himself to the treatment of sick people, no matter what their wealth or circumstances. All religions develop an esoteric side, and the Rosicrucian movement can be seen as a mystical slant on Christianity—and yet when one looks at the doctrines of the organization closely, they deviate significantly from orthodox Christian teachings.

The Rosicrucian movement began with the appearance of three documents known as the *Rosicrucian Manifestos*. The first of the manifestos appeared in 1614, the next in 1615, and the third in 1616. In all probability the manifestos were actually written by a man named Johannes Valentinus Andreae (1586–1654), a renegade priest from Germany. It has been said that the Rosicrucian movement was a reaction against Catholicism and that it was essentially a Protestant institution, but whether or not this is the case, Rosicrucianism quite clearly carries doctrines that do not sit comfortably with either branch of Christianity.

Legend asserted that the probably mythical Christian Rosenkreuz had studied in the Middle East, that he had spent considerable time in Jerusalem, and that he had been inspired by an esoteric Muslim sect known as Sufism. Wherever it came from, the Rosicrucian movement soon gained ground across Europe and was especially strong in Germany, Holland, and eventually Britain. The best way to understand what Rosicrucianism was really about is to read the third of the manifestos, *The Chymical Wedding of Christian Rosenkreuz*. This is a fascinating document about a man's search for truth and spiritual liberation. It is filled with allegory and replete with alchemy, and in its form it closely resembles Chretien de Troyes' story of Percival and also many of the later Grail legends.

What stands out clearly in *The Chymical Wedding of Christian Rosenkreuz* is the presence of the feminine, not least of all because the hero's guide throughout large parts of the narrative is a beautiful woman. The goddess Venus also appears significantly as part of the plot. Although it might take a lifetime to truly understand what the essential message of *The Chymical Wedding of Christian Rosenkreuz* actually is, its association with courtly love and with an appreciation of the feminine within spirituality is undeniable.

The Rosicrucian movement became extremely popular, and it was the preferred religious slant of many of the first immigrants from western Europe to what would eventually become the United States. Parts of its doctrines have been embraced by some branches of Freemasonry, and it seems to parallel some of the less well-understood aspects of the Knights Templar.

What *The Chymical Wedding of Christian Rosenkreuz* shares with Freemasonry, and presumably with the mystical core of Templarism, is that it sees life as being a journey, the ultimate destination of which is spiritual and moral liberation but through an understanding of the feminine principles at work as part of the Godhead.

The first Rosicrucians and the earliest Freemasons who found a foothold on the coast of North America would have a profound bearing on the way the United States would develop. However, in terms of their ultimate aspirations and beliefs, they were not the first to reach the New World. There is extremely strong evidence that they had been preceded there by members of the Knights Templar order at a period long before Christopher Columbus was even a gleam in his great-grandfather's eye. What is more, it is now certain to us that the most accomplished and intelligent of the Knights Templar—the most esoterically inclined and trustworthy of the Freemasons and those who best understood the true ideals of the Rosicrucian movement—were members of another and as yet mysterious organization. Janet rightfully referred to these people as the foot soldiers of an ancient association that Scott Wolter first named and that we also have chosen to call the Venus Families.

7

THE KNIGHTS TEMPLAR AND THE VENUS FAMILIES

At dawn on Friday, October 13, 1307, the doors of all Knights Templar properties on French territory were opened to the forces of King Philip IV, either voluntarily or with the aid of a battering ram. This terrible morning was the beginning of the end of the officially sanctioned order of the Knights Templar, and the situation had come about as a result of the caprices of fate together with the greed of a cruel and avaricious king and his tool, Pope Clement V. The pope's birth name was Bertrand de Got, and he was a childhood friend of King Philip IV of France.

Philip despised the Templars for a number of different reasons. Sometime earlier he had sought honorary membership of the Templars and had been refused. It is likely that this incensed him, because other monarchs, such as England's Richard I, had been granted honorary Templar status. This might have been bad enough, but the fact was that Philip, like many other crowned heads of Europe, owed the Templars a fortune. They had made extensive loans to the French crown and at one time held the economy of the kingdom in their hands. Philip must have reasoned that if the lender disappears, then so does the debt. He was far from being alone in this situation, because most of his fellow kings and emperors were also deeply in debt to the Templar order, which had grown phenomenally rich.

On his own, Philip IV was not powerful enough to destroy the Templar order. They owed allegiance to no king, but they were directly responsible to the pope—in theory at least. Numerous historians have pointed out that in all probability Philip had the previous two popes killed and then used his power to force his own man onto the throne of the Vatican. European kings getting rid of inconvenient popes, though not routine, was far from extraordinary during the whole of the Middle Ages. Not content with this, he made Clement V move his headquarters from Rome to France just to make sure his ally would not betray him once he was beyond Philip's grip. Philip also had one other card up his sleeve—a circumstance delivered by fate but which in itself probably assured the Templars of a swift demise.

By the last quarter of the thirteenth century the office of the count of Champagne had passed into the holdings of the kings of Navarre. The last of these was Henry I of Navarre. Henry's only son had died in a tragic accident while still an infant, which left him with only a daughter, whose name was Joan. When Henry of Navarre died in 1274, his infant daughter became queen regent of Navarre and also countess of Champagne. This made little Joan very popular with kings and princes all over western Europe, and there was a definite lunge from several directions to secure Joan and also her vast estates. In desperation and fear, Joan's mother sought sanctuary and protection at the court of King Louis IX of France. It was a terrible mistake, because it soon led to young Joan being betrothed to Louis' eldest son, Philip, who in the fullness of time would become King Philip IV.

Even though he was Joan's husband, Philip could not get his hands on Champagne—a prize he clearly coveted. That title could only go to their eldest son, and until he came of age his mother, Joan, would rule in his place. So covetous was Philip with regard to the acquisition of Champagne, and of course Navarre, that more or less as soon as there were enough children from the marriage to satisfy his dynastic needs he either got very lucky or else found a way to get rid of Joan. She died in

1305, supposedly in childbirth, but it was rumored at the time and in our opinion is probably the case that she was poisoned by her husband. This would not have been at all out of character for Philip, who even by the standards of the age in which he lived was manipulating, calculating, and sadistic.

From this point on Philip had complete control over Champagne, because he was the regent there for his son, another Louis. Since the headquarters of the Knights Templar were and always had been in Troyes, Champagne, the Templars themselves must have realized their time had come to an end as soon as Joan of Navarre breathed her last.

It is a matter of observable fact that from the moment Champagne came into the hands of the French crown the place began to change dramatically. Within a few years the Champagne Fairs had lost many of their regular customers, and the cities of Champagne were soon shadows of their former selves. What had once been a shining star in Europe soon became a quiet, rural backwater. It seems as though everyone of consequence had relocated to other areas, especially the merchants, who now concentrated on the markets in Flanders and Italy.

If it had not been obvious to the Templars that their tenure in Champagne was now looking extremely precarious they could hardly have failed to realize it when Bertrand de Got became pope two months later. In truth the Templars were extremely astute and would have had spies in every European court. Philip was tyrannical but not intelligent and undoubtedly communicated his intentions well in advance.

To anyone who has studied the Templars in detail the idea that they were taken by surprise in October of 1307 seems fanciful. All the same, most Templar personnel found in France were imprisoned, including their Grand Master, Jacques de Molay. The Grand Master, along with other Templars, was tortured and not surprisingly admitted to the charges that had been brought against the Templar order. Most of the charges related to various heresies such as spitting on the crucifix, carnal relationships between brother knights, worshipping an idol, consorting with the enemies of Christianity, and cowardice.

A few years later when he discovered he would be imprisoned for life, Jacques de Molay recanted and made an impassioned attack on his accusers. Eventually he was slowly roasted to death over a charcoal fire near Notre Dame Cathedral in Paris. It is suggested that just prior to his burning Jacques de Molay called upon both Pope Clement and Philip IV to join him before God within a year to answer for their crimes. Strangely enough, before twelve months was up both had died.

The Templars were almost certainly the richest and most powerful institution of their day. Philip IV was not only anxious to rid himself of his own debt to them but also to get his hands on all their property and gold throughout his domains.

Philip had visited the Templar Church and commandery in Paris on many occasions; in fact he had lived there for a while in order to protect himself from the angry Parisian mob that wanted to tear him to pieces. The Templar Church is said to have been magnificent, with many impressive artworks and fabulous Flemish stained-glass windows. Philip would have taken in the opulence and seems to have assumed that somewhere in the depths of this building was a fortune in gold. Indeed this may have been the case—prior to 1307—but at the same time King Philip did not fully comprehend how the Templar organization functioned. It was rather like a modern, multinational company, and its assets were spread across every part of its trading empire. Medieval monarchs such as Philip were famous for keeping their wealth in huge chests at the very center of their most impregnable fortresses, but the Templars behaved in a very different way.

As an example: If a merchant from Paris wished to travel to Jerusalem, either on pilgrimage or more likely to involve himself in trade, it would have been both foolish and dangerous for him to take a great purse of gold on his journey. The roads were dangerous, and thieves were everywhere. But what could he do? He needed the money to complete his business. This is where the Templars cornered the market and built up their fantastic wealth. The merchant could go to the Templar headquarters in Paris and hand over his gold there. In exchange he would be given a note written in cipher. Even if this note were stolen it would be of no use to the thief because he would not be able to read the details and probably the passwords that the merchant would have to offer when presenting the note. Should the merchant by some misfortune lose the note he had been given, he could redeem his money later at the establishment where he had placed it.

Taking the note to Jerusalem he would hand it over at the Templar headquarters there. In exchange for the note he would be given his money in the local currency and could complete his transaction. According to Christian law at the time it was wrong and punishable for anyone to charge interest for such a service, but the Templars got around this by manipulating the exchange rate between one currency and another so they always got their cut for handling the transaction. They were, in effect, the first bankers who made it possible for money to be deposited in a Templar establishment in one city and then withdrawn in a different city or even another country—and all using nothing but a ciphered letter.

This meant that money was constantly flowing throughout the Templar area of influence, which was vast. They also loaned money—sometimes in huge amounts—so not everything the Templars owned in terms of wealth was ever immediately available. In this respect they were like a modern bank that could never pay back all the savings of its clients at one time. The Templars were behaving in a way that would seem totally natural in the modern age, but it was positively revolutionary at the time.

Much of the Templars' wealth also lay in their infrastructure. It is known that the Templars had a large fleet of ships because they were great transshippers of cargo, which they had the military might to protect. As far as France was concerned, most of the Templar ships were moored in their port of La Rochelle, on the French Atlantic coast. On Friday October 13, 1307, King Philip did not simply send his soldiers to all the Templar commanderies in France, he also sought to seize the Templar fleet at La Rochelle. He must have been incandescent with rage when he was told that the entire fleet of Templar ships had quietly slipped away the night before and were nowhere to be found.

As far as the gold was concerned, King Philip IV must have been very disappointed, because no great treasure was ever found. Anything of real value had clearly been removed from France before the October 1307 attack took place. Relocating their wealth must have presented the Templars with a significant problem, because the accusations brought against them were enforceable in every country that fell under the sway of Roman Catholicism. Virtually nowhere was safe—but there were exceptions.

Alan and the Canadian writer and researcher Stephen Dafoe pointed out in their book, *The Warriors and the Bankers,* that a significant amount of Templar gold could have been taken over the Alps to what would eventually become Switzerland. However, the Templars certainly could not sail their ships into the Alps. Some of them were sent south to Portugal, where they fell under the protection of the Portuguese king. Once in Portugal the Templars simply changed their name to the Knights of Christ and continued much as before. Meanwhile, items that were held sacred by the Templars more likely found their way to the remotest western part of Catholic Christianity: Scotland.

In 1306 the king of Scotland was Robert the Bruce. Primarily because he had killed an opponent on the altar of a church but mainly to please the English king, Edward I, Robert the Bruce was excommunicated by the pope, together with the whole of Scotland. This excommunication was not officially lifted until 1328, and during this period the Scottish monarch was not bound by any laws the pope might impose on the Catholic world.

Clearly this would have been of interest to the Templars once they began to realize that the writing was on the wall. They had enjoyed good relationships with successive Scottish kings, and the very remoteness of Scotland—especially its western parts—would have seemed attractive as places of refuge. The fact that the Scottish king was at odds with the pope and not subject to his commands would have made the country even more attractive to the Templars. They could approach Scotland from the western coast of Ireland without encountering the English navy, and they were likely to have been sending ships on this route on a regular basis, loaded with whatever they did not wish the French king to get his hands on.

The willingness of King Robert the Bruce to shelter at least some of the Templars during and after 1307 was not a one-sided affair. It is more than likely that the Templars assisted him in his ongoing battle against the old foe, England. Generally speaking the much larger England was gaining the upper hand against what it considered to be the renegade upstarts in Scotland, but all of this came to an end in 1314 with the Battle of Bannockburn in which the Scots routed an invading English army. In this strategic and quite brilliant victory Robert the Bruce was assisted by a contingency of unknown and unmarked knights whose decisive actions helped to win the day. It has always been rumored and is probably the case that these knights were former Templar knights who had taken refuge in Scotland. Not only would their presence have been of assistance to Robert the Bruce, but also they were buying themselves time because they were safe in Scotland as long as the country stayed out of the clutches of the English.

As we have already seen, some of the most significant of the Templar treasures had been hidden in Scotland for a protracted period before 1307, first in a series of Tironensian abbeys—culminating in Kilwinning—before finding their way to Rosslyn Chapel. Despite the fact that the Templars had almost certainly transported some of their most important artifacts to North America at a much earlier date, it is possible that some items did not leave Scotland for the United States until as late as the nineteenth century. All of this effort could only have been to one end: the abandonment of Europe and the establishing of the New Jerusalem in North America.

What has gradually become obvious during research spanning the past two decades is that the Templars, like the Freemasons, were ultimately responsive to a much less well-known but extremely long-lived group. We know this to be the case, because the very origination of the Knights Templar was part of a plan that had emerged in and around Champagne, as indeed was the Cistercian order. A whole skein of decisions and actions, starting in the eleventh century, went into the temporary possession of the Holy Land and in particular Jerusalem. The people who were ultimately responsible for the planning are those of the Venus Families. We gave them this name because in both a practical and a mythological sense the planet Venus had always been important to them, but pinning down where and when the Venus Families commenced is as good as impossible. Venus is also perhaps the best-known name of the Great Goddess. It is important to mention at this juncture that the group in question almost certainly does not refer to itself as the Venus Families. Its very nature is to remain silent and as anonymous as possible. In previous books that Alan has written and coauthored the same group has been called the Golden Thread and also the Star Families, but it was the continued importance to this group of the planet Venus and also Venus the goddess that ultimately caused Janet, Alan, and also Scott Wolter to adopt the name Venus Families. The Venus Families seem to have existed in one form or another since truly ancient times. Seeing the same beliefs and incentives cropping up at irregular periods throughout countless centuries, Alan Butler and Stephen Dafoe regularly referred to "the golden thread through the tapestry of time," which could be seen clearly among the normal background of historical events in their book, *The Warriors and the Bankers,* first published in 1998.

It is possible that the Venus Families gradually evolved from a number of different times and from different places, but there are certain facts about them that remain consistent. It is clear that no matter in what shape or form the Venus Families have appeared; they have retained a particular reverence for the feminine in religion. Through their various guises they have also stuck rigidly to a belief in the cycles of nature as being representative of the lives of people as espoused in virtually every one of the Mystery religions that were once so important to humanity.

Another distinguishing feature of the Venus Families is their absolute belief in self-determination and freedom. Wherever and whenever they have been evident, it has been with the ultimate objective of destroying feudal systems, dictatorships, and oligarchies. Organized religion also seems to be something that the Venus Families have always worked against, especially where that has meant the emergence of subjugation, the perpetuation of superstition, and the predominance of a powerful priesthood. On the other hand, since truly ancient times the Venus Families have shown a distinct reverence for astronomy and geometry, both as practical and sacred subjects.

As unlikely as it may appear, it seems that the Venus Families have perpetuated since extremely ancient times. They proved this once they began to build their New Jerusalem in North America, not least of all because they based the federal capital of Washington, D.C., on a measuring system that had been in use in Britain and parts of France before 2000 BCE and then disappeared from use until it reappeared in modern times. What we may never know is whether this knowledge remained in the Venus Families or, perhaps more likely, was rediscovered by the Templars as part of what they recovered in Jerusalem. This system of measurement, which Alan and Christopher Knight christened the "megalithic system," had been used to construct some of the most ancient and enigmatic structures, many hundreds of which still occupy the landscape of the British Isles and France—for example, the stone circle of Stonehenge and the extensive stone avenues of Carnac in Brittany, France. When these structures were created the most important deity to these truly ancient peoples was the Great Goddess. Alan and Chris found ample evidence to demonstrate that those who had built the megalithic wonders of the British Isles had been worshippers of this incredibly early and very pervasive deity. Her worship perpetuated among human beings for many thousands of years, prior to the rise of the much more recent paternal religions, such as Judaism, Christianity, and Islam. It is evident that through countless generations the Venus Families have retained this reverence for a supreme goddess.

During a research period that spans the past twenty years, those we now refer to as the Venus Families have also been called the Continuum and the Star Families. In other places and by other researchers and historians they have also been known as the Illuminati. Among their distinguishing features when their presence makes itself known is their interest in a New Jerusalem. The Venus Families also retain an interest in the patriarch Enoch and have endeavored to retrieve knowledge that dates back thousands of years.

Although the Venus Families have often used Christianity in its present form as a cover for their own individual beliefs, they by no means repudiate the story of Jesus. On the contrary, we have seen in chapter 5 how the Knights Templar rediscovered the Talpiot tomb, some of them leaving the skulls of their departed brothers to guard it while at the same time almost certainly removing relics from the ossuary of Jesus and his wife, Mary Magdalene. It is not the message of Jesus that the Venus Families repudiate but rather the power the organized church has had over its followers for the past two millennia. Jesus is viewed by the Venus Families as being representative of the dying and reborn god of all the Mystery religions, while his wife, Mary Magdalene, and possibly also his mother, Mary, are synonymous with the Great Goddess herself. Their teachings included a balance between the male and female, working in unison as they undoubtedly believed reflected the nature of God and Goddess. There is every evidence the Venus Families disbelieve the patriarchal version of the Jesus story that the Roman Christians manufactured.

One of the most famous Venus Family members we can definitely identify was Thomas Jefferson, an author of the American Declaration of Independence and third president of a free United States. Although Jefferson openly despised the despotic methods adopted over the centuries by the church, he was supremely moved by the ministry of Jesus. He even went as far as to create a revised version of the Christian scriptures from which he removed all the elements that related to superstition and dogma. This was a task that took him years to complete, which sounds a very strange occupation for someone who has been labeled an atheist.

Probably the most significant fact about the Venus Families is that generation after generation they remain incredibly patient. They clearly recognize that creating the idealized version of the New Jerusalem that is described in the Book of Revelation was never going to be something that could be achieved in a short amount of time. They have undoubtedly realized all along that their efforts would take centuries to mature.

The Venus Families have always been clever enough to either create the organizations they needed to further their aims or else to hijack ones that already existed. They have regularly infiltrated and manipulated the Catholic Church, for example, in the case of the Cistercian monastic order. Groups such as the Knights Templar and the Freemasons seem to have been built with the specific intention of espousing Venus Family beliefs and as a means of influencing society directly. This is not to suggest that the majority of those involved had or have any real idea of what lies behind the group to which they belong. The Templars, the Freemasons, Rosicrucians, and many other groups have provided the foot soldiers the Venus Families needed, but usually without appreciating the cause they were ultimately serving.

It is in the very nature of the Venus Families to remain in the shadows. There is probably a degree of heredity involved, but it also seems self-evident that new Venus Family members are sourced from very specific parts of the groups that they have created or co-opted. Sometimes Venus Family members briefly shine like the sun in the annals of history. This includes individuals such as Count Hugh of Champagne, Bernard of Clairvaux, Leonardo da Vinci, Sir Francis Bacon, George Washington, Thomas Jefferson, and Franklin D. Roosevelt, as well as many others. But in general those serving the Venus Families are harder to locate or to recognize.

One fact remains certain. When the Venus Families appreciated that the inequalities, corruption, and entrenched beliefs of Europe were never going to allow their ideal of a genuinely fair and equitable society to develop there, a decision was taken to look elsewhere. Probably from as early as the twelfth century the Venus Families were already looking far across the sea, in the direction of America.

It is also as good as certain that part of Venus Family belief centers on a continuing bloodline that goes right back to Jesus and Mary Magdalene. This bloodline was enshrined in the Merovingian dynasty of kings from the time of Clovis and has existed in secret since the Merovingians were replaced by the Carolingian dynasty of French kings. It is likely that a desire to preserve this bloodline was one of the major factors that led to the actions of the Champagne counts from as early as the eleventh century. Not all Venus Family members can trace their heritage to this unique genetic source, but recognition of its existence has been fundamental to Venus Family planning and actions.

8

THE KENSINGTON
RUNE STONE

In 1898 an immigrant farmer of Swedish origin by the name of Olof Ohman was clearing land on his farm near Kensington, Douglas County, Minnesota. Olof was a hard worker, a family man, and a no-nonsense farmer committed to building a better life for himself and his family in this new and developing country. For specific information about Olof Ohman we are grateful for the extensive work undertaken by Scott F. Wolter in his book *The Kensington Rune Stone: Compelling New Evidence.*

It was late in the year, and Ohman was clearing trees and stumps prior to plowing areas of his farm that had previously been inaccessible for growing food. The land in question was an eighty-acre lot that had formerly been in public domain, and now Ohman wanted to incorporate it into his gradually growing farm. Some of the land was wet, but there were slightly higher, drier areas, and it was on one of these drier areas that Ohman found, among the roots of a felled tree, a large inscribed stone. He could never have realized on that fateful day just how much controversy this discovery would cause, or how important it would come to be in terms of research into the Europeans who were early visitors to this part of North America.

Fig. 8.1. The medieval Kensington Rune Stone found in 1898 in
Minnesota by immigrant farmer Olof Ohman describes a journey
taken by a party of thirty Scandinavians far into the interior of
North America, on "acquisition business or taking up land" in 1362.
Photo courtesy of Scott F. Wolter

Ohman's find soon became known as the Kensington Rune Stone. It is roughly rectangular but somewhat irregular. It measures approximately 30 × 16 × 6 inches (76 × 41 × 15 cm). Almost at once his son noticed the markings carved onto its surface. Ohman at first believed that they had something to do with the indigenous people of the region. The stone was ultimately taken to the local town of Kensington, from where the stone received the name and was put on display. Once winter came, Ohman took the time to make a hand-drawn copy of the inscription on the stone, which by this time was recognized as being written in a runic alphabet that was Swedish.

Early interpretations of the writing suggested the following translation.

8 Gotlanders and 22 Northmen on [this?] acquisition journey from Vinland far to the west. We had a camp by two [shelters?] one day's journey north from this stone. We were fishing one day. After we came home, found 10 men red from blood and dead. Ave Maria save from evil. There are 10 men by the inland sea to look after our ships fourteen day's journey from this peninsula [or island]. Year 1362.

It did not take long for the rune stone's problems to begin. Many historical experts refused to take it seriously from the start. They reminded anyone who showed the remotest interest in the Kensington Rune Stone that it does not fit the mainstream historical time line. Something along the lines of: "History tells us that the first European to set foot in the Americas was Christopher Columbus. This happened in 1492; therefore, there were no Europeans in North America in 1362 and so the stone and its inscription has to be a fake."

It is our experience that academics are naturally cautious and conservative thinkers. For all manner of reasons they shy away from controversy. Nevertheless, during a significant period the Kensington Rune Stone was examined by archaeologists and linguists. A few accepted its validity, while many others came up with various reasons why it must be a fake or a hoax perpetrated by the farmer. Most of the objections to its validity were based on linguistic considerations, but what could not happen in those early days was a scientific examination of both the stones and the inscription from a purely physical point of view, at least not with the armory of technological devices and accumulated knowledge that is available today. However, as Scott Wolter pointed out in his book on the Kensington Rune Stone, the Minnesota state geologist, Newton Winchell, did examine the stone and declared it a genuine artifact based on the weathering of the inscription.* However, the scholars, historians, and the Minnesota Historical Society did not embrace his conclusion.

The Kensington Rune Stone eventually came into the possession of a museum in Alexandria, Minnesota, while arguments passed back and forth for decades, and no definitive consensus as to the stone's authenticity could be established. In a further attempt to establish the truth, in 2001 the museum approached Scott Wolter, who is a forensic geologist. Technology has come a long way since the end of the nineteenth century, and Scott Wolter would be in a position to look at the rune stone in a way it could not have been studied before.

From the outset Wolter was naturally skeptical and made it plain to the museum that his report would be based *entirely* on his forensic observations. In other words he might be able to prove definitively whether the Kensington Rune Stone was a hoax. Despite this he was told to proceed.

As Wolter described in his 2006 book, *The Kensington Rune Stone: Compelling New Evidence,* exhaustive tests followed. At this stage Wolter was not remotely interested in anything the inscriptions may or may not say. Rather he examined the stone itself and the marks that had been made on its surface from a mechanical and chemical standpoint and the degree of weathering of the marks.

Having established that the stone itself was of a local origin, Wolter then began to look at the individual letters carved into it. These stood out in a lighter color than the background stone itself, which seemed at

---

*Scott Wolter, *Kensington Rune Stone: Compelling New Evidence,* 413.

first to be an indication that they were of a fairly recent origin. However, when he examined the runes using a powerful microscope he could see that the shapes were constructed from V-shaped channels and that only the bottom of these trenches showed the lighter color that seemed so obvious with the naked eye. The V-shaped sides of the runes themselves looked undisturbed. This particular puzzle was solved when Wolter discovered that when the stone had first been found, Olof Ohman had carefully scraped along all the letters with a nail to better see what they might be and to clean out the dirt. This nail had scratched only the bottom of the grooves, leaving the sides of the V's untouched. The sides of the grooves showed heavy weathering and were of the same dark color as the stone itself, which would be virtually impossible to replicate fraudulently.

What Wolter needed now were comparisons. Having established that the stone was local, he looked around to find stones of the same type with carvings that were as comparatively old. These turned out to be tombstones that he located in Maine. The tombstones had a mineral composition and a grain size extremely similar to the Kensington Rune Stone. Just as helpful was the fact that the Maine tombstones had endured more or worse weathering than the rune stone. This was important because it allowed Wolter to analyze the weathering rates of this type of stone over a protracted period, and of course the dates on the tombstones gave him a very accurate time frame.

Wolter ultimately discovered that it took at least two centuries for specific minerals exposed by carving of the rock to begin to erode from the exposed surface of the rock. He had plenty of comparisons to work with and accurate dates for each, so he could be quite confident in the results. When he analyzed the grooves on the Kensington Rune Stone he discovered that the same minerals had disappeared altogether. There was no doubt that the minerals in question had been present in the V-shaped grooves when they were first made, so the fact that they were no longer present at all definitely pushed the carving of the rune stone back beyond two hundred years. Because the stone had been kept indoors since it was found, and bearing in mind that it was discovered in 1898, the inscriptions therefore had to date back to at least 1698. At that time only indigenous people and a few French fur trappers and explorers were present in the area where the rune stone had been found in Minnesota—in other words, nobody with the skill, the linguistic knowledge, or the incentive to create a hoax.

Later in 2001, Wolter was asked by the museum to explain his findings at an archaeological conference. Because the dating evidence was now irrefutable, he was happy to turn over the investigation to archaeologists and linguistic experts, but he was stunned at the reaction of at least half of those present: "Don't you know that the Kensington Rune Stone is a hoax?" It seemed incredible to him that nobody took up the baton and wanted to run with it. History said that no European had set foot in North America before Christopher Columbus in 1492 and no matter what Wolter had proved to the contrary, that was that.

Fig. 8.2. The enigmatic Hooked X character carved
twenty-two times on the Kensington Rune Stone and also
seen on four other rune stones found in North America
Photo courtesy of Scott F. Wolter

Being the type of man he is, this astonishing reaction made Scott Wolter all the more determined to continue the investigations himself, even though that meant traveling a great deal and also making himself an expert in disciplines far beyond his original remit as a forensic geologist. It was the start of an adventure for him that continues until the present time.

Wolter began to collect all the information he could regarding the Kensington Rune Stone that had been written in the past century. He studied this resource very carefully. He knew that the message on the stone was in Old Swedish, and he learned that some experts had declared it to be a hoax because some of the characters used were unknown in the runelogical record of Sweden. All the same, logic told Wolter that there had to be an explanation for this because the geology of the stone informed him that the inscription had to be extremely old.

Wolter took a total of seven trips to Scandinavia, where he talked with numerous experts as well as with members of Olof Ohman's family who still lived there, for verification regarding the integrity and character of the man who found the stone and also regarding family knowledge of the circumstances.

Ultimately, Wolter visited Gotland, where he was able to track down many of the runes that had been used on the Kensington stone. Talking with experts who had specific knowledge of Gotland, he learned that inscriptions in the region were datable as a result of something known as the Easter table. This was a table that the clergy used to determine when Easter would fall on any given year. Tombstones and church bells were often dated using this very medieval practice and, in fact, were often double dated, using numerals in Arabic placement as well, the way we use numbers today (tens, hundreds, thousands, and so forth). The year carved on the Kensington Rune Stone was 1362.

A great breakthrough was the discovery of the medieval use of a dotted *R* in Gotland. This same dotted *R* was present on the Kensington Rune Stone. No modern forger would have had knowledge of its existence, because it was not discovered anywhere in Sweden until after the Kensington Rune Stone was found.

During his investigations in Gotland it became obvious to Wolter that the only people there who would have been literate as early as the fourteenth century would have been those involved in a religious life— either the clergy or monks. This was a very important clue, because in conjunction with the use of the Easter tables, which was also the pre- rogative of those educated in the church, it showed that whoever carved the Kensington Rune Stone was likely to have been a monk, and the only monks in Gotland at that time were from the Cistercian order. The conclusion had to be that the runic inscription on the Kensington stone had been carved by a Cistercian monk who was present with a sizeable group of travelers from Northern Europe.

It remained to try to establish who this group of travelers—in the heartland of North America more than a century before Columbus— could have been and also what the purpose of the message on the rune stone actually was. Thanks to exhaustive research and consultations with those who knew a great deal about medieval Gotland inscriptions, Wolter and his coauthor Richard Nielsen were able to offer the most accurate interpretation of the message on the rune stone up to the pres- ent. It said, line by line:

> 8 Gotlanders and 22 Northmen upon this acquisition business from Vinland far to the west, we had camped by two shelters [?] one day's journey north from this stone. We were fishing one day. After we came home found 10 men red from blood and death. Ave Maria; Save from evil. [There] are 10 men by the inland sea to look after our ships. A fourteen-days' journey from this peninsula/island. Year 1362.*

With the latest interpretation of the message it became obvious to Wolter that the words on the rune stone represented a land claim. In other words, *someone* in the fourteenth century had been laying claim to land in North America—and in a very remote part of it. This could not have been some accidental visit by a crew blown off course and

---

*In the translation of the runes shown here the question mark represents an educated guess regarding specific runes, and the brackets denote a word added to allow the inscrip- tion to make sense in English.

hurled by storms across the Atlantic. The people concerned had come to this spot intentionally. But who could they have been? The possibilities were limited, particularly since they had with them at least one literate Cistercian monk, giving the impression of a deliberately planned expedition and probably not the first of its type.

Alongside the Kensington Rune Stone another puzzle had come to light that may or may not have had a bearing on the stone and its inscription. In the same region where the stone was found people had reported finding hand-pounded, triangular-shaped holes in large rocks spread across the landscape in an apparently haphazard way. Some locals believed that Viking sailors had visited the area in the remote past and that these holes had been used to hold metal pins to which the Viking boats had been moored. Being a geologist, Wolter was aware that water levels had not changed significantly in the area, and because many if not

Fig. 8.3. An example of a hand-pounded stone hole made
with a straight chisel. Notice the slightly triangular shape.
Photo courtesy of Scott F. Wolter

all of the stone holes were in places that had never been flooded, the boat-mooring theory clearly did not fit the circumstances.

As is often the case with this sort of puzzle, Scott and Janet Wolter put the matter on the back burner and concentrated on other things. One night Janet was suddenly roused from sleep by a realization. She shook poor Scott into wakefulness and announced excitedly, "The stone holes. It's sacred geometry!" She had realized the stone holes were more numerous around the rune stone discovery site.

It did not take long for Wolter to understand what she was saying. By this time he was certain that the Kensington Rune Stone represented a land claim on behalf of those who had carved it, but he had not yet figured out how a returning party would relocate it to exercise their claim. Perhaps the stone holes were the answer.

If the Kensington Rune Stone had been a land claim there was a good chance that it had been buried rather than having been stood upright as in the case of a tombstone. This was normal practice. Wolter's analysis of the stone had shown this to be the case, because stone underground weathers at a different rate to stone above ground. In other words, if the stone had been set upright there ought to be two areas of different weathering, making a "ground line," and there was not. In addition the physical location of where the stone was found was indicative of a land claim. It became the habit of those exploring this huge part of North America to place land claims near the headwaters of rivers. In this way all the land associated with a particular river's drainage basin could be claimed as well as the river and all its tributaries. The Kensington Rune Stone was associated with three drainage basins, the Red River of the North, the Mississippi River, and the western edge of the Great Lakes watershed, all originating there in the center of the continent in what is now Minnesota. A land claim placed here would result in a claim for about half the North American continent. Suddenly, a party coming all the way here to this remote area did not seem so strange after all.

All the same, this was virgin territory with few natural, enduring landmarks. If the stone had been buried so that it was not visible, how on earth would those who made the land claim ever be able to find it again? Could the answer be that they used geometry to make the stone holes, which are still evident, in the area that are such a puzzle? Perhaps something was placed in the holes, but more probably not. Finding the Kensington Rune Stone would be reliant on those who knew the pattern that the stone holes formed, probably across a significantly large area. Discovering the position of one stone hole would lead to its companions and then eventually to the rune stone.

Scott and Janet already knew that there was one group of likely candidates who had practiced this sort of tight, geometrical placing of objects. The authors Erling Haagensen and Henry Lincoln had written a book titled *The Templar's Secret Island* in which they had demonstrated that the Knights Templar had placed churches across the island of Bornholm in the Baltic Sea with unerring geographical and geometrical skill. The area covered was large, but the sacred geometric patterns created by the positioning of the churches were incredible. Irrespective of the meaning of the patterns, the work of Haagensen and Lincoln showed the Templars to have been peerless surveyors and great mathematicians.

It began to look more and more likely that those who had left both the Kensington Rune Stone and the triangular stone holes were members of the Knights Templar. Not only had sacred geometry been used to mark the position of the Kensington Rune Stone, but the Templars had always had a close relationship with the Cistercian order of monks, and all the evidence suggested that a Cistercian monk had carved the runes. Additionally, it also became apparent that what the rune stone did *not* say was indicative of the Templar order. The claim was *not* made in the name of a particular monarch. The only Europeans not under the fealty of a monarch in the feudalistic system were the Templars and their brothers, the Cistercians. One more feature found in the Kensington Rune Stone inscription was the use of codes, something the Templars had become masters of. A series of unusual punch marks and strokes on certain characters led Wolter to a dating code, which, when used in conjunction with the Easter table, confirmed the date 1362, already carved on the stone. It was an ingenious way to protect the date from alteration, the most important thing on a land claim.

But would such visitors be likely or possible? Although the Templars had been officially disbanded by the pope in 1312, we have already seen that in many different ways this had certainly not ended the order. All the pope and Philip IV had managed to do was to cut off the head of a hydra. The Templars were so deeply enmeshed in society across such a vast area it would have been impossible for them to be entirely destroyed. In Portugal they had simply changed their name to the Knights of Christ, and there were plenty of dark corners on the edges of Europe where Templars could have continued to function.

It is known that until 1307 the Templars were definitely looking for a place to call their own. One of the rumors that had worried Philip IV so much was that the Templar order was thinking of creating its own domains in southern France, and Philip would most certainly not have wanted them as a neighbor. However, experience had proved that western Europe was not a good place for the Templars to be, and it is entirely likely that they had been familiar with the New World for a protracted period of time prior to their official demise. Had this been earmarked as their new home?

The Templars were the best sailors of their day and had drawn their captains and crews heavily from the people of Scandinavia, who themselves are now recognized as having visited North America on a number of occasions. The Norsemen were adept at navigating by the stars and at land-hopping across the Atlantic via Iceland and Greenland. Neither is there any real doubt that the Templars knew about North America, even back in the days when they were a legal, monastic order. One of their chief ports on the west coast of England was Bristol, where even the fishermen knew of the continent to the west long before the time of Columbus. Fishing vessels from Bristol were fishing the Grand Banks off Canada for cod probably back in the thirteenth century or earlier.

The fact that none of this is well represented in the historical records is hardly surprising. Even in modern times nobody is anxious to kill a goose that is laying golden eggs. Rumors that the Templars were bringing silver out of America are legion, but as secretive as they always were there wasn't much chance they were going to make this fact known and thereby open up the routes they were using to the avaricious crowned heads of Europe.

Even when Christopher Columbus made his own famous voyage in 1492 it is plain he was not setting out on the sort of speculative voyage generally reported to schoolchildren even today. He sailed on three ships with red crosses on their sails. His father-in-law had been a Grand Master of the Knights of Christ (the Templars by a different name), and he was using charts that already existed and that he had secured from his wife's father and other sources. Columbus was in on the secret, which, in fact, was not so great a secret in any case by the time of his voyage.

Scott Wolter became an expert in his own right on the Kensington Rune Stone; he eventually uncovered other facts from this marked stone and others found in various parts of North America along with a very unusual eight-columned stone tower in Newport, Rhode Island: all indicating the same story. Europeans had come and gone for a considerable period—to trade in precious metals and other commodities that were deemed valuable back in Europe. And foremost among these visitors had been the Knights Templar.

Anyone doubting these assertions should read *The Hooked X: Key to the Secret of North America* and *From Akhenaten to the Founding Fathers: The Mysteries of the Hooked X*. They might also choose to obtain and watch all the excellent documentaries in which Scott Wolter has been the host. These appear under the titles *America Unearthed* and *Pirate Treasure of the Knights Templar* on the H2 and History networks. It was from appearances on *America Unearthed* that led to the meeting between Alan and Janet, which ultimately led to the research and writing of this book.

Further information regarding Templar activities in North America have been forthcoming from what at first might seem to be a very unlikely source. Scott and Janet established strong bonds with elders from some of the indigenous American tribes that have occupied large areas of the continent in the North and West. Although these people have been reticent in the past to say much about the situation, they know only too well that the Templars were there and that they established good relations with the local people—even to the extent of intermarriage. Aspects of Templar beliefs and practices are safeguarded among those whose business it is to keep tribal history, and there are ceremonies still practiced that reflect the relationships that developed in those far-off days. There is a high degree of secrecy relating to aspects of Algonquin practices that are not for the eyes of outsiders, but Scott and Janet have been in a privileged position and there are discussions of these topics in Scott's books, as mentioned previously.

When Thomas Jefferson became the third president of a free United States (in office 1801–1809) he showed a great interest in the vastness of the continent that lay beyond the borders of the thirteen original states. The new republic was able to purchase a vast area of land from the Napoleonic government of France, which became known as the Louisiana Purchase. This took place in 1803. Almost immediately Jefferson dispatched his personal secretary—a man by the name of Meriwether Lewis—along with William Clark to lead an expedition into the newly acquired area and to discover all they could about the tribes living there and the nature of the land.

Many aspects of the Lewis and Clark expedition are shrouded in mystery. Lewis's journal of their travels and discoveries is missing a number of pages or else falls silent at significant points in the narrative. It is likely that the expedition had orders from Thomas Jefferson that were never published and that one of their objectives was to search for particular "objects of a durable kind" and to make contact with specific tribes with whom the Templars had formerly enjoyed good relations. One such tribe was the Mandan; they had formerly lived farther east, on the St. Lawrence River. Before the Lewis and Clark Expedition the Mandan had migrated up the Missouri River. Because of earlier outbreaks of smallpox, the Mandan were much reduced in numbers by the time Lewis and Clark encountered them, but they were still different from other tribes in the area.

There had been little if any contact between the Mandan and Europeans around the time Lewis and Clark overwintered with them, yet it was reported that many members of the tribe were fair skinned. Some had blond hair, and blue or gray eyes were common. The Mandan were predominantly farmers but also hunted buffalo. One of the strangest aspects of these people is that they appeared to understand a significant number of Welsh words. It was suggested that they had been much affected by the arrival in their midst of Prince Madoc of Wales, who legends said made two expeditions to North America, the first of which was around 1170.

No such character is listed in historical documents in Wales for the relevant period, and there is some doubt as to whether such a person ever existed. However, that does not necessarily mean that the voyages never happened. The Knights Templar was officially sanctioned as a fighting monastic order in 1129, at which time it began to grow very rapidly. It is known that by 1145 the Templars had extensive properties in Bristol, which is an important seaport in the west of England. Bristol is located just across the Bristol Channel from South Wales, and it is likely that the growing Templar settlement at Bristol was staffed, in part at least, by men of Welsh origin. The Templars also had a commandery on the River Usk, not far from Bristol, at a place now called Kerneys Commander. It is more than feasible that Welsh Templars from this location staffed the new Templar port of Bristol.

Although it is somewhat unlikely that an expedition to the New World could have been staged by a Welsh prince—at least not without having a greater degree of evidence left in the historical record—the same would not be true of such a voyage undertaken by Templars. From the very start the Templar order was shrouded in mystery, and because their ships would have been coming and going to and from Bristol all the time it would have been an ideal starting point for such a venture, which could have been kept entirely under wraps.

We will never know what Lewis and Clark told President Jefferson in private concerning the Mandan, although they had certainly spent enough time with the tribe to learn anything they might want to know.

The Mandan had originally lived on the St. Lawrence River, and this would undoubtedly have been the place where the Templars from Bristol would have come into contact with them. Over time this tribe and many others had migrated farther and farther west, which was why by the time they were encountered by Lewis and Clark they were living on the Knife River, a tributary of the Missouri River in North Dakota.

The question arises as to why the Knights Templar should have wanted to visit the New World in the first place. This would not be hard to answer. In the first place the Templars soon amassed a sizeable fleet of ships. They were not simply in the business of being a holy army; they were bankers, shippers, and traders. From early in their history Templars could be found as far east as Constantinople or the Black Sea. They made it their business to obtain state-of-the-art technology, including the latest in navigational aids, and they had staff from the best seafaring nations that Europe could offer. The Templars would have followed up on any potential business opportunity that presented itself, and if they had learned of America from fishermen in Bristol, it would not be in the least surprising for them to set out and travel there themselves. The important thing is that they would never have divulged the fact to any of the rulers of the countries from where they drew their strength and resources. To do so would have been commercial suicide.

Perhaps right from the start the Templars, or more to the point the Venus Families they ultimately served, were looking for the New Jerusalem or at least a place where they could build it. The Templars lived from start to finish in precarious times, and in any case they were part of an agenda that had begun in Champagne, which was always under threat of being invaded by France. The most precious of the objects and scrolls that the first Templars found in and around Jerusalem were doubtless brought to Scotland, but even that remote country would eventually not be far enough away from the avaricious thrones of western Europe and from the jealous Catholic Church. It may be no coincidence that the west of Scotland faces out across the Atlantic, in the direction of the New World. Anything precious that was in Scotland could be moved out quickly and transshipped across the Atlantic. It seems that when things began to get difficult, this is exactly what happened.

In 1999, while at a conference in Nova Scotia, Scott Wolter met a Canadian writer and researcher named William Mann, who subsequently became a good friend. Bill (as he is generally known) has a unique perspective on life: on the one hand he is a high-ranking Freemason, as many of his family have been, but he also has Algonquin blood and is very familiar with the history, culture, and practices of his people.

Mann has written extensively, both fiction and nonfiction, about pre-Columbian North America and has been able to demonstrate Templar influence there from a number of different perspectives.* Perhaps most persuasive is the anthropological evidence. Mann was in a unique position to demonstrate just how closely related are some of the ritual practices of the Algonquin with aspects of Masonic knowledge and ritual that were themselves derived from Templarism. He is also keenly aware of the oral traditions of his people, which speak about the associations the tribe had with the Knights Templar, long before Christopher Columbus made his famous journey to the New World.

Bill Mann claims that the Knights Templar were in possession of information that had made them peerless navigators; this information having been derived from ancient sources. In his books he demonstrates a series of longitudinal meridians that he claims were known and followed long before the time of Jesus. These, he asserts, were used by a number of different seafaring peoples in their voyages, including the Phoenicians, the Minoans from Crete, the Carthaginians, the Greeks, and the Romans. One inference of this is that visitors to the New World had been coming and going for a very long time, and because the Templars were in possession of this navigational understanding, it is not surprising that they also traveled there.

Bill Mann suggests that for three hundred years, between 1150 and 1450, Templars regularly visited North America, usually from their

---

*Mann's books include *The Knights Templar in the New World: How Henry Sinclair Brought the Grail to Acadia, The Templar Meridians: The Secret Mapping of the New World,* and *The 13th Pillar.*

main port on the French Atlantic coast at La Rochelle. Further to this, Mann asserts that the trade that took place between the Templars and the indigenous population of North America was cemented by strategic intermarriages and that the Templars passed a great deal of information to the indigenous people, including aspects of the unique religious perspectives held within Templarism.

The original Templar points of contact with the locals, which were close to the East Coast, eventually became known to others, particularly representatives of the Catholic Church. As a result the Templars, who by now were an illegal organization, moved their base of operations farther inland, following the same meridians that had allowed them to become such accomplished sailors.

A good deal of the information Bill Mann possesses regarding the interactions of the Templars and the Algonquin is set out in his novel, *The 13th Pillar,* which is not only a fascinating story but also a very informative book. Scott Wolter drew from Mann the confession that part of the reason he chose to place this information in a novel was because of his high-ranking Masonic status. No matter what researchers such as ourselves may draw from the book, Bill Mann is always in the position of claiming it is a work of fiction.

Bill points out that many of the spiritual and physical elements of the Native Mide'win, or the Great Medicine Society can actually be found within modern Masonic-Templar rituals. Because these go back to a time long before modern Freemasonry could have touched the indigenous people, they can be traced back to the original interaction between the Templars and the tribes. In addition the Algonquin know that many of the most important of the Templar's treasures were brought to the New World and were hidden at specific, ritually important places on the meridians used by the Templars.

Much of the relevant information regarding the interactions of the Templars and the indigenous population of North America, with whom they had such good relations, is itemized in Scott Wolter's book *Akhenaten to the Founding Fathers.* What is important about Bill Mann's observations from our point of view is that they coincide perfectly with what was happening in Europe during the same period. They mesh particularly well with our observation that the first Templar visits to North America took place during the second half of the twelfth century and our conviction that some or all of what the Templars brought back from Jerusalem and the area surrounding it was eventually transshipped to North America. We will explain in due course where many of the Templar treasures found their final home.

9

SIR FRANCIS BACON'S
NEW ATLANTIS

By now it has become obvious that North America had been visited by Europeans for a very long period of time. Exciting revelations such as those provided by the Kensington Rune Stone and also the observations of Bill Mann regarding the Knights Templar and indigenous peoples in the Americas painted a picture of a place awash with travelers. The fact that all of this is not better known is partly due to the fact that many of the early visitors, such as the Templars, had a vested interest in keeping quiet about their travels to the New World. It is also a response to the unwillingness of orthodox historians to accept any alternative to the Christopher Columbus view, even when faced with overwhelming evidence to the contrary. We have lost track of the endless range of pre-Columbus European artifacts found on American soil that have found their way into the Smithsonian and other museums, never to be seen again. In something akin to a paradox it seems to be a fact that historians in particular do not like change.

This is an unfortunate state of affairs, but as far as the Venus Families and their exploits are concerned it is not a disaster; significant historical evidence of the Venus Families' existence and influence has been just as strong since the accepted visits to North America began.

The first *official* visit of a British expedition to the New World took place in 1497 and was led by a captain of Genoese origin. The anglicized version of his name is John Cabot, but his real name was probably Giovanni Caboto. Among a number of other ventures, Cabot had been involved in sailing merchant craft into the eastern Mediterranean, and he also claimed to have been in the Middle East, where he suggested he had visited Mecca.

Cabot arrived in England in 1495 with the express intention of leading an expedition to find new land west of England and across the Atlantic. Although he received permission from King Henry VII of England to fly the English flag and sail in the name of England, Cabot seems to have been sponsored from mainly private sources. Some of the money he needed came from Italian bankers in London, but it is likely that his primary backers were wealthy merchants from Bristol. It was from Bristol that Cabot set sail. This is probably not surprising since people from the port had known for a long time about the large landmass across the sea. The Bristol merchants who accompanied Cabot were particularly interested in what they called "brazilwood," from which a precious red dye could be obtained. The name of this wood related to the general name used for the New World, which was "Hy-Brasil." The reader will note, as do we, that hardheaded merchants would hardly lay out good money and risk a lengthy sea voyage in order to obtain something as specific as a source of red dye unless they knew it actually existed. It appears that brazilwood had been brought to Bristol at an earlier time than Cabot, but it was said that Bristol sailors had forgotten how to find the mysterious land of Hy-Brasil. (The country now known as Brazil got its name from brazilwood, because that was the place where the tree in question grew most readily.)

Only one ship took part in Cabot's first expedition; it was named the *Matthew,* and it arrived in America on June 24, 1497. Exactly where the *Matthew* landed is open to argument, but it is likely to have been Newfoundland, though some have argued that it was actually Nova Scotia or even the coast of Maine. According to later accounts, Cabot went ashore only to take on fresh water, and no contact was made with local people.

On his return, John Cabot went straight to see the king, who granted him a pension of £20 per year, which was a considerable sum at the time. It was reported that he was treated as a hero, that he was high in the estimation of the king, and that he went around London dressed in silk. All of this sounds very odd for a man who had embarked on a voyage that actually achieved nothing. Even odder is the fact that Henry VII was willing to substantially finance a second voyage with Cabot in charge, this time with five ships. The flotilla departed at the beginning of May 1498 and apparently simply disappeared from history. One of Cabot's ships had to turn back and dock in Ireland for repairs, and it was thought that the other four must have been destroyed in storms.

One odd fact relating to this voyage is that a man who was listed as being with Cabot, one Lancelot Thirkill, is recorded as living in London in the year 1500. In addition, evidence has recently been found that suggests Cabot's second expedition did return—after a two-year voyage—sailing down the East Coast of North America. Unless further documents come to light it is unlikely that the truth will ever be known. But it is certain that Cabot's son, Sebastian, also led an expedition to North America, specifically to search for the Northwest Passage. Many modern researchers accept that Cabot did return from the second voyage. The mere fact that he set out with five ships surely demonstrates that he intended to come back with a sizeable cargo. All in all it seems there were secrets associated with Cabot's voyages that have never fully come to light. Once again, vested interest and secrecy were almost certainly the reasons for the silence.

From this point on there was no longer any secrecy regarding America, and numerous voyages began, undertaken by the English, the Spanish, the Portuguese, and the French. During the following century various colonies appeared across the Americas, some of which were successful and others of which fared badly. Life for those who chose to try their luck in the New World was initially very hard. Many British who undertook the journey did so for religious reasons—trying to get away from oppression—because they belonged to Christian minorities that were not well tolerated by the Church of England. Few of these people were farmers, and on more than one occasion an embryonic settlement either failed entirely or survived only because of the generosity of the indigenous population.

It is likely that the *real* father of an English-speaking United States was Sir Francis Bacon, a truly extraordinary man who was a statesman, a scientist, a writer, a philosopher, and almost certainly a member of the Venus Families.

Bacon was born in London in 1561 into a good family. He was the nephew of William Cecil, the first Baron Burghley, who had been first minister to Queen Elizabeth I and probably the most important man in England during her reign. Bacon was privately educated and then entered Trinity College, Cambridge, while still only twelve years old, before going on to study at the University of Poitiers in France. After that he studied law at Gray's Inn in London before setting off to the Continent again, partly to learn about statecraft, certainly as a royal courier, and undoubtedly also as a spy.

Francis Bacon was an extraordinary man. He was deeply intelligent and a humanitarian. In matters of religion Bacon was certainly not run-of-the-mill. He would undoubtedly have prospered better if he had fully supported the Church of England, but he showed a great regard for Puritanism—even though he was never actually a Puritan himself. Like all Venus Family members we have encountered he was staunchly opposed to feudal privileges, and he had no respect whatsoever for dictatorial powers, either in the state or the church.

It is evident that Francis Bacon was a man of conscience. There was more than one occasion in which his sense of fair play got in the way of his elevation. He was a member of Parliament on several occasions but did not succeed in achieving the office of the attorney general in 1594 because his opposition to certain acts of Parliament had upset Queen Elizabeth. As a judge he was noted as being a man of compassion and utterly free from malice.

Bacon's chief problem in life was that he had become enmeshed in debts early in life and struggled to remedy the situation as time went on. He did eventually become attorney general and then lord chancellor, but in 1621 he was briefly thrown into prison for debt, and he was accused of corruption, mainly as a result of political infighting in the court of King James I. Bacon was released after a few days by the personal intervention of the king, but his reputation was irretrievably damaged.

During his time in public office Bacon worked strenuously on behalf of the fledgling English-speaking colonies in North America and was instrumental in founding some of them. He was particularly committed to Virginia and in fact played such an important part in encouraging and supporting the colonies in general that he has been described as one of the fathers of the United States.

In some ways Francis Bacon came closer to disclosing his Venus Family credentials to the world than others have. This is because of a story he wrote, titled *The New Atlantis*. This work was first printed in English in 1627, shortly after Bacon's death, and has been described as a utopian novel. It deals with the finding of an isolated island in the Pacific that is called Bensalem. Those who find the island have only done so because the inhabitants of the place have allowed themselves to be discovered. The narrative tells us that Bensalem is an enchanted place, which is never located by chance, and which has deliberately kept itself separate from the world.

At the heart of Bensalem is an institution known as Salomon's House, which functions in many ways like a modern university. Those who are employed in Salomon's House do not govern Bensalem, but it is made obvious in the plot that they have a very strong influence upon it. Scientific study and methodology are the paramount virtues of Salomon's House, which is described in detail.

Not surprisingly (because of the age in which he lived and *where* he lived) Bacon suggests that most of the inhabitants of Bensalem are Christians, having learned about the Bible as a result of the intervention of St. Bartholomew, one of the original disciples of Jesus. However, Bacon also makes it plain that there are people of all races and beliefs who dwell as absolute equals on Bensalem. Bacon explains at length that Bensalem is a place of fairness, equality, piety, and public spirit. Bensalem sends out ships to all parts of the world in order to learn as much as possible about advances in science and about humanity in general, but it always does so using ships that carry the flags of other nations and never divulges its own existence. In other words, Bensalem interacts with the wider world but never betrays itself. Under most circumstances the entire island of Bensalem is invisible.

The significance of *The New Atlantis* cannot be understated. It had a profound bearing on the thoughts and actions of Thomas Jefferson, who suggested that Francis Bacon was one of the three most important influences on his life. It is also suggested that the book ultimately led to changes in equality of the sexes—despite the fact that the subject is not mentioned directly. The book also seems to have been significant in the struggle that led to the ultimate abolition of slavery.

In some ways the story is reminiscent of *The Chymical Wedding of Christian Rosenkreutz,* though Bacon abandons the strictly alchemical nature of the Chymical Wedding in favor of a more modern approach to science. The name of Salomon's House is clearly a reference to King Solomon (in fact Bacon states that this is the case), who was deeply important to the Knights Templar and ultimately to Freemasonry. Whether Bacon himself was associated with either organization cannot be ascertained, but as we have said repeatedly, institutions such as Templarism and Freemasonry were the servants of something much deeper but infinitely more secret—which is what the whole topic of Bensalem suggests.

It is not surprising that Christianity is mentioned in conjunction with Bacon's Bensalem, because at the time he wrote the work he occupied a significant role in the English government. He had to uphold the values of his nation in anything that was intended for publication. In the story he suggests that knowledge of the Bible came to the island in a wooden ark that appeared in a pillar of light. This was supposed to have happened around 100 CE, but the ark also mysteriously contained books of the Bible that had not been written at that time. The Book of Revelation is prominent among these.

The New Atlantis is filled with thinly veiled allegory, and Bensalem itself is undoubtedly a description of the Venus Families. Like the island, they existed (and still exist) out of sight of the world at large but could interact with it "under the flags of other nations," as Bacon puts it; in other words, through the medium of specific organizations such as Templarism and Freemasonry. Just about every aspect of Venus Family philosophy and its ultimate objectives fall within the remit of the story, although Bacon was very careful not to stray into the sphere of the feminine component within religion. Given the religious circumstances present in England during Bacon's life this is hardly surprising. He could not use the old technique of bringing the Goddess to the fore in the guise of the Virgin Mary because she had been marginalized with the arrival of Protestantism, though his own reverence for the Goddess was shown in other ways.

All the same there are times when Bacon comes very close to making reference to the unseen but pivotally important Goddess. In one section of the story the narrator makes reference to a celebration taking place in Bensalem called the Feast of the Family. As this ceremony begins the male head of the family, known in the story as the Tirsan, leads his family into the place of celebration.

> The Tirsan cometh forth with all his generation or linage, the males before him, and the females following him; and if there be a mother from whose body the whole linage is descended, there is a traverse placed in a loft above on the right hand of the chair, with a privy door, and a carved window of glass, leaded with gold and blue; where she sitteth, but is not seen.

This sounds uncannily like the presence of the Goddess, which is all-important but not recognized, except to those who are in the know. In other words the Goddess can see everything and yet remain unseen.

It is very likely that it was Francis Bacon who first coined the name "Virginia" for the most important of the new English-speaking communities on the East Coast of North America. This was something he could get away with because it supposedly related to Queen Elizabeth I, who was on the throne of England at the time. She was known as the Virgin Queen because she had deliberately chosen not to marry. However, what the name of the colony *actually* meant to Francis Bacon is probably something else entirely. In all probability it related to the constellation of Virgo, which is also known as the Virgin and is the group of zodiac stars most commonly associated with the Goddess. The sun occupies the sign of Virgo at harvesttime—something that was particularly significant to the Mystery religions, in particular that of Demeter.

Because Thomas Jefferson had so much personal respect for Francis Bacon it is probably not surprising that aspects of Bacon's *The New Atlantis* are close to the heart of the Declaration of Independence, which Jefferson drafted. It is also worth mentioning that although in the story Bacon suggested that Bensalem was located in the Pacific Ocean, the very name of his book *The New Atlantis* leaves little doubt that he was referring to North America, which is of course in both the Pacific and the Atlantic.

Francis Bacon himself never visited North America, but some of his descendants did. An extremely famous man who made very early demands for American independence was Nathanial Bacon. Nathanial was English-born and, like his relative Sir Francis Bacon, was educated at Cambridge University.

Nathanial Bacon traveled to Virginia in 1673, and because of his family background he was at first welcomed by the colonial ruling elite. Even at this early date the mother country was imposing restrictions and taxes upon the citizens of Virginia that they were unwilling to accept. Probably in recognition of what he knew his relative Sir Francis had wanted for Virginia, Nathanial Bacon became a leader of the disaffected faction and was ultimately involved in what could only be described as a battle for freedom from oppression. Bacon and his compatriots managed to get Governor Berkeley to implement new laws regarding voting rights, but Berkeley repeatedly went back on his word, which ultimately led to armed rebellion. Unfortunately Nathanial Bacon died of dysentery in 1676, leaving his followers without his charismatic

leadership. The rebellion soon collapsed, and full colonial rule was rees-
tablished. It would take two other Virginians, George Washington and
Thomas Jefferson, together with other outraged colonist leaders to pick
up the baton Nathanial Bacon had first carried, albeit a century later.

At the very center of colonial Williamsburg, which was for some
time the state capital of Virginia and a place Nathanial Bacon knew
well, is a fairly ordinary-looking church with a very fascinating past.
It is known as Bruton Parish Church, and it stands not far from the
famous College of William and Mary, which itself was significant in
the lives of some of the United States' first presidents. The present
church was dedicated in 1715, but this was the second building on the
site that served the citizens of Williamsburg. The first structure was
completed in 1683, and it occupied a position to the west of the present
church. The foundations of the old Bruton Church became of interest
in the 1930s, when it was announced by the philosopher, mystic, and
writer Manley P. Hall and his wife, Marie Hall, who was also a writer
and investigator, that a secret vault lay beneath its altar.

It was suggested by the Halls that a ten-foot by ten-foot cubic vault
had been created beneath the old Bruton Church during 1676, when the
contents of an earlier vault under a church in Jamestown were transferred
to Williamsburg. The creation of the new vault had taken place under
cover of the rebellion of which Nathanial Bacon had been the leader.

It was Marie Hall who undertook most of the research relating to the Bruton vault, and it was a cause she championed from the
1930s until her death at the grand old age of one hundred in 2005.
The suggestion that such a vault existed had been present for generations in Williamsburg, together with the belief that tunnels led from
the old church to various buildings in the settlement—in particular
the William and Mary College. Marie Hall investigated these stories,
and—partly as a result of ciphers on some of the tombstones in the
churchyard, as well as information from a book written by an author
named George Wither—she was able to find the lost foundations of
the old church in their entirety. The Wither book also offered her the
information she needed to locate the hidden vault, which was said to

contain all manner of documents. The books in the vault were supposedly stored in copper cylinders and included works such as *The New Atlantis* by Francis Bacon (in this case a complete version of the story, which in its published form is incomplete), as well as other documents related to the deliberate founding of the Virginia colony as the site for the New Jerusalem. In addition it was suggested that there were truly ancient texts included.

The Wither book written in 1635 is titled *A Collection of Emblemes, Ancient and Moderne.* The strange thing about this book is that it carries woodcut illustrations of many of the buildings of Williamsburg—years before any of them had actually been created! It also gave Marie Hall the information she needed to locate the hidden vault, informing her, in a sort of pictorial code, how large it was and how far below the old altar it was located.

In the 1920s the whole of historic Williamsburg was adopted by the Rockefeller Foundation, which runs it to this day. When seeking permission to have the old church ruins excavated, Marie Hall came up against all manner of excuses, sidelining, and misdirection. The result was that nobody ever dug down the suggested twenty feet in the place where the vault is supposed to be. A very early form of ground radar, developed in the 1930s to detect copper deposits, was brought to the site and apparently showed that there was a void at the supposed depth and of about the right size, but this information never led to any further investigation.

One of the problems of mysteries such as this is that the story often grows in the telling. We have been very careful to relate only what seems to us to be valid with regard to Bruton Church, but in any case we have a very important additional reason for being interested in this location, which has to do with its physical distance from Washington, D.C. We will explain this fully in chapter 10. It will also become apparent why we estimate that anything of significance that once was in the Bruton vault was probably removed from it just prior to the Civil War—probably around 1861—and is now housed in another vault under the center of Ellipse Park, just south of the White House in Washington, D.C.

The significance of the free United States of Sir Francis Bacon cannot be overstated. It is abundantly clear from his book *The New Atlantis* that most likely, together with a group of other influential people in early seventeenth-century England, Bacon already had very clear plans regarding what North America should be—and this more than 150 years before the American Declaration of Independence was signed. On the other hand, we have to bear in mind that Bacon's invention of the island of Bensalem may have been specifically referring to the secret presence of the Venus Families within society rather than to a specific location. It seems strange that a direct family member of Francis Bacon should have been the leader of an extremely early effort to gain independence from Britain by pure chance, and we are left wondering what would have happened to United States history if Nathanial Bacon had not so unfortunately succumbed to disease.

As it was, the Venus Families would have to wait a considerable period before the time was right to gain the independence of not just Virginia but all thirteen colonies. This is another indication of an organization that has shown almost unbelievable patience when it came to achieving its objectives.

There is one factor that may demonstrate that Nathanial Bacon was jumping the gun when he attempted to wrest Virginia from British rule. The Book of Revelation is quite specific about what the dimensions of the New Jerusalem will be. It suggests a huge square with sides of 12,000 stadia, which in modern terms is around 1,400 miles or 2,200 kilometers. Although the thirteen states that formed the free United States when taken together did not represent a square, it is odd that the general measurements of the original United States are close to being the same as those for the New Jerusalem as they are quoted in Revelation. If this is a coincidence it is indeed a very strange one, and perhaps it was always the intention of the Venus Families to hold back the thrust for independence until the area involved approximated that of the New Jerusalem of Revelation. There would have been good method in this, because by the time of the Declaration of Independence there was sufficient manpower to launch an effective campaign against the British. It is unlikely that Virginia alone could ever have held out against the British forces.

Could it also be a coincidence that when disaffection by the colonies regarding British rule eventually came to a head two of the men who had the strongest influence on the Declaration of Independence were very familiar with Williamsburg and Bruton Church? Both George Washington and Thomas Jefferson had often been present in the church, and Jefferson had studied at the College of William and Mary for some time. There are persistent rumors that both George Washington and Thomas Jefferson had explored the tunnels under Williamsburg and that they knew the contents of the Bruton vault.

In *Archaeological Conspiracy at Williamsburg: The Mystery of Bruton Vault,* published in 2007, David Allen Rivera reviews the whole Bruton story in a full and fair way. It is probably the most complete and well-researched appraisal of the Bruton vault story we have found. Toward the end of the report Rivera suggests that the Rockefeller Foundation may have already gained access to the Bruton vault and removed its contents. Rivera suggests that if this is the case the foundation would hardly allow an empty vault to be excavated, since this would lead to acute embarrassment and awkward questions. This is a plausible assessment but would only apply if there was indeed anything still in the vault when the Rockefeller Foundation began its commitment to Williamsburg in the 1920s. A counter suggestion might be that from the very start someone associated with the Rockefeller Foundation was well aware of the existence of the Bruton vault and equally aware that it had been empty since the nineteenth century.

Despite the criticism and suspicion surrounding the Rockefeller Foundation, especially on the Internet, it is possible that Williamsburg has been protected since the 1920s primarily because it is one of the most significant locations regarding the United States' journey to independence and freedom. The true importance of the colonial settlement may only become evident in the future, at which time its safety from overdevelopment and exploitation will be appreciated. To some extent it may also be seen as a convenient diversion, preventing researchers from looking in the direction where Bruton's original treasures are now located.

Part Two

WASHINGTON, D.C.: THE CITY OF ISIS

10

WASHINGTON, D.C., AND
THE MEGALITHIC YARD

In 2010, together with British writer and researcher Christopher Knight, Alan published *Before the Pyramids*. When research for this book began it was intended to detail the similarity between the three major pyramids on the Giza Plateau in Egypt and an arrangement of three extremely ancient henges in the North of England. It seemed to Alan and Chris that both groups of structures were representations on the ground of a group of stars known as Orion's Belt. A henge is a circular structure comprised of a deep ditch and a mound made from the ditch material. It has one or more entrances, and the ditch is almost always inside the mound, making henges unlikely to have ever been intended for defensive purposes. The Thornborough Henges date back to around 3500 BCE.

As it turns out we will have more to say about Orion's Belt, this time in connection with the United States. As far as *Before the Pyramids* was concerned, research for the book unexpectedly took Alan and Chris from the windswept hills of Northern England to the capital city of the most powerful nation in the world: Washington, D.C. The connections between what is known as the Thornborough array of henges and Washington, D.C., seemed little short of ridiculous at first, and yet the evidence could not be denied.

What had led Alan and Chris to look closely at the henges of Northern England in the first place was their interest in the Megalithic system, an ancient form of geometry and measurement. They had investigated this in their 2009 book *Civilization One,* which had first introduced the public to the Megalithic system. Aspects of the Megalithic system had been uncovered by a Scottish professor of engineering named Alexander Thom. In addition to his professional qualifications (he held a chair at Oxford University) Professor Thom was a keen amateur astronomer and also an enthusiastic sailor.

As a young man sailing around the islands and lochs of western Scotland, Thom had become fascinated by the many stone circles from antiquity that overlooked the sea routes in this part of Scotland. He began to wonder if the stone circles had actually been used as a way for the Megalithic people of the British Isles to better understand the cycles of the moon. Because the moon has a bearing on ocean tides, a good knowledge of its cycles would have been invaluable to the Megalithic people of the New Stone Age (ca. 2000 BCE), who were themselves accomplished sailors.

Once employed at Oxford University after the Second World War, Alexander Thom began to spend most of his spare time carefully surveying the stone circles of his native Scotland and then expanded his investigation to other areas of the British Isles, as well as parts of France. He also surveyed groups of standing stones, stone avenues, and other apparent alignments from the Megalithic period. This research continued for more than fifty years until Thom eventually had a wealth of data at his disposal.

Alexander Thom was able to demonstrate that the builders of the stone circles had indeed been studying the cycles of the moon, as well as the stars and planets. For this research he was applauded and is probably rightfully often called the father of astroarchaeology, which is a discipline dealing with the way our distant ancestors viewed and often used the heavens, both for practical and religious reasons. Unfortunately, Thom's reputation was virtually ruined because of a chance discovery he made on the way. He could not avoid noticing that a series of very specific linear measurements fell out of the statistics he had collected. The first such unit was 2.722 feet in length (82.966 cm), and Thom christened it the Megalithic Yard. He also found another unit that was equal to 2.5 Megalithic Yards. This measured 6.805 feet (207.415 cm), and he called this unit the Megalithic Rod. From site to site these measurements varied by only the tiniest amount, and from a statistical point of view there was no doubt whatsoever that they were real. The inference was that the Megalithic Yard and the Megalithic Rod had been standard linear units used by all the builders concerned and probably across well over 2,000 years—just as we use the foot or the meter.

These discoveries did nothing to endear Thom to the archaeological community. Archaeologists wanted to know how apparently primitive people had managed to create and then replicate unbelievably accurate units of linear measurement. Logic asserted that over time any such unit should have drifted, since keeping accurate track of them across such a large area and during so much time should have been impossible, especially bearing in mind the sort of technology available to Stone Age farmers. Thom could not answer these criticisms, but for the rest of his life he went on demonstrating that both the Megalithic Yard and the Megalithic Rod were *real* units. So meticulous was he in his calculations that he was awarded a specially struck gold medal by the British Statistical Society.

Alan Butler and Christopher Knight thought it was outrageous that such a careful and persistent researcher as Alexander Thom should be vilified and was often accused of cheating. As a result they set out to discover what the Megalithic Yard and the Megalithic Rod actually were and how it was possible that they had remained so accurate for such a long period of time.

The ultimate conclusion, laid out in *Civilization One,* was that the Megalithic Yard was a linear unit that had been re-created on any site where it was required. It never had to be copied and passed from one location to another. The methodology was simple. It involved the use of a pendulum (effectively just a stone suspended on a piece of twine), a few logs of wood, and a good view of the planet Venus during a specific period of its cycles across the sky. It was a method of turning the passage of time into a linear unit of length. A full description of the way the Megalithic Yard was produced can be seen in *Civilization One*. There was an implication that the original "base" linear unit of the system had been half of a Megalithic Yard, and it was five times this unit that made the Megalithic Rod.

At the same time as the Megalithic Yard was being used in the British Isles and France, another linear unit was being employed by the Minoan civilization on the island of Crete in the Mediterranean. This was a shorter unit that closely approximated a modern foot, but not quite. It was 0.9962 statute foot, or 30.365 cm, in length, and it was called a Minoan Foot by the man who rediscovered it, the Canadian archaeologist, J. Walter Graham. A comparison between the Megalithic Yard and the Minoan Foot showed that both had been part of a widespread European geometric system based on the polar circumference of the Earth, and it was possible to figure out how this geometry had worked.

Megalithic geometry differed from modern geometry in that it assumed all circles were composed of 366 degrees and not the modern 360 degrees. In Megalithic geometry each degree could be subdivided into 60 minutes of arc, each minute of arc could be again divided into 6 seconds of arc, and each second of arc of the Earth's polar circumference was equal to 366 Megalithic Yards. It is not our intention in this book to go into detail about how Alan and Chris arrived at these figures. That information can be found in *Civilization One* and in their subsequent books, including *Before the Pyramids*. What was demonstrated was the almost unbelievable but irrefutable fact that people living as long ago as 5,500 years were fully aware of the size of the Earth, with accuracy comparable to our present estimation!

As Alan and Chris put the final touches on *Civilization One,* they made a number of predictions regarding future possible findings. Included among these was the expectation that if Megalithic geometry had been a genuine system, units of 366 Megalithic Yards and 366 Megalithic Rods could be expected to have been used by our ancient ancestors in the structures they created. As it turned out, even before *Civilization One* reached the bookshelves of the world the prediction was realized.

Further research showed that most of the instances of the use of units of 366 Megalithic Yards or Megalithic Rods were not related to the stone circles, the majority of which were too small to require a linear length equal to almost 1,000 feet, but instead were restricted to henges, which in general were considerably older than any of the stone circles, and many of them were much larger. The best example of all was in the case of three massive and related henges near the little city of Ripon in North Yorkshire where units of both 366 Megalithic Yards and Megalithic Rods were present all across the large site. Not only had Alan and Chris proved how the Megalithic Yard had been created wherever it was needed, they had also introduced the world to an incredible form of geometry that was already extremely old before the people we call the ancient Greeks existed and was being used a thousand years or more before any pyramid was built in Egypt.

This might have been the end of the story had it not been for Alan happening to watch a television documentary about the beautiful city of Bath in southern England. Most of Bath was created in the eighteenth century where Georgian masterpieces built in the warm, honey-colored local stone create one of the most elegant cities in Britain.

The documentary focused on a particular structure in Bath called King's Circus. It is a circular structure composed of regal terraced houses, all facing each other across a grassy interior. The narrator of the television program happened to mention the dimensions of King's Circus, and immediately Alan's ears pricked up: he recognized the diameter of 317 feet (96.65 meters), which he knew was also the diameter of Stonehenge, probably the most iconic standing-stone circle and henge anywhere. A circle with a diameter of 317 feet would have a circumference of 996 feet, which is equal to 366 Megalithic Yards! In the case of Stonehenge this measurement does not relate to any of the circles of standing stones on the site but rather to the henge after which the structure is named. This henge was constructed maybe a thousand

Fig. 10.1. Masonic symbols on building in King's Circus, Bath, England

years before any stone was brought to the site, and it has a circumference of 366 Megalithic Yards: exactly the measurement Alan and Chris had predicted they should find.

King's Circus had been designed by a man called John Wood (1704–1754), who had also created some of the other iconic structures in the city of Bath. Alan and Chris soon discovered that John Wood was an early Freemason and that he also had a deep interest in the ancient structures of the region in which he lived. This included Stonehenge, which he had surveyed. The question now was had John Wood created King's Circus as a direct copy of the measurements of the henge at Stonehenge without having any idea about the reality of the Megalithic Yard, or had he somehow been in possession of knowledge relating to Megalithic measurements and geometry? Although it had ancient roots, as far as its eighteenth-century builders were concerned, Bath was a "new city." John Wood was one of the men who first envisaged creating a new Regency town to serve the mineral spa that had been known since Roman times. Unfortunately, Wood died at a comparatively young age, and many of the buildings he had hoped to create in Bath were never built. Alan and Chris had no way of knowing if he would have used the Megalithic Yard again.

Custom-built cities in the eighteenth century were rare. Major changes were made to existing cities, such as London and Paris, but what Alan and Chris really needed was a place that had been totally planned and built at this time—and preferably by people like John Wood, who had Masonic connections. In the end there was only one candidate and that was Washington, D.C.

A few very hectic days followed during which Alan and Chris were rarely out of contact with each other. When maps of Washington, D.C., were carefully measured, it soon became apparent that not only had a unit of 366 Megalithic Yards been used in the planning of Washington, D.C., but in fact the whole of the historical heart of the city was based on this unit of linear length. Underpinning the whole of Washington, D.C., and radiating out from the very center of a huge park south of the White House, which is called Ellipse Park, every major intersection, ceremonial square, and circle of the city plan as it was first devised equaled an even number of units of 366 Megalithic Yards from this one particular spot. Ellipse Park is often referred to as President's Park these days.

It then became apparent that the center of Ellipse Park was also the center of the inverted square with ten-mile sides, which defines the District of Columbia, in which Washington, D.C., is situated. There was absolutely no doubt about it; Alan and Chris were faced with deliberately planned and meticulously accurate sacred geometry! When all the major intersections that had existed since the city was planned were connected to the center of Ellipse Park, what appeared was a very large and most elaborate arrow, pointing directly at the very center of the Ellipse. The Ellipse itself also measures 366 Megalithic Yards across its widest axis.

All of the findings were included in *Before the Pyramids,* but Alan

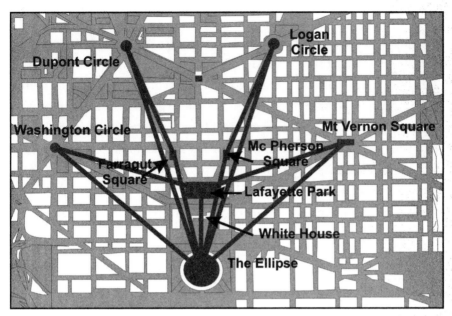

Fig. 10.2. The Megalithic Arrow in Washington, D.C. Each line taken from the center of the Ellipse to one of the original intersections of the planned city is made up of a number of full units of 366 Megalithic Yards.

then went on to write and publish a solo book *City of the Goddess: Freemasons, the Sacred Feminine, and the Secret Beneath the Seat of Power in Washington, D.C.* This book went into the subject of Washington, D.C., in much greater detail. In particular it drew attention to the tremendous number of goddess statues to be found throughout the city. Goddesses are to be found at almost every intersection, throughout the public spaces of the city, and on most public buildings there. Taken individually these do not appear particularly surprising, especially when it is born in mind that the predominant building style used to create Washington, D.C., was classical revival. This was a type of architecture that became immensely important in the eighteenth century, and its buildings were closely copied from those of ancient Greece and Rome. As a result, statuary was not unusual in architecture at the time, but nevertheless the proliferation of representations of goddesses in Washington, D.C., must be considered excessive.

The largest and most important of all the goddess statues is that of *The Goddess of Armed Freedom,* which is a colossal bronze statue 19.5 feet in height. She stands on the very top of the dome of the Capitol; therefore, apart from the Washington Monument, she occupies the highest position in Washington, D.C. There were political reasons why this statue acquired the name she has and also regarding her appearance and clothing, but in truth the real name of the statue should be "Columbia."

Most of the major countries of the world have a patron goddess. For example, in Britain she is called Britannia, and France has the patron goddess Marian. An independent United States would be no different with this regard, and even prior to the American War of Independence the goddess of the United States was Columbia, which is also the name of the district in which Washington, D.C., stands. Her representation on the dome of the Capitol looks east, to where the sun rises each day over the city. This is entirely appropriate, because the whole of the original, civic heart of Washington, D.C., is a giant astronomical observatory

Fig. 10.3. The Capitol, Washington, D.C.
Photo courtesy of Scott F. Wolter

running from east to west, with the Capitol at the eastern end and the Lincoln Memorial now at its western extremity. These are joined by a wide, green avenue, known as the Mall. It is on the National Mall, as it is formally named, and to either side of it that many of Washington, D.C.'s most enigmatic and beautiful structures were created.

How Washington, D.C., came to be what it is and where it is represents a fascinating story in its own right. Armed rebellion by the colonists of North America against Great Britain began in 1775, and the issue was not resolved until 1783. Eventually Great Britain capitulated, and the United States became the first truly democratic republic in the world. The cooperation of the original thirteen colonies in the prosecution of the war against Britain was often an uneasy one. Just because the states had banded together to throw off the colonial yoke did not mean they always agreed. Each state had its own agendas, and welding so many disparate factions into a workable unit was never going to be easy. This was a task that fell to General George Washington, the man who had so carefully led the American forces throughout the Revolutionary War. He was voted into office as the first president of a free United States in 1789, and together with an administration that contained a number of the original Founding Fathers he began to lay down plans for his nation's future.

Something the new United States lacked was a capital city. The legislature met in a number of different places in the first days of the republic, but the job of finding a suitable site for the capital and planning its creation was given to President Washington himself. This was going to be no easy job. There were already serious divisions between the northern and southern states, and political expediency showed that it would be unwise to place the new capital in any of the northern cities, such as Philadelphia or New York. Realistically a new capital city had to be built from scratch, and it was necessary to place it between the northern and southern states.

The compromise came with the adoption of a location that at the time was little more than a swamp beside the Potomac River on the border between Maryland, which considered itself a northern state, and Virginia, which had always leaned toward the southern states. Congress voted on the issue, and Washington was told that the new capital should be placed in a "district," which stood apart from all the states, and that this district should be no bigger than a hundred square miles. Within this district the capital city itself would be built. The fact that it was placed between the states named *Mary*land and *Virgin*ia was undoubtedly intentional, as was the designation that it be shaped as a square or a diamond.

George Washington knew a great deal about surveying, but it would have been neither practical nor politically expedient for him to design the new city himself. He turned instead to a man whom we will meet again and again as our story unfolds. His name was Pierre Charles L'Enfant, and he was a French citizen who had come to America to fight in the Revolutionary War. L'Enfant was an often difficult, irascible character, but he was a staunch supporter of both George Washington and the United States. His background lay in art and he had studied extensively in Paris.

Together with a committee appointed by the president to oversee the planning of the capital, L'Enfant began "inventing" the very heart of the New Jerusalem in 1791. What L'Enfant envisaged was little different from the city of Washington visitors see today, though some of his more grandiose ideas were modified by George Washington and Thomas Jefferson. For example, L'Enfant had envisioned a veritable palace for the president's house, which was soon discounted and became the much more modest White House. Exactly how much L'Enfant was working to his own ideas or was being manipulated by forces behind the scene will never be known. What is apparent is that from the very start Washington, D.C., was going to be a place replete with symbolism and based, from start to finish, on sacred geometry.

The heart of the city was built around a right-angled triangle. The long base of this triangle would represent the length of the Mall, running from the Capitol at the east end to a projected grand monument, which would be dedicated to George Washington. Running north from this the apex of the triangle would be the site of the president's house, and then the hypotenuse would run southeast, back to the Capitol. On L'Enfant's original plan, just south of the president's house is what appears to be a thinly disguised drawing of an eye. This would eventually become the site of Ellipse Park, though between the founding of the city and the end of the American Civil War the area was surrounded by a picket fence and was simply called the White Lot.

Around this central triangle L'Enfant envisaged a stately city with wide boulevards that came together in large circles and squares. Most of the intersections envisaged on L'Enfant's original plan dividing up the gridiron nature of the new city still exist. What is absolutely apparent is that underpinning the map created by L'Enfant is another map, based on Megalithic geometry and Megalithic linear measurements. Under a very definite Freemasonic influence, because after all L'Enfant himself, President Washington, and indeed many of those involved were Freemasons, the symbolic city of Washington, D.C., was hidden in plain sight beneath the visible plan.

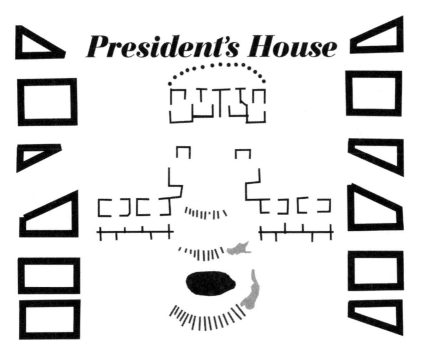

Fig. 10.4. The All-Seeing Eye, placed just below the president's house on L'Enfant's original plan for the city of Washington, D.C., and disguised as a landscape feature. This is the area now known as Ellipse Park.

The controlling influence of the Venus Families was evident from the start. Knowledge of the Megalithic system of geometry and measurement goes far beyond Freemasonry itself and is never mentioned in Freemasonic ritual. As far as we can tell, between circa 2000 BCE and the building of King's Circus in Bath, England, the Megalithic system of measurement was never used, although it does seem to have been retained by a regularly used Spanish linear unit called the *vara,* and it is also evident in some of the Mesoamerican structures of Central America. The inference has to be that although the Venus Families retained a very accurate knowledge of Megalithic geometry and measurement, they had chosen not to use it until it could be employed for the most important building project undertaken by these extraordinary people. It is most likely that as far as the underlying measurements of the capital city were concerned, Pierre Charles L'Enfant was told what to do. It is even possible that he personally failed to understand the ancient implications of his design. Where these instructions came from is unknown, but we would probably have to look in the direction of George Washington and Thomas Jefferson to find the answer.

While L'Enfant was drawing up his plans, a small group of hand-picked surveyors was marking out the new district surrounding the capital, which took the form of a square, with its points facing the cardinal points of the compass and with each of its sides measuring ten miles in length. L'Enfant's plan for the city ensured that the center of the White Lot, where he had drawn the mysterious eye on his original plan, would also mark the center of the square. Almost immediately the district formed by the square was named Columbia after the matron goddess of the United States.

When we bear in mind the central position of the eye—which, in time, would become Ellipse Park—relative to the District of Columbia, and when we also see the large and impressive "arrow" that points to it (see figure 10.2 on p. 155), we can be certain that this spot was earmarked from the start as being the most important location in the new capital.

Events that followed proved that L'Enfant was far from being the easiest of men to deal with. He was fiery by nature and absolutely set on making certain that everything the city would become would reflect in minute detail the plan he had so carefully created. When this involved him tearing down the brand-new house of an influential politician simply because it crossed one his sacred boulevards, George Washington had no choice but to dismiss L'Enfant and replace him with the more sanguine Andrew Ellicott, who took over responsibility for the city plan. Ellicott made slight alterations, but these in no way affected either the original Megalithic arrow or the importance of the center of the White Lot, where L'Enfant had drawn the eye.

Every use of the 366 Megalithic Yard unit in Washington, D.C., was in truth a miniature representation of the entire Earth: 366 Megalithic Yards, which is 996.2 feet, or 303.65 meters, divides into the polar circumference of the Earth precisely 131,760 times. In turn, 131,760 represents the number 366 multiplied by 360.

The conclusion that at least some of the Founding Fathers were well aware of this is proved by the fact that when Thomas Jefferson proposed a new decimal system of measurement for the United States in 1790, he hid the Megalithic Yard within his plan. It would have been impossible for him to propose the Megalithic Yard directly as the basic unit of linear measurement for the United States because he lived in an age in which the 360-degree circle was the norm. This had been the case since before the time of the ancient Greeks. Had Jefferson proposed a change in the very nature of geometry to circles based on 366 degrees he would have been considered a madman. Nevertheless, he proposed a system of measurements in which the Megalithic Yard was as safe and secure as it was beneath the street plan of the capital city. As it turned out, Jefferson's plans for a new measuring system were never adopted, possibly because it betrayed the underlying Megalithic system too well.

Because many of the citizens of the brand-new Washington, D.C., were Christians, churches and even cathedrals were eventually built there. What is obvious, however, is that no such structure appeared on L'Enfant's original plan. Had this been the case, one might have expected a glorious cathedral to stand at the end of one of L'Enfant's boulevards or to have been shown taking pride of place somewhere on the central Mall. Most observers would probably suggest that the reason this was not the case was because from the start the Constitution of the new United States made it abundantly clear that no religion would be allowed to influence the republic. The government of the republic would be totally secular in nature. This is absolutely true, but the fact that no provision was made for any religious structure in the original conception of the city also relates directly to the Book of Revelation and its description of the New Jerusalem. It specifically stated in Revelation 21:22:

> I did not see a temple in the city, because the Lord God Almighty and the Lamb are its temple.

The Venus Family members who were ultimately responsible for the creation of Washington, D.C., took this quite seriously. Although the vast majority of those who have lived in or visited Washington, D.C., were and are totally ignorant of the fact, the whole city is a temple, dedicated to the beliefs of the Venus Families.

The Book of Revelation refers to the New Jerusalem as "the wife, the bride of the Lamb." In Venus Family–speak the meaning of this is quite clear. The Lamb is the sacrifice—the god of the cereal grain—who is sacrificed annually at harvesttime so that humanity can eat and survive. The wife, the bride of the Lamb, is therefore the Great Goddess, the essence of nature and the Earth itself, who gives birth to the god each year. Washington, D.C., as the heart of the New Jerusalem, is the personification in stone of the Goddess, so it is not in the least surprising to find representations of her at virtually every street end.

With all the skill and dedication that could be mustered, the new city began to take shape, sandwiched between a northern and a southern state. The names of both Virginia and Maryland were entirely appropriate for what was taking place, because each had a resonance with the Goddess. Meanwhile the federal district within which the city stood also bore one of the thousand names of the Great Goddess—Columbia. Although apparently relating to Columbus, who is credited with first visiting the New World, the truth behind the name Columbia is that it signifies *Columbidae,* which is the Latin word for "dove." This particular bird has been closely associated with the Goddess since remote antiquity and also represented the Holy Spirit, which is the feminine aspect of Christianity, carefully hidden at the heart of the faith.

The creation of the New Jerusalem, which of course was not merely Washington, D.C., but the whole of the original United States, was far from easy, and old smoldering animosities that had existed from the start between the northern and southern states burst into the flames of war in 1861. It was a dark time for the relatively new republic, and little was accomplished in Washington, D.C., while the Civil War was being fought. Perhaps the only advantage of the conflict was that when it was over there was a large force of army engineers that could be put to work, finishing parts of the capital that had been put on hold.

One of the first jobs was the creation from the White Lot, south of the White House, of a large, elliptical park. This took place under the supervision of Thomas Lincoln Casey, a general of the engineers and a veteran of the Civil War. The work was undertaken from 1877 to 1880, and during the construction Casey passed regular reports to Congress. In one of these, at the end of 1880, he reported that the grading was complete for the Ellipse, except in the very center, where he was unable to concentrate his efforts because a hole had been dug that had nothing to do with his own work. He suggested that this was under the control of the city authorities. His report said that during the past year very satisfactory progress had been made on the Ellipse. He reported that the grading, soiling, and seeding of the central ellipse had been completed, except for a small area at its center, left by reason of an incomplete sewer under the control of the district commissioners.

It is hard to understand why a sewer would be required in that particular location, and though we remain confident that there was indeed a sizeable hole at the center of the Ellipse in 1880, we are equally confident it had nothing to do with sewers. In this place, at the very center of the District of Columbia and in the most sacred place within Washington, D.C., a chamber was created, where some if not all of the greatest treasures collected over centuries by the Venus Families were deposited.

Fig. 10.5. Center of Ellipse Park, looking south with the Washington Monument to the left and the Jefferson Memorial in the center distance. The fence on the right was a *temporary* structure, but on numerous visits it has *always* been there!

The very center of the Ellipse is only evident these days to anyone who is willing to look very carefully and probably do a little probing. Just below the surface of the grass they will come across a small and insignificant square stone. All that is written on the stone are the words "US Meridian" and the date "1890." This stone was placed at the center of the Ellipse to mark what was originally planned by Thomas Jefferson to be the unique prime meridian of the United States, a line of longitude from which all other distances in the country could be measured. In the end the U.S. Meridian was never adopted, but the small stone at the very center of the Ellipse remains. It is interesting to note that on three separate visits to Washington, D.C., across five years, Alan was never able to access the very center of the Ellipse because it was always fenced off. This situation prevailed when we visited the Ellipse together in 2013.

Further investigations showed that the preoccupation of the planners of Washington, D.C., with the Megalithic Yard had not been restricted to the period during which the city was under construction. Southwest of the city and across the Potomac River is the Pentagon, which at the time of its construction was the largest office block in the world. As the 1930s drew to a close it became increasingly obvious that the United States would most likely find itself drawn into a war that seemed inevitable in Europe. It was decided that all of the armed forces, the headquarters of which were spread throughout Washington, D.C., should be brought together in one location. As a result a giant building was planned. The structure was at first intended to be located in Arlington, but at the last minute President Franklin D. Roosevelt decided to place it instead on the site of the old Hoover airport.

President Roosevelt was a 33rd-degree Scottish Rite Freemason and undoubtedly also a member of the Venus Families. Despite a punishing schedule as president he virtually took control of the design and planning of the new military headquarters, which, because of its ultimate shape,

Fig. 10.6. The Ellipse in Washington, D.C., showing the fence that almost permanently prevents access to the center of the Ellipse. Photo courtesy of Scott F. Wolter

was called the Pentagon. It was to become the largest and most prominent building within the vicinity of Washington, D.C., and virtually every one of its dimensions relates to the Megalithic measuring system.

All regular pentagons are created within circles, and the circle from which the Pentagon in Washington, D.C., was derived had a circumference of 5 × 366 Megalithic Yards. Its footprint owes more to one of the giant henges of Stone Age Britain than to any structure in the modern world, and it represents a positive icon of Venus Family knowledge in a city already replete with Megalithic measurements. No structure with dimensions such as this had been built for more than 5,500 years, and the Pentagon remains to this day as proof positive of the connection between the modern United States and the Megalithic culture of the British Isles.

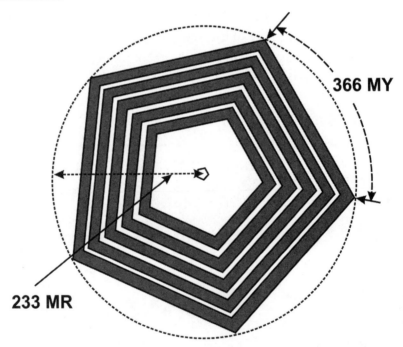

Fig. 10.7. The Pentagon in Washington, D.C. The circumference of the circle within which the Pentagon was created is 5 x 366 Megalithic Yards, and the radius of the circle is 233 Megalithic Rods. The Pentagon is therefore closely related in terms of its dimensions to the giant henges of Northern England.

The Pentagon betrayed its Megalithic origins in other ways. It had been very carefully placed on the landscape so that its center was exactly 10×366 Megalithic Yards from the center of the Ellipse and 15×366 Megalithic Yards to a position below the dome of the Capitol. Because the distance from the Capitol to the center of the Ellipse is 8×366 Megalithic Yards, the three structures create a triangle with a total length of 33×366 Megalithic Yards. The Pentagon itself and its placement on the landscape have very definite Masonic overtones and relates specifically to the 32nd and 33rd degrees of Scottish Rite Freemasonry. The ritual of the 32nd degree relates to the willingness to put one's own needs to one side in order to fight for others, as indeed the United States did, even before the Pentagon was completed. The 33rd degree is that of Grand Inspector General, which, in this case, refers to the role of the United States after World War II as the "policeman of the world."

Fig. 10.8. The Ellipse in Washington, D.C., showing the White
House in the background
Photo courtesy of Scott F. Wolter

During the research for both *Before the Pyramids* and *City of the Goddess,* of all the iconic structures at the heart of Washington, D.C., the only one that did not appear to have any particular Megalithic associations, either in its position on the landscape or in its dimensions, was the iconic Washington Monument. In the end this proved to be the most significant structure of all, but it would take the combined ingenuity of both of us to uncover this most incredible of all Washington, D.C., secrets.

11

THE WASHINGTON MONUMENT

The Stone Sentinel

In the late summer of 2013, Alan returned to his desk one afternoon to find he had received an e-mail from Janet. A few months earlier we had been together in Washington, D.C., where Alan was the guest on H2's documentary series *America Unearthed*.

The shoot was due to last a week, but because there was one clear day during which Alan would not be required, Janet flew down to Washington, D.C., to spend some time with Alan, checking out leads regarding D.C. that required their physical presence in the city. Janet recounts spending a few hours walking along the Mall, which is a long, grassy avenue approximately 650 feet in width that runs the 2.2 miles from the Capitol in the east to the Lincoln Memorial in the west. It is on the Mall, about 1.4 miles west of the Capitol that the Washington Monument pushes its mighty bulk up into the air, its pyramid point standing 555 feet above its base.

During our walk along the Mall we had plenty of questions regarding the Washington Monument, but at that time very few answers to offer. As the name implies, the Washington Monument was built to celebrate the

United States' greatest general and first president, George Washington. It was not commenced until nearly half a century after Washington himself had died, but once finished it became the tallest freestanding stone structure in the world.

Despite all the investigations undertaken by Alan alongside Christopher Knight for their book *Before the Pyramids,* and Alan's own research for *City of the Goddess,* the Washington Monument remained deeply enigmatic. Both of us knew that there were some strange facts regarding the structure that deserved explanation, but the truth of the monument escaped us on that particular visit. However, the e-mail from Janet, later in the summer, started a chain reaction that would bring us to our most surprising findings regarding both the monument and the people who have been responsible for running Washington, D.C., since its creation.

We had noticed during our walk along the Mall how frequently the shadow of the monument changed throughout that sunny day, but it was Janet who had really thought about the situation and who had decided to look more deeply into obelisks and the shadows they cast. The Washington Monument is a perfect example of an obelisk and has the distinction of being the tallest one ever created. Obelisks built in ancient Egypt where such monuments were first raised were tiny in comparison; they were generally constructed from one solid piece of stone, whereas the Washington Monument is comprised of many blocks.

Egyptian obelisks became very popular in the West from the eighteenth century on. Two specific and very genuine obelisks were brought to Britain and the United States from Egypt in the nineteenth century. The British example, now generally known as Cleopatra's Needle, is to be seen on the Embankment in London; the American obelisk, also often referred to as Cleopatra's Needle, is to be found in New York City, a structure that will become quite important later in our story. Janet had been reading about these and also about another example originally from Egypt, which now stands in the Vatican in Rome and forms part of an elaborate sundial created at the time of the Renaissance. This had caused her to think more about the nature of obelisks generally and the fact that even modern ones have often been erected to form a part of shadow clocks. She wondered if there was any information to suggest that the Egyptians had ever used them in this way and also whether the shadow's behavior had originally been part of the intention of those who planned and built the Washington Monument.

These questions started us on a quest that led to the most incredible findings regarding the beliefs—and also the power—of the people who had planned Washington, D.C., from the start, and especially those who designed and built the Washington Monument. What makes our findings about the Washington Monument so unique is that there is no conjecture involved. What the monument does, and when it puts on its regular shadow-play shows, are matters of astronomy and mathematics. What we discovered is unequivocal and yet until we revealed the truth it was completely unknown to the world at large. We are certain that when we reveal our findings to you, our reader, you will be just as astounded as we were that this information has somehow been kept totally secret from all but an incredibly small group for well over one and a half centuries!

The idea to create a monument dedicated to George Washington is as old as Washington, D.C., itself. This is hardly surprising. No person who has been a United States citizen since the founding of the free republic in the late eighteenth century has ever enjoyed the prestige of the United States' savior and first president. Although the most unassuming of individuals, George Washington was an amazing general and a peerless statesman who sacrificed a large chunk of his life to ensuring that the British-American colony would gain its independence and then guiding it through its first tentative steps.

Washington was already a national hero when the city that bears his name was first suggested, and indeed it was George Washington who ultimately chose the land for the federal city and who employed those who would design and build it. As we have seen, the first of his town planners was a French engineer, artist, and architect by the name of Pierre Charles L'Enfant. It was this capricious and often awkward individual who decided, presumably in cooperation with George Washington, how the city should be laid out and where its principle buildings should stand.

As we explained in chapter 10, Washington, D.C., was built around a right-angled triangle. The base of the triangle ran west from the proposed Capitol building to a point directly below and therefore south of the intended president's house. It then ran up to the site of the president's house before turning south and east, with the hypotenuse of the triangle running from what is now the White House back down to the Capitol. It was at the corner of the triangle immediately south of the White House and west of the Capitol that the proposed monument to George Washington was originally intended to stand.

For some years after Washington's death in 1799 it was hoped that his mortal remains could be buried under the rotunda of the Capitol,

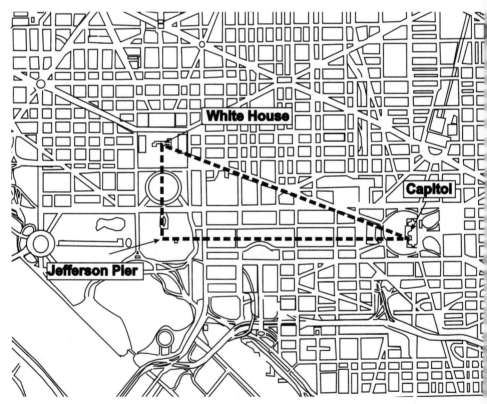

Fig. 11.1. The so-called Federal Triangle upon which all the geometry of Washington, D.C., was based. It ran from the Capitol, west to the Jefferson Pier, then north to the White House before turning south and east again, back to the Capitol.

but Washington stated in his will that he wished to be buried at his home at Mount Vernon, and his family complied. There were also political differences that delayed Washington's body from being immediately buried under the rotunda, and by the time these were resolved it appears that most parties agreed it was better to leave him at Mount Vernon. Therefore, it was some decades after his death that those wishing to create a fitting tribute to the first president began to make serious suggestions about the monument that L'Enfant had envisaged from the start.

Due to differing political affiliations, a lack of resources, and a host of other issues, nothing concrete happened regarding the proposed monument—which L'Enfant had wanted to be an equestrian statue—until nearly a century after George Washington's birth. With popular sentiment pushing for the tribute to be created, it was in 1832 that a committee was formed and public subscriptions began to roll in. But what sort of a monument should be created? It was well known that George Washington had been an enthusiastic Freemason. It was also common knowledge that although he paid lip-service to Christianity, like many of the Founding Fathers he was more in line with a Deist view of religion. Doubtless the Freemasons of the United States would have loved to create a fitting tribute to one of their own, but it just so happened that Freemasonry was under severe attack in the United States at this time. There was even a political party that canvassed very successfully on an anti-Masonic platform.

To appear fair to all concerned, a contest was held to find a designer and architect for the intended project. The competition was won by Robert Mills, who was probably the first great American-born and American-trained architect. Mills proposed a high, square, tapering central shaft with a flat top, surrounded by a colonnade that would contain statues of people who had contributed significantly to the freedom of the United States. However, as elaborate and elegant as this monument would undoubtedly have been, there is good reason to believe that right from the start both Mills and those who had chosen his design had something quite different in mind.

Fig. 11.2. The original design for the Washington Monument
as proposed by Robert Mills

The monument was commenced with an elaborate and deeply Masonic ceremony on Independence Day, July 4, 1848. As far as almost everyone was concerned, the finished monument, which was commenced on the back of the $87,000 contributed by enthusiastic citizens, would end up looking exactly as Mills had proposed when he entered the competition.

As can be seen from this artist's impression of the period (see figure 11.2), although generally similar to a true obelisk, the monument had no pyramid top, as all true obelisks do. It was therefore simply a square, tapering shaft. It would be surrounded by a classical Greek colonnade replete with statues of the Founding Fathers. The height of the shaft proposed by Mills was 500 feet, and herein lies the proof that all was not what it seemed to be at the time the monument was commenced: Mills had proposed that the base of the shaft should have sides of 55 feet.

The truth of the matter only came to light some decades later. A problem arose because the money raised to build the monument ran out in 1854. Some effort was made to continue the project, but the whole issue became bogged down in opposing political wrangles and eventually had to be shelved because of the commencement of the Civil War. It was not until 1879 that construction began again, but not until there had been furious arguments regarding what the finished monument should actually look like.

By this time anti-Masonic feeling had abated, partly because so many of the combatants on both sides of the Civil War had joined army lodges and become enthusiastic Masons, but also because the anti-Masonic politicians who had been so powerful when the monument was commenced had either died, retired, or switched their political allegiance. Meetings were held in the Capitol to decide if Mills's original blueprints should be followed, but it had suddenly occurred to almost everyone that the proposed design, with its large colonnade, would prove to be prohibitively expensive to build.

Advice was sought from a number of different individuals, some of whom knew about history, art, and architecture, and others who were totally ignorant of such matters but simply wanted their voices heard. Two individuals who did make their feelings known were Norton P. Chipman, who as secretary to the District of Columbia was a high-ranking civil servant, and George Perkins Marsh, a highly respected statesman and the United States ambassador to Italy. Marsh was something of an expert when it came to ancient architecture, and he did not beat about the bush when he told Congress what the finished monument should look like.

According to Marsh, the Washington Monument should be a plain, unadorned obelisk. He maintained that in terms of dimensions, all ancient Egyptian obelisks enjoyed a height—including the pyramid on top—that was ten times the length of the sides of its base. Norton P. Chipman agreed and added that there was something special in a simple, majestic obelisk. As far as the colonnade was concerned, this was part of what George Perkins Marsh called the "gingerbread," and he proposed that anything other than the obelisk itself should be abandoned.

With the benefit of hindsight, it is now possible to determine that this result was exactly what Robert Mills had indirectly decided upon decades before. Ostensibly, Mills proposed a square section shaft of 500 feet, with base sides of 55 feet. Mills was an excellent architect, and therefore he must have known that such a structure would be out of proportion and would look distinctly odd. However, if a 55-foot pyramid was placed on top of the flat topped shaft he had proposed, the height of the monument would become 555 feet high and the sides of its base would be ten times less at 55 feet. In other words, it would be a perfect, proportional copy of all the genuine Egyptian obelisks.

In all probability Robert Mills knew very well that the cost of his proposed monument would prove to be prohibitive and that at some stage during the initial build, the colonnade would be abandoned in favor of a simple shaft. Robert Mills was an enthusiastic Freemason, and it is certain that he was looking back to ancient Egypt in his design for the monument. This would be quite understandable, because obelisks were already being used as part of the adornment of Masonic graves.

Fig. 11.3. Washington Monument from Ellipse Park
Photo courtesy of Scott F. Wolter

Also, despite his original design having a flat-topped pillar, Mills had proposed placing a large, winged sun on the side of it—a motif that is just about as Egyptian and also as Masonic as it could be. The winged sun was eventually dropped, but what Washington, D.C., got was the largest obelisk in the world.

With the end of the American Civil War and the resumption of work on the monument, management of the project passed to the army. The Union had employed many engineers during the war, many of whom were still in uniform and short of something to do. Probably the most intriguing of these was Lieutenant Colonel Thomas Lincoln Casey, a professional soldier from New York and also a trained engineer who had proved his abilities during the recent conflict. It has been impossible for us to ascertain whether Casey himself had Masonic credentials, but it seems entirely possible that he did.

Casey was already in Washington, D.C., when the Washington Monument was recommenced. With the end of the Civil War it had been decided that parts of the capital were looking distinctly shabby, and Casey had been charged with working on the Mall. His primary task had been to lay out and build the Ellipse, mentioned in chapter 10.

Casey was put in sole charge of finishing the Washington Monument, a task that he managed very ably and in good time. Before we look in detail at the results of his efforts, it is first necessary to deal with another issue that had plagued Alan for some years prior to our common discoveries about the monument's true history.

When the monument had been planned, as early as 1847, its positioning on the landscape came into question. This had been governed from the start by the right-angled triangle upon which Pierre Charles L'Enfant had based Washington, D.C. Indeed, its proposed position had been the subject of some research and effort on the part of the United States' third president, Thomas Jefferson, who had come to power in 1800. Jefferson was the first president to live exclusively in the White House while in office. He had previously been a surveyor and took a great interest in the development of Washington, D.C. He had personally surveyed the line running down from the center of the White House to the place on the Mall where it met another line coming west from the center of the Capitol. Where the two converged he had placed a short, stone monolith that in the course of time became known as the Jefferson Pier. This was the spot where the memorial to George Washington was intended to stand.

However, when the monument was commenced it actually began to rise 389 feet east and slightly south of the Jefferson Pier. The discrepancy was explained as being because the land on which the monument was supposed to be placed was too marshy and unstable to support the proposed weight of the structure. From the start we suspected that this was not the truth of the matter. Forensic geologist Scott Wolter was the ideal person for us to ask about this situation. We wanted to know if the land where the monument was actually built was any different from the place where it was *supposed* to be. Scott considered the situation and eventually told us that in his opinion there was no tangible difference. If anything, the site east and south of the Jefferson Pier was likely to be less stable because it was closer to the tidal basin of the Potomac.

This opinion was born out by another contact of Alan's, architectural expert Ray Sheller. It seemed as though the suggestion about the insecure foundation was an excuse and that those planning the monument wished it to be in its alternative position for some other reason. This was a situation that started us thinking deeply, because although the difference between the Jefferson Pier and the present monument was only about 389 feet it had significant implications for Washington, D.C., as it had originally been planned.

On L'Enfant's original plan it was clear that the Mall was intended to run from due east to due west. This was partly because Washington stands within the District of Columbia, which is a square with sides of ten miles with its corners facing the cardinal points. There were probably other considerations, because building a city that responded absolutely to the four cardinal points of the compass would have been a very Masonic procedure. Since it now becomes obvious that the Washington Monument was a Masonic and indeed a Venus Family construction from the very start, it seems odd that the sacred Masonic geometry employed to design the city was being subverted—and for no apparently good reason.

The part of the Mall west of the Washington Monument did not exist until the start of the twentieth century. Much of this had indeed been extremely marshy ground, and some of it was actually under water. Land was drained to accommodate the Lincoln Memorial, which was commenced in 1914.

With the help of Google Earth we discovered that if we extend a line westward from the middle of the Capitol and take it through the middle of the Washington Monument, we eventually come to the middle of Lincoln Memorial. However, the compass bearing of such a line is not strictly due east to due west but rather from 1 degree north of east to 1 degree south of west. In other words, once the Washington Monument was built, someone made the decision to change the whole orientation of the center of Washington, D.C., by 1 degree. It doesn't sound like very much, but we were to discover that this change had tremendous implications

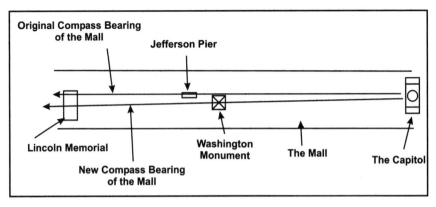

Fig. 11.4. The addition of the Washington Monument changed the orientation (compass bearing) of the Mall. Originally it had run from due east to due west, but after the Washington Monument was built the Mall ran from 1 degree north of east to 1 degree south of west.

for the Washington Monument and and its importance to the design of Washington, D.C.

The ultimate position of the Washington Monument, which had always puzzled us, was thrown into sharp relief once we had gathered all the information relating to its construction and positioning on the landscape, and it tended to support our hypothesis that it was placed where it is for a very definite reason. Once all this information had been amassed it then remained for us to try to discover what its true purpose might be. We decided that the best place to start on this quest was to look at possible shadows from the monument, as Janet had originally suggested in her e-mail.

12

DEMETER AND
CONSTITUTION WEEK

If the Washington Monument was going to produce a meaning-
ful and intended display, it seemed to us it must surely do so around
September 17 each year. There were a number of reasons why we saw
this time of the year as being so significant. Not least among these is
the fact that the United States Constitution was ratified and signed on
September 17, 1787. This was the day that the United States truly came
into existence as a free republic. Until the country had a constitution
of its own it was, officially at least, still nominally a series of colonies
belonging to Great Britain.

The delegates who represented the states that had willingly become
part of the battle gathered together in Philadelphia in May of 1787, and
they remained in session for almost four months. Clearly there was a
great deal to discuss, but we were not the first observers of this gathering to wonder why it took so long to formulate the Constitution.
After all, the states concerned had been fighting for several years to
gain their freedom. There had already been plenty of time to work out
what the United States should be once victory was won. It eventually
became obvious to us that the reason the gathering was in session for
so long was because its members (or at least some of its most influential

members) deliberately intended that the Constitution should be signed at a particular part of September.

The days between September 17 and September 23 are now listed in the calendar of the United States as Constitution Week, though this is a recent designation, having only been sanctioned as recently as 2002 by President George W. Bush. However, the fact that the signing of the Constitution is celebrated not by a single day, but across a whole week, is actually very telling.

As the whole of this book demonstrates, there was at the heart of the formation of the United States, and there still remains in certain circles, a venerating for the feminine within religion, which has broadly been forgotten by both Christianity and Islam, the two most significant religions of the modern world. For those who know where to find it, this recognition of the feminine rests at the very core of Freemasonry, and Freemasonry had a great part to play in the various stages of the United States' fight for independence.

Although Freemasonry does not espouse any specific religious creed, we have more than enough evidence to show that at its core it represents significant elements of what were once known as the Mystery religions. The Mystery religions flourished in the centuries leading up to the rise of Christianity and were phenomenally important, not only in Greece, Rome, and ancient Egypt but also across the known world. In one way or another all of the Mystery religions sought to introduce their followers to a personal experience of enlightenment, which came about as a result of specific rituals and ceremonies, the most famous of which took place each year in Eleusis, Greece.

Across many centuries countless thousands of acolytes experienced a ritual death and rebirth ceremony of the most profound sort in a huge temple specifically built for the purpose and dedicated to the Greek goddess Demeter. Like the other Mystery religions, that of Demeter was well named because the secrets of what happened during the initiation were kept totally secret on pain of death. As a result we are short on specifics regarding the actual ceremony, but some details are known, and it is clear that the mystery celebration at Eleusis was of supreme importance and that in its day the whole cult was just as powerful and persuasive as Christianity and in some ways more so.

What the Mysteries all shared in common is that they were an expression of truly ancient human beliefs. They dealt with the yearly death and rebirth of not only human beings but also nature as a whole. In the Mysteries humanity was associated with the seasons during which crops were planted, carefully tended, and eventually gathered—specifically cereals of all types but especially barley. The cutting down of the barley and the sowing of new seed were the pivotal points of reference, so it is not in the least surprising that the ceremonies at Eleusis were practiced at harvesttime in September. Because nature itself was synonymous with the Goddess of the Mystery rites, the Goddess herself was seen as being eternal, whereas her consort, who was also her son and was represented by the barley, died and was reborn each year.

The rites of Demeter were celebrated at Eleusis each September, at the same period as is now set aside in the United States as Constitution Week. For several days those taking part gathered and performed specific rituals around Athens before parading to nearby Eleusis, where the celebration of the Mystery took place. A day later they dispersed and returned to their own countries and homes. The rites of Demeter were available to all—both men and women and even to slaves—which at such an early date was most unusual.

As the reader will learn throughout this book, Washington, D.C., positively reeks of Goddess awareness and is filled with imagery that makes perfect sense in light of the personal reliance many of the Founding Fathers had on Freemasonry, which, as a creation of the Venus Families, retains many elements of the Mystery religions at its core. Indeed, the 3rd degree of Freemasonry represents the same kind of symbolic personal death and rebirth ceremony that lay at the heart of all the Mystery religions, while in the symbols of Freemasonry we find much of the imagery that would have made eminent sense at Eleusis. In addition, many of the Founding Fathers steadfastly refused to commit themselves to Christianity and positively insisted that the free United States should be a secular country. Obviously none of the Founding

Fathers spoke openly about a direct belief in a Goddess as opposed to a God. Such an approach would have met with abject horror among the deeply religious Christian communities throughout the former colonies. Instead, many took a Deist stance, which although suggesting a belief in a divine creator, steadfastly refused to name such a being or even to specify its gender.

It is for these reasons that we consider that the particular part of September during which the Mystery rites of Demeter took place in the ancient world was held as special to many of the leaders of the new United States at the time they met with their counterparts in Philadelphia in 1787. There they drew out the proceedings until they extended into September and set the date for signing the Constitution as September 17, as close as they could get to the same day of the year upon which the acolytes of Demeter took part in her rites.

It is not difficult to see why they arranged things this way. The United States, as it had been under the British Crown, met its ritual and actual death at the time the Constitution was signed, to be reborn at the same time as the free United States of America.

It is no surprise and no coincidence to note that when the cornerstone was laid for the Capitol in Washington, D.C., a building that represents the republic, the ceremony was organized by Freemasons and undertaken by free America's first president, George Washington, who himself was an enthusiastic Freemason. Nor is it anything other than logical that the event took place on September 18, 1793—only one day later in September than the date on which the Constitution was signed six years earlier. The reason that September 18 was chosen instead of September 17 was most likely because that day was a Friday, and Friday is named after the Norse goddess Frigg. Frigg was the closest approximation in Nordic mythology to the Greek Demeter. Had the cornerstone ceremony been celebrated on September 17, 1793, it would have taken place on a Thursday, which is named after the Nordic god Thor, who was responsible for war and storms. Symbolically speaking this would not have been a good choice for a country that wished to look forward to peace and prosperity—

predominantly through farming—which was one of the prerogatives of Frigg and her Greek counterpart, Demeter.

Such a stance might sound unnecessarily superstitious to us, but such considerations were still of the utmost importance in the late eighteenth century, especially to those of an esoteric bent as the planners of Washington, D.C., certainly were.

The Congress that spent four months considering the United States Constitution was reported on regularly throughout all the states involved, and there was one fact that had stayed at the back of our minds from the newspaper reports of the proceedings. The chairman of the meetings was George Washington, who sat at the head of the room with his own table and chair. The chair on which he sat throughout all the proceedings was not part of a normal suite of furniture. It was specifically created in Philadelphia during the war against the British.

The chair was of exquisite quality, deeply carved, and it had an extremely high back. The chair still exists in Philadelphia. At the top of the back, facing forward, it has a carved and gilded representation of a rising sun. Above this is a mushroom, which represents the famous Phrygian cap of freedom, a symbol that was so important to the American Revolution. The sun would have stood immediately above the head of George Washington when he occupied the chair. Indeed, one of the delegates, the incredibly clever Benjamin Franklin, said later that he had seen the sun above George Washington's head each day and had wondered whether, as far as the United States was concerned, it would turn out to be a rising or a setting sun. He was ultimately pleased to be able to state categorically that it had indeed been a rising sun. At the time we had first seen the chair and learned of its design it had seemed interesting, but it did not become truly significant until we were researching the Washington Monument and its shadow patterns.

What we now had to ascertain was whether the size and positioning of the Washington Monument had been orchestrated to ensure that something significant and possibly spectacular took place on Constitution Day, September 17. To do this we had to make ourselves conversant with the way shadows behave and how the sun, changing its

Fig. 12.1. A sketch of the gilded sun from the Rising Sun Armchair, occupied by George Washington during the Constitutional Proceedings in Philadelphia in 1787

position throughout each day and across the seasons, affects the shadow of a massive structure such as the Washington Monument.

The sun always rises at dawn at some point on the eastern horizon. In the Northern Hemisphere it then climbs and travels south until it reaches its highest point in the middle of the day. After this it begins to fall toward the west and sets at some place on the western horizon. The place at which the sun rises and sets is determined partly by the latitude of the location at which the observation takes place and is also very much affected by the seasons.

In Washington, D.C., the sun rises around 30 degrees north of east at midsummer and 30 degrees south of east at midwinter. It sets at 30 degrees north of west at midsummer and at 30 degrees south of west in midwinter. Throughout the year the points of sunrise and sunset gradually change, with the sun rising due east and setting due west on March 21 and September 21. Not only does the sun rise much earlier in the day in the summer, it also climbs much higher into the sky, whereas in winter it sticks fairly close to the horizon throughout most of the short days. This is due to the position of the Earth on its orbit around the sun during any part of a given year.

All of this means that accurately predicting the point of sunrise and sunset and the height to which the sun climbs on any given day would have been a fairly complicated procedure for the planners of the Washington Monument, whereas it is now a relatively simple task thanks to astronomical computer programs. The length of a shadow cast by the sun is dependent on the sun's height above the horizon at any given time, together with the height of the object casting the shadow. By using calculators dedicated to measuring the size and angles of right-angled triangles in conjunction with an accurate assessment of the sun's position and altitude at any moment in time, it is possible to predict how long a given shadow will be at a specific time on a particular date. We were also aided greatly in this task by Google Earth, the use of which allowed us to measure easily and accurately the distance between the Washington Monument and other structures on and around the Mall.

There is another factor regarding tall objects and the sun that became abundantly clear to us at the start of our investigations. If an observer walks to the end of a shadow and looks back at the object casting the shadow, he or she will observe the disk of the sun apparently positioned on top of the object (there will always be a slight discrepancy due to the height of the observer, but to all intents and purposes this happening is a fact).

After careful calculations this is what we discovered. As long as the sky is clear, each year, on September 17 at 6:45 p.m., anyone standing outside the center of the western doors of the Capitol and looking west down the Mall will see the sun's disk standing on the point of the Washington Monument. Meanwhile, the shadow of the monument will pass eastward up the Mall and the point of the shadow will reach the western doors of the Capitol. This is an inevitability brought about because of the position of the monument relative to the Capitol, the height of the monument, and the height and azimuth (compass bearing) of the sun at this particular time of this specific day.

The perfect nature of this happening does not occur on any other day of the year except March 25 (which will be explained later). The event becomes possible because the monument was built at 1 degree

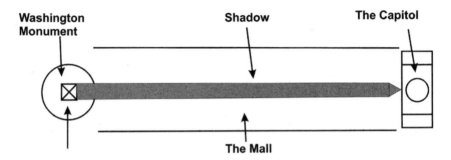

Fig. 12.2. The point of the shadow of the Washington Monument touches the western entrance of the Capitol at 6:45 p.m. on September 17, as seen by an observer standing at the entrance.

south of west as seen from the Capitol, and because of its height of 555 feet. Had the monument been built due west of the Capitol—where it was *meant* to be—it would only have replicated this happening if it had been just over 300 feet in height, because of the amount the sun drops toward the horizon between its azimuth of 1 degree south of west and due west. Such a situation could easily have been made to work, but, as we will presently see, there are other shadow and solar phenomena from the monument to other specific locations that could not take place if this had indeed been the case. In addition, the monument would have looked much less impressive than it does if it had been 200 feet shorter in height.

Because the sun also sits on top of the monument when seen from the Capitol on March 25, the odds of this event taking place on September 17 are 182:1 against random chance. However, we have to remember the Rising Sun Armchair and the fact that its gilded carving of the sun could be observed over George Washington's head for four months in Philadelphia and of course during the actual signing ceremony. In addition, it is important to bear in mind the true significance of September 17 to the United States calendar. Taking all of this into account we would suggest that this happening was most certainly planned and that the Washington Monument was placed where it is and built to a height of 555 feet to create the event.

To understand why such a situation might even be seen as relevant, we have to look at the significance of obelisks in a historical sense. The ancient Egyptians were building these structures from earliest times. Few if any explanations exist as to what obelisks were specifically meant to represent to those who first created them, but it is safe to say they were seen as a representation of the god Osiris.

The association of the god Osiris with obelisks undoubtedly came from a story about his death at the hands of a competitor god, Set. Set had sealed Osiris into a sarcophagus, which he threw into the River Nile. The coffin came to rest among reeds and trees, and the body of Osiris, together with the sarcophagus, became entombed by the growing trunk of a large Acacia tree. The tree was cut down and used as a great pillar in a local palace, where Isis, the grieving wife of Osiris, eventually found it. This part of the Osiris story undoubtedly encapsulates truly ancient tales about tree trunks and stone pillars that are "possessed" by spirits or deities. Many early cultures worshipped stone pillars, for example the pre-Hebrew peoples of the Near East and also the Minoans on Crete. Devotees treated the pillars as if they were either actually alive or were periodically inhabited by supernatural agencies. Britain and France still have thousands of standing stones, which also exist across other areas of Europe and on the islands of the Mediterranean. Most of these date back thousands of years, and all of them might well have been considered to be possessed at certain times or to represent specific individuals or gods.

Osiris was one of the most important of the ancient Egyptian deities and was the god solely responsible for death and the afterlife. It was said that Osiris dwelled in a part of the sky where the stars of Orion's Belt can be seen. The Egyptians believed that in this region of the sky there was an exact replica of Egypt to which souls could travel after death. This journey was not without its perils, however, and in between the real Egypt and its divine counterpart were a host of tests and horrors that had to be undertaken by the departing individual. With the right preparations the departed could face all the ordeals and be reborn into a life that was very similar to the one they had previously enjoyed. In other words, they would be reborn.

Obelisks have been described as "frozen sunbeams" and this is undoubtedly one of the ways the ancient Egyptians viewed them. The sun was all-important to ancient Egypt, because it was the source of all life but could also be a great destroyer. Among the earliest civilizations high stone pillars—the forerunners of obelisks—had already enjoyed a solar association. Such pillars represented the phallus of the sun. Buried deep into the ground they represented the sexual union of Sun and Earth, and it is more than likely that the Egyptians viewed them in a similar way. In this sense there is almost certainly another connection with the god Osiris. In addition to Set sealing Osiris into the sarcophagus that eventually became a pillar, Set later tore the body of Osiris into fourteen parts, which he spread throughout the world. Isis found all of the parts of Osiris except one: his phallus. It is possible that the ancient Egyptians associated obelisks with the missing phallus of Osiris, which was replaced by Isis with an artificial one.

We do not know for sure what part the shadows of obelisks played in the beliefs of the Egyptians, but there are many theories, especially when the obelisks were placed in pairs at the entrance to temples. During the day different shadows would be cast from the obelisks onto the open temple floor, where they undoubtedly had ritual significance. Devotees standing at the end of an obelisk shadow would be able to look up and see the disk of the sun standing on the point of the column, and they probably believed that the sun was passing its power down the column and along the shadow.

It is easy to see the fascination shadows might have for an unscientific mind. Shadows could easily be viewed as the stuff of the spirit world, because although they can be seen, they have no substance. Like rainbows they are elusive and no doubt puzzling if the mechanisms that create them are not understood.

It is quite conceivable that the Egyptians considered the shadows of obelisks to be associated with the afterlife, about which they were virtually obsessed and on account of which they all gave a great deal of time, thought, and wealth. Thus the power of the sun, passed along the shadow from obelisks, may have been seen as feeding the observer's "ka," which is the ancient Egyptian version of what we would today call a person's soul. Clearly obelisks were extremely important to the Egyptians— it was even said that some obelisks could speak and give prophecies.

We were very impressed at the precision of the nineteenth-century engineers who had managed to negotiate the sun's altitude and azimuth together with the height and position of the Washington Monument in order to have it offer such a memorable show each year on Constitution Day. Its meaning was quite clear. On the day the Constitution was signed the United States died to its old past and was reborn as a free and independent republic. Like all those devotees at Eleusis and similar to the souls of the Egyptian dead, it had conquered death and been reborn to a better world. This historical happening was highlighted on every Constitution Day on the same day in the calendar that the many thousands of devotees of Demeter had undergone the symbolic death and rebirth ceremony at Eleusis. Those who had planned all of this were not only commemorating the true start of their own free nation, they were also paying homage to Demeter, who as we have already demonstrated was a significant presence across Washington, D.C., as a whole.

Had this been the end of the story of the Washington Monument it would have been interesting enough, but it turns out that it was merely the start of a series of realizations that, when taken together, are truly extraordinary.

13

INDEPENDENCE DAY AND
THE WINTER SOLSTICE

It occurred to us that there is one day in the United States calendar that is even more iconic than Constitution Day. This is the Fourth of July, the day in 1776 on which the American colonies unilaterally declared independence from Great Britain. The Declaration of Independence led to the bloody war during which the former colonists fought like Trojans to secure their freedom, and as a result of which Great Britain was soundly beaten and humbled.

Americans in general hold the Fourth of July as being almost sacred. The Declaration of Independence was a bold and beautiful statement made by individuals who considered that to fight and possibly to die for freedom was preferable to living under the yoke of colonial rule, with all the embargoes, taxes, onerous responsibilities, and implied servitude it represented.

Was it possible, we asked ourselves, that the people who had so carefully planned and erected the Washington Monument had included the same sort of solar event that marked Constitution Day, but this time relevant to that memorable statement of the human right to freedom and dignity?

By this time we were becoming quite adept at carrying out the calculations necessary to show where the shadows of the monument fell throughout any particular day, so it did not take us too long to come up with the answer. When we did, it was so perfectly and so obviously planned that half a dozen excited e-mails passed back and forth across the Atlantic Ocean on the day it fell into place.

At the point on the ground where the Washington Monument was meant to be placed there is a small, squat stone. It goes unnoticed to most visitors, but it does have a great significance. In fact it is a replacement for an earlier stone that was somehow lost when the Mall was being renovated after the American Civil War. As we mentioned in chapter 11 it was and is called the Jefferson Pier. The word *pier* in this context means an upright stone, usually a mooring post for boats. This was exactly the Jefferson Pier's original use, because there was formerly a canal that ran from west to east below what is now Constitutional Avenue, and the owners of merchant craft somewhat irreverently used the Jefferson stone as a mooring post.

The original Jefferson Pier had been erected at the instruction of Thomas Jefferson when he was the third president of the United States. Jefferson had formerly been a surveyor. He was anxious to establish a prime meridian for the United States, which was to be a line of longitude from which all other measurements in the United States could be measured. The prime meridian was to run through the very center of the White House and would divide the rotated square that is the District of Columbia into two equal parts. Jefferson's prime meridian was never actually adopted by the United States, but while he was surveying it he marked out, very accurately, the point at which the east–west line from the Capitol met the north–south line from the center of the White House. It was at this point that the Jefferson Pier was placed, and it marked the position where Pierre Charles L'Enfant had intended the memorial to General and President George Washington to be placed.

As we have seen, the Washington Memorial was placed east and south of this location, primarily, we believe, so that it would provide the solar disk and shadow show on Constitution Day. However, those who designed and placed the Washington Monument were much more clever than we had originally given them credit for being. At 10:55 a.m. on each July 4 when the sky is clear, the point of the shadow of the Washington Monument touches the face of the Jefferson Pier. Prior to July 4 the shadow falls short of the Jefferson Pier, and after July 4 the shadow of the monument extends beyond the stone. It is only on this one day each year when the light and shadow show takes place at this spot. It also follows that anyone standing by the Jefferson Pier when this event takes place would see the solar disk apparently standing briefly on the point of the monument.

Once again this could be a random chance event, but there is a very important reason why it is unlikely to be a fluke. Until the Jefferson Memorial was built in the twentieth century, this small and unpretentious stone was the only commemoration on the Mall of one of the most significant people in the history of the United States. Next to George Washington himself, Thomas Jefferson was probably the most important individual throughout the formative years of a free United States. Even more to the point, he was the man who first put the immortal words of the Declaration of Independence onto paper, because although the full declaration was amended and sanctioned by a small committee, nobody doubts that the words came from the mind and pen of Thomas Jefferson.

In other words, Thomas Jefferson could reasonably be called the father of the Declaration, so it is absolutely appropriate that the shadow celebration from the Washington Monument should point to the stone that still bears the name of Thomas Jefferson on July 4, the day the Declaration was officially made in 1776.

An interesting side issue here is the realization that for fifteen to seventeen years at the end of the Civil War, the Jefferson Pier was "lost" during remedial work on the Mall. It was replaced in 1889 with a new stone, but we have no way of knowing whether the new stone stands *exactly* where the old one did. In other words, its final position may have been slightly manipulated to ensure that the July 4 light and shadow show took place precisely. Even a few feet could make a difference in the result, and it is known that the new Jefferson Pier stands more than two feet from the true meeting of the north–south line through the middle of the White House and the east–west line from the center of the Capitol. Of course this could simply be a mistake, but it is equally likely that when the new Jefferson Pier was erected its position was tweaked to take account of the Fourth of July event. By this time the Washington Monument had been finished for five years, and it would have been simplicity itself to place the new Jefferson Pier exactly where the shadow of the monument reached at the critical moment on July 4. Indeed, this could be the very reason why it was "lost" during the remedial work on the Mall—it was probably never actually mislaid at all but removed for a period until the Washington Monument revealed its exact shadow position for July 4.

After exploring the two major days in the United States civil calendar we thought it worthwhile to see if the builders of the Washington Monument had also marked any of the astronomically important days of the year. We were both aware that there are many connections between Freemasonry and the solstices and equinoxes, and we wondered if these too might be represented by the monument's shadow shows. The summer and winter solstices are the two days at which the sun alternatively reaches the most northerly and southerly points it achieves at dawn each year. In Washington, D.C., the sun rises 30 degrees north of east at the summer solstice around June 21, and it rises at 30 degrees south of east during the winter solstice around December 21. The equinoxes are the two days of March 21 and September 21 when the sun rises due east and sets due west.

All of these dates were particularly significant to our ancient ancestors, especially the solstices. Through the advancing days of autumn, sky watchers would have observed that the days were getting shorter and that the sun was rising ever farther south each morning. This coincided with the onset of winter and the dark days when famine lay just around the corner. It would be quite natural that the earliest farmers especially would take special note of the day on which the sun appeared to halt its southerly course along the horizon at dawn and when it began to move north again. Many cultures held great celebrations at the winter solstice, and there is some evidence that ritual sacrifice—even sometimes human sacrifice—formed a part of these celebrations.

Similar ceremonies were doubtless held on the summer solstice, when the days were at their longest and the promise of an upcoming harvest would have brought joy to communities all across the Northern Hemisphere.

The equinoxes were celebrated because they represented the onset of spring and the arrival of autumn with its promise of abundance. The equinoxes were also important because they represented a fixed point from which astronomical calculations could be made.

What we discovered when we studied the shadow of the Washington Monument on December 21 surprised us even more than the happenings on Constitution Day and Independence Day. To fully appreciate it we need to look again at that enigmatic area south of the White House that is known as the Ellipse. For decades after the founding of Washington, D.C., the area of land that is today covered by the Ellipse was nothing more than a meadow surrounded by a white picket fence and known as the White Lot. As we showed earlier, Pierre Charles L'Enfant, and presumably his boss, George Washington, clearly intended something special for this lot. On his original map of the projected Washington, L'Enfant drew what could only have been intended to represent an eye, very similar to the All-Seeing Eye that is so familiar to Freemasonry and which can also be found on the American one-dollar bill. This eye is said to represent the Great Architect of the Universe, which is the name Freemasonry gives to the Deity.

There are other factors that make the Ellipse important. Alan demonstrated that—like the distance between many of the junctions, landmarks, and public buildings of Washington, D.C.—the Ellipse is distinguished by displaying an ancient unit of measurement equal to 366 Megalithic Yards (996 feet, or 303.6 meters), which is the distance across its widest part. In addition, we know for sure that when it was being created from the White Lot, just after the Civil War, a large hole was dug at its center. What we don't know is who dug the hole and what its purpose might have been. We will have more to say about the possible contents of the resulting chamber at the center of the Ellipse in due course, but for the moment it is only necessary to understand that there is something deeply sacred and special about the Ellipse, even though for all intents and purposes it is nothing more than a very large public park. Even the fact that it is an ellipse and not a circle turns out to be highly significant, especially in terms of its relationship with the shadow cast by the Washington Monument.

What we discovered taking place on the day of the winter solstice, December 21, each year is little short of sensational and so absolutely pagan that it simply cannot be dismissed. It speaks of ideas and ceremonies that must have taken place for many thousands of years, involving a multitude of cultures across our planet. The December 21 event is replete with symbolism impossible to dismiss; yet until we rediscovered

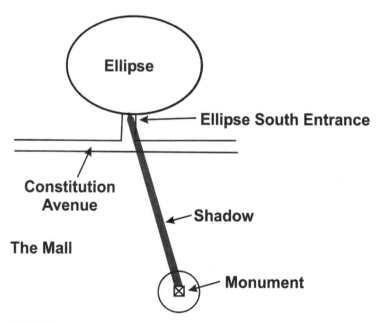

Fig. 13.1. Taking into account the height of the sun and its position on the horizon at 10:58 a.m. on December 21, the shadow of the monument would extend 1,250 feet. The point of the shadow would *just* break into the Ellipse at the center of the south entrance. It takes little imagination to understand what is taking place here in a symbolic sense.

it, hardly anyone can have been aware that it was taking place. Figure 13.1 on page 197 is a simplified image of the event.

It is important to mention that this happening in Washington, D.C., ties in perfectly with observations made by Scott Wolter at the Newport Tower, a fascinating structure located in Newport, Rhode Island. All manner of ideas have been put forward to try to explain what the Newport Tower might actually be, and he is not the only researcher to claim that it is very old indeed.*

Wolter puts forward the theory that the Newport Tower was originally created by members of the Knights Templar who visited North America long before Christopher Columbus made his own journey. Wolter and other researchers demonstrated that the Tower was very carefully created and that it contains astronomical alignments. One of these takes place at 9:00 a.m. on December 21, the winter solstice. As the sun rises above the horizon it shines through one of the tower's windows and illuminates an egg-shaped keystone opposite. This is simply a slightly different version of what takes place on the same morning in Washington, D.C., as the shadow from the Washington Monument subtly penetrates the southern entrance of Ellipse Park. It is our contention that the same ultimate group of people—the Venus Families—were responsible for both happenings, even though their creation was centuries apart.

Ancient peoples often viewed the cycles of nature as being synonymous with the cycles of human beings. They knew very well that birth in human females took place nine months after conception. This was one of the reasons why the winter solstice celebrations were so important. Not only did the sun cease to travel south at dawn on this day and begin to move north again, but the solstice was seen as being the time when Nature herself conceived. The birth that followed nine months later was the harvest, so the parallels with human beings were obvious.

Of course, several thousand years ago nobody fully understood the

---

*Anyone who wishes to know more about Scott Wolter's painstaking research into the Newport Tower should read *The Hooked X: Key to the Secret History of North America.*

mechanism of conception. Even the physical act that led to conception may not have actually been connected with birth in the minds of ancient hunter-gatherers, but by the time farming had been adopted and the breeding of animals began, with the necessary knowledge that was gained it would not have taken long for the relationship between sexual intercourse and birth to be understood in human beings as well as livestock. By the time the Washington Monument was built in the nineteenth century science was moving ahead rapidly, and the mechanism by which male sperm penetrates the egg of a female had been studied in detail.

In a symbolic sense, the Ellipse was created to represent a female egg, specifically that of the Earth Goddess (and therefore of nature itself). The shadow of the monument can be seen as a human sperm: the longest cell in the human body. At the time of conception a single sperm, which following sexual intercourse has traveled up the woman's birth canal, makes contact with and ultimately penetrates the egg that is waiting. If all goes smoothly once fertilization has taken place, a child resulting from the union of the sperm and the egg will be born nine months later.

At the time of the winter solstice, for two or three days it appears that the sun has stopped its journey south and retains the same rising point on the horizon at dawn. This is in stark contrast to the spring and autumn, at which times the sun alters its rising point on the horizon by a full degree of arc each day. For this reason, the point of the shadow of the monument penetrates the Ellipse at around 11:00 a.m. for two or three days, though its most significant incursion into the Ellipse occurs on December 21, the winter solstice.

This is potent symbolism, interpreted partly through the eyes of a physiological understanding of the happenings inside a female that ultimately lead to birth. Symbolically speaking, the Washington Monument is a phallus, the potency of which is supplied by the sun. The winter solstice was often referred to as the "triumph of the sun," because it was at this time that the sun ceased its southward journey and once again began to travel north to achieve its full potency the following summer. So, at its moment of greatest triumph, the sun charges the phallus that is the obelisk with its potency, creating the shadow that represents the sperm that carries the seed of new life to the Earth, the waiting egg that is represented by the Ellipse. The nine-month wait for a human mother leads to a child, whereas in the case of the Earth, the result is the life-giving harvest of autumn.

As any scientist worth his or her salt knows, a theory is just a theory until it is tested in the field. While we were very confident the programs and calculations used to determine the shadow play of the monument were correct, we had yet to see it happen for ourselves in Washington, D.C. In an effort to witness the shadow perform as we had predicted, Janet and her husband, Scott, decided to be the agents in the field and took a three-day trip to Washington in December 2014, just prior to the winter solstice of December 21. Alan was unable to join them but was as physically present as modern technology could allow him to be. While the actual penetration by shadow into the southern side of the Ellipse was not due to happen until December 21, they could still verify on December 18–20 that the shadow was in its predicted location for those days. Because the weather was particularly cloudy that time of year, they hoped for clear skies at least on one of the days they were there. A holiday event was planned for December 21 back home, so they would not be able to be present on the actual solstice.

Tension ran high the first morning Janet and Scott set out to witness the shadow near the Ellipse—as all scientists must feel when they are about to prove or disprove their theory. The weather was not cooperating with high but rather thin clouds, but just enough sun was peeking through most of the time to cast weak shadows. Poor Alan had to wait all day to hear the results, he being six hours ahead in England.

Janet and Scott arrived at the parking lot that surrounds the southern side of the Ellipse to find that the shadow from the Washington Monument was invisible—in the weak sunshine the farther from the monument the shadow went the more it was obscured. They could see their own shadows on the ground, however, and quickly figured out that when they moved into the zone where the shadow should be, their own shadows disappeared! It was quite strange to see. The other clue as to where the shadow tip was on the ground was to look up at the monument and see where the sun was in relation to the top of the monument. The partial cloudiness allowed them to be able to look directly at the disk of the sun where it sat perfectly on the tip of the monument. It was spectacular. As 11 a.m. approached, and the shadow moved to its nearest position to the southern end of the curb of the Ellipse, they both began snapping pictures with cameras and phones of the incredible sight of the sun on top of the monument. They moved with the sun, and it moved fairly quickly, all the while testing the visibility of their own shadows on the ground by waving their arms as their body shadows stayed in the monument tip's shadow. When she was about four feet from the curb of the Ellipse at 11 a.m., Janet snapped another photo of the sun on the tip of the monument, turned around to photograph how far from the curb she was, and e-mailed them to Alan on her phone. She knew their calculations were correct for where they had predicted the shadow would be for that day and time! She and Scott

Fig. 13.2. The sun appears to sit on top of the Washington Monument on December 18, 2014, at 11 a.m., as viewed from near the southern edge of the Ellipse in Washington, D.C., indicating the photographer was standing at the tip of the shadow. The partial cloud cover gave the sun a moonlike appearance. Photo courtesy of Scott F. Wolter

could practically hear the whoops of excitement across the Atlantic as Alan viewed the photos.

Security is very tight around the area of the Ellipse, being just south of the White House, and there were several police officers who inquired as to what Janet and Scott were doing. To their credit and our great relief they took a polite interest in the explanation about the way the shadow points to things on the ground on certain significant days of the year. While the police kept a watchful eye on them the entire hour they were there, Janet and Scott greatly appreciated their patience and tolerance in allowing them to gather the evidence they needed.

But as the shadow moved away from the Ellipse, Janet soon realized that what they needed to do next was get a photo of the shadow from the top of the monument. The second day was cloudy, and there would be no shadow that day. In the mean time she found out that the elevator in the Washington Monument was broken, but the park ranger she spoke to hoped it to be fixed by the next day. To get tickets, she would have to wait in line early in the morning and hope some were available for the 10:30 a.m. tour.

On their last morning in D.C., Janet and Scott again awoke to clouds, but they seemed to be thinning and showed promise of breaking up later in the day. Janet called the number the park ranger had given her to see if the elevator was working, and, to her great relief, it was. The date was December 20, and if the clouds broke by 11 a.m., they should be able to get some great photographs of the monument shadow just touching the edge of the Ellipse. That is IF they could get tickets for the 10:30 a.m. tour allowing them to be at the top of the monument for the 11 a.m. event. Alan was once again set to waiting all day until the predicted time arrived and he would see the results of his friends' quest.

Janet arrived in the ticket line for the Washington Monument tours and patiently waited while the ticket distributors crossed off the available tour times on a sign above the window. There were still several people ahead of her when 10 a.m. was crossed off, and the next one to go would be 10:30 a.m. She held her breath and was thrilled when she arrived at the window and was able to get two tickets!

She and Scott arrived at the appointed hour, and as they rode the elevator to the top of the monument they hoped the skies would clear in time. Once at the top, they were free to stay as long as they wanted and admire the lovely views of the capital city from each direction. As 11 a.m. approached, the time when the monument's shadow was due to reach the Ellipse, the clouds were still present. There were ribbons of brighter streaks in the clouds where the sun was trying to peak through, but the hour came and there was no shadow. Janet stayed in the north-facing viewing window for another few minutes while Scott wandered off and went to snap photos in other directions. As she stood alone in the window looking over the Ellipse and the White House, she wished one more time for the sun to come out. Suddenly at 11:05, the shadow

Fig. 13.3. The shadow of the Washington Monument (outlined) appeared far below the monument's observation deck, reaching to a point just past the southern edge of the Ellipse on December 20, 2014, at 11:05 a.m. The shadow made only a weak, brief appearance that morning, just after it would have briefly touched the southern edge of the Ellipse at 11:00 a.m. Photo courtesy of Scott F. Wolter

appeared like a ghostly apparition on the ground 555 feet beneath her. She started to snap photos with her phone and yelled for Scott to come take photos with his good camera. He heard her, and soon they were both taking photos. The sun never shone strongly, but it was enough to get good photos. On a clear day, they had no doubt it would have been a spectacular sight. It was clear from the shadow's position, five minutes past when it would have just crept over the curb of the Ellipse, that Alan and Janet's theory was correct. She e-mailed the photos to Alan, who was as thrilled as she was to see them.

Washington lies within its own district, which is called Columbia. As far as those who laid out and created the District of Columbia were concerned, the center of the Ellipse was also the very center of Columbia. In reality they were very slightly wrong, but that was a fault in eighteenth-century surveying. As we have shown elsewhere in this book the intention was clear. Columbia was the name by which the Goddess of the United States was known. But Columbia was only one name of a Goddess who had a long legacy; she was simply one version of the Great Goddess, who literally *was* the Earth.

Whoever dreamed up this happening each winter solstice was motivated partly by ancient symbolism and partly by medical knowledge that was developing at the time: it is the perfect merging of belief and knowledge, the same fusion of mythology and fact upon which Freemasonry itself is founded.

Having discovered this behavior of the monument's shadow on December 21, it became clear to us why the Ellipse could not have been created as a circle instead. If its measurements north to south had been identical to its size from east to west, which would certainly have been possible, the shadow of the monument would have driven deep into the resulting circle at the time of the winter solstice instead of subtly penetrating its membrane as does a human sperm when it encounters a waiting female egg. The ultimate shape of the ellipse was carefully calculated to make sure the subtle penetration took place on the correct day of the year.

By this stage of our investigations we had begun to understand in much greater detail the way in which the shadow of the Washington Monument behaves throughout the year, and it seemed clear to us that providing a suitable show for the summer solstice would have been extremely difficult for the planners of the monument—at least without making the situation so obvious that people would have been bound to work out what was taking place. This is because by the summer solstice the sun dawns well north of east and then rises very quickly, achieving its highest altitude of the year on that day. When the sun is high, shadows are much shorter than they are at times when the sun is low in the sky. This means that close to noon on the day of the summer solstice, the shadow of the monument would be virtually nonexistent.

It appears that the monument planners understood this fact all too well and did not initially attempt to mark the summer solstice on the ground close to the monument's base. However, it was at this point in our investigation that we began to understand that the knowledge that had led to the Washington Monument's height and placement on the landscape was definitely not simply a nineteenth-century matter. Old aerial photographs of the monument show that the base around it was quite plain. The system of paths that surrounds the monument at present was not created until as recently as 2005. Once the paths were laid down in their present form, the paths allowed for a summer solstice show from the monument that is every bit as potent as the one taking place at the winter solstice.

Figure 13.4 on page 206 is a simplified drawing of the major paths surrounding the Washington Monument, as of 2005. At 12:10 p.m. on June 21 each year, the shadow from the monument would be extremely short—in fact only about 140 feet. It would extend to the point shown in the drawing, which is the top intersection of a version of a Vesica Piscis.

The Vesica Piscis is a common geometrical figure formed from two interlocking circles, as shown in figure 13.5 on page 206. The term *Vesica Piscis* is Latin and means "the bladder of a fish," because this is what the symbol resembles. It is created when two circles of the same diameter are interlocked in such a way that the edge of each circle runs

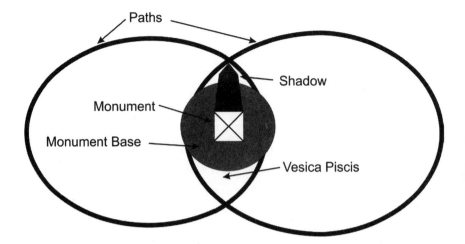

Fig. 13.4. Shadow from Washington Monument, June 21, 12:10 p.m.

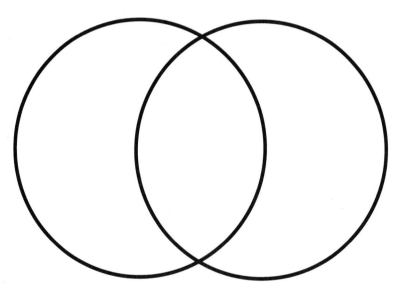

Fig. 13.5. The geometrical figure known as a Vesica Piscis

through the center of the other circle. In a true Vesica Piscis it is possible to create two equilateral triangles within the shape created, as shown in figure 13.6. The mathematical ratio between the height of the Vesica Piscis and its width is equal to the square root of 3, a fact

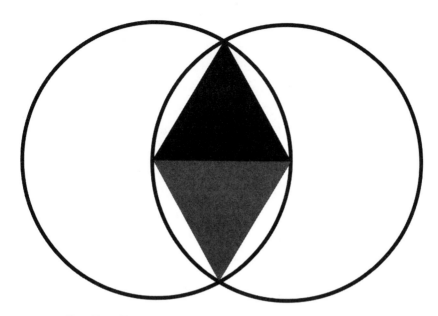

Fig. 13.6. Two equilateral triangles within a Vesica Piscis

that fascinated ancient mathematicians. Despite this, for many centuries the Vesica Piscis has been not simply of geometric interest but has also been a shape of tremendous spiritual and religious importance. The Vesica Piscis represents the feminine, most likely because it was taken to resemble a human vagina. For thousands of years it has been used in iconography from East and West and is still as popular as ever, especially among modern Pagans. The symbol has also figured prominently in Freemasonry, where it is displayed on the collars of lodge officers during certain ceremonies. Probably more than any other symbol it is taken to represent the feminine principle in religion and spirituality.

In the case of the monument the two ellipses that create the Vesica Piscis are set within a larger ellipse, which has the same width as Ellipse Park, in other words 366 Megalithic Yards. This surely indicates an intended connection on the part of whoever planned these paths, associating the monument and the Ellipse itself. The summer solstice shadow from the monument splits the Vesica Piscis in two and points directly to the northern intersection of the two ellipses. This could hardly fail to be significant, because at the time this happens the sun is as high in the sky as it ever gets in Washington, D.C. No shadow formed directly north of the monument on other days can ever be shorter, and in all other cases the point of the shadow falls outside of the Vesica Piscis.

No shadow cast by the monument could be used to define either the vernal or the autumnal equinox directly because at these times the sun rises due east. This means that by the time it clears the horizon it has already moved slightly south of east. In any case, with the sun directly on either the eastern or western horizon, the shadow cast by the monument would be of a finite length. However, in a sense the whole of Washington, D.C., was created with the equinoxes in mind. Although the axis of the city was changed very slightly in the nineteenth century to accommodate the Washington Monument, Washington, D.C., itself was always intended to have an east–west axis.

So in addition to being planned to commemorate both the American Constitution and the signing of the Declaration of Independence, the Washington Monument was also designed to perform a very specific task at the time of the winter solstice. In addition, the ground around

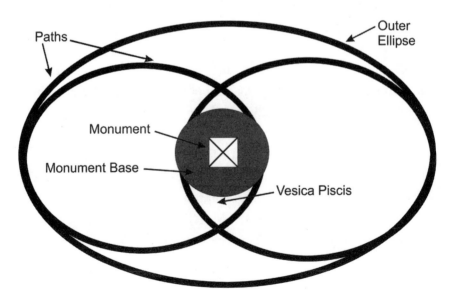

Fig. 13.7. Paths around Washington Monument including outer ellipse

the monument has been altered as recently as 2005 so that an equally impressive display takes place on the day of the summer solstice.

All of this is remarkable indeed, not least of all because no acknowledgment of any of this has ever been forthcoming from those within Washington, D.C., who are responsible for urban planning, either in the nineteenth century or far more recently. These happenings remain as secrets hidden in plain sight. What is even more incredible is the fact that major structures created on the Mall in very recent times were also carefully locked into the magic of the monument.

14

Sun and Shadow on
the U.S. Capitol

At the close of the twentieth century there was still no national monument in Washington, D.C., to commemorate the involvement of the United States in the Second World War, though this was a matter that was already under review as the millennium approached.

As early as 1987, Congress had been approached about the possibility of creating a National World War II Memorial, but it took some time before the suggestion introduced in December of 1987 by Marcy Kaptur of Ohio was acted upon, and in fact it was 1993 before a bill was passed and work began on finding a suitable site. An advisory board was set up, and ideas were sought for a suitable location. All manner of suggestions were forthcoming, but in the end it was decided that the new monument should be placed on the National Mall, between the Washington Monument and the Lincoln Memorial. An existing feature, the Rainbow Pool, was incorporated into the stunning design of the new memorial, and building began in September of 2001.

We visited the site together during the early spring of 2013, though at the time we had no idea of its connection with the Washington Monument, which stands around 1,500 feet to the east. All the same, we were quite conversant with the importance of the WWII Memorial

Fig. 14.1. The National World War II Memorial on the Mall
in Washington, D.C.
Photo courtesy of Scott F. Wolter

in terms of the sacred geometry upon which the whole Mall area of Washington, D.C., is based. Readers will find plenty to explain Washington's sacred geometry elsewhere in this book, but suffice it to say that the position chosen for the WWII Memorial was far from arbitrary and conforms to the secret ground rules laid down for Washington, D.C., first established at the end of the eighteenth century. Bearing this in mind, we wondered if it was possible that the WWII Memorial also had a deliberately planned relationship with the Washington Monument.

The United States WWII Memorial is indeed a stunning and fitting epitaph to American citizens who died or were injured during the Second World War, as well as to all the people who survived but whose lives were forever changed as a result of their involvement in the conflict. This was a pivotal point in human affairs because if the black threat of Fascism had not been confronted or the Japanese Empire had been allowed to continue expanding, the world in which everyone reading this book grew up would certainly have been radically different. These were considerations we spoke about on that spring day when we looked up at the high pinnacles surrounding the central fountain and pool at the center of the structure. It was also impossible from this location to avoid noticing the huge bulk that is the Washington Monument, which dominates the landscape to the east, but we remained at that time totally unaware of its significance to the memorial.

As we had done at other times and locations, we used several computer programs to work out what relationship the shadow of the Washington Monument would have to the WWII Memorial throughout the year. In reality the shadow of the monument can only make direct contact with the WWII Memorial in the summer. This is because between September 21 and March 21 the sun in Washington, D.C., rises south of east and sets south of west. This means that by the time the sun rises high enough to cast a discernible shadow, such shadows will always appear farther north than the Mall itself. Shadows can only be cast along the length of the Mall between March 21 and September 21.

The operative date for the shadow point of the monument to make contact with the western center of the plaza surrounding the WWII Memorial is August 15. This takes place at 7:16 a.m., and the moment we came to realize this fact it became clear that there was nothing

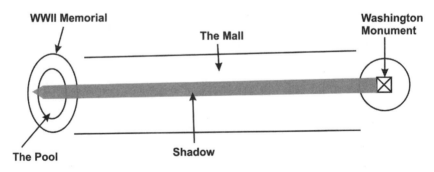

Fig. 14.2. At 7:16 a.m. on August 15 the point of the shadow of the Washington Monument contacts the western side of the National World War II Memorial.

remotely arbitrary about the place where the WWII Memorial had been built. It was on August 15 in 1945 that the misery and carnage that was the Second World War finally came to its end. Seeking to avoid the probable catastrophe in terms of allied lives having to invade the Japanese home islands, the United States dropped two atomic bombs on Japan, the first on August 6 and the second on August 9. This forced the reluctant Japanese government to accept unconditional surrender.

Although August 15—which is known as Victory in Japan Day, or more commonly VJ Day—marks the end of the Second World War overall, it is still only half the story. This fact is emphasized by the very design of the WWII Memorial. The structure is an ellipse, with its long axis positioned from north to south. At either end is a high arch, or pylon. The southern arch is dedicated to the war in the Pacific, while the northern arch was built to commemorate the war in the Atlantic and also in Europe.

We knew from the start that a shadow cast from the Washington Monument to the WWII Memorial must occur twice during any given year, once as the sun is passing on its journey to midsummer and again as it returns from midsummer back toward winter. The VJ Day shadow is the second of these events, but what we never expected was that the first of the shadows each year would also have been calculated to match events at the end of the Second World War in Europe. By carefully studying an astronomical computer program it was possible to ascertain when the spring-occurring shadow would hit the entrance to the WWII Memorial, which is situated on 17th Street. The date in question that fit best was May 7. This was not an exact copy of the August 15 event, because the point of the Washington Monument shadow in this case would have pointed directly at a small, rectangular stone plinth that stands at the very center front of the WWII Memorial as seen from 17th Street. Imagine our sense of wonder and disbelief when we realized that May 7 was the date on which the German forces had surrendered to the allies in 1945 in Reims, France! The official date celebrated as Victory in Europe Day (VE Day) is May 8, when the German forces in

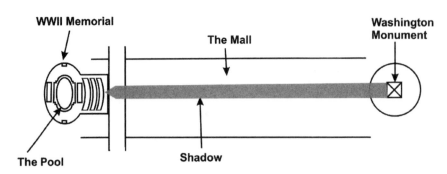

Fig. 14.3. At 7:25 a.m. on May 7 the point of the shadow of
the Washington Monument contacts the eastern entrance of
the National World War II Memorial.

Berlin surrendered, but peace occurred on May 7. There were in effect
two World Wars being fought, one associated with the Pacific and the
other with the Atlantic.

If we had experienced any doubts about the solar disk and shadow
events previously, there could be absolutely no argument about what
takes place each year at the WWII Memorial. Those Americans who
fought in Europe against the Germans and their allies could stand at
the WWII Memorial entrance on May 7 and see the solar disk standing on the point of the Washington Monument at the same time as
its shadow swung around slowly from the south to point directly at
the memorial entrance. Three months later, veterans of the war in the
Pacific could have the same experience, but this time from the western
side of the plaza. This is entirely appropriate, because the Atlantic and
Europe are to the east of the United States and of course the Pacific is
to the west.

It is worth pausing to reflect how such a state of affairs was brought
about. Not only did the WWII Memorial have to be placed in exactly
the right position on the National Mall relative to the Washington
Monument, it also had to have exactly the right dimensions from east
to west if the two shows were to take place on the appropriate days. We
then have to remember that the memorial's actual design was decided

by way of a competition and that the winning design was one of more than four hundred entries. Bearing this in mind, the word conspiracy cannot possibly be avoided. The notion of the winning entry fitting the criteria necessary by chance is preposterous—the more so because the memorial also had to be placed in exactly the right position on the Mall. Either the winning architect, Friedrich St. Florian, had been told what the dimensions of his design should be, or else changes were made to it later to accommodate the sun and shadow shows on the correct dates. As far as the positioning of the memorial was concerned, that was decided by the memorial committee and so could have been manipulated from the start.

It became obvious to us why the two arches, or pylons, representing the Atlantic and Pacific spheres of the Second World War had been placed at the northern and southern ends of the memorial. Logic asserts that they should actually have been placed in the east and the west, but this would have ruined the shadow display from the monument on the two significant days. In fact the whole design of the WWII Memorial was quite clearly handled so as to offer an unimpeded view to the east and west. All of the many pillars and arches that make up the memorial were placed around the northern or the southern arcs of the ellipse that forms the structure with absolutely nothing to obstruct the view of the Washington Monument at one end of the Mall or the Lincoln Memorial at the other.

It is important to make one fact clear. On any day of the year when the sun rises north of east in Washington, D.C., at some time during that morning, the sun will stand at 1 degree north of east. This means that a shadow will be cast along the Mall west of the monument. What matters in terms of our observations is that the shadow in question will be of different lengths on different days because of the sun's altitude as it passes 1 degree north of east. During the period in question, from May to September, the sun appears to change its position on the horizon at dawn very quickly. The only two days when the point of the shadow from the monument touches the west center of the WWII plaza or the memorial's entrance are August 15th and May 7th. respectively. For a day or two either side of these dates the shadow will *almost* replicate the phenomenon, but not quite. What matters most here is that anyone who stands at the WWII Monument on either day, at the correct time, will see the disk of the sun standing on the point of the Washington Monument and will observe the shadow's point touching a point very close to their position. (In fact the difference between the observer's position and the actual point of the shadow will be equal to the distance between their eyes and their feet.)

Of course it is unlikely that anyone would make this observation by chance. To do so on either day one would have to be present at the WWII Memorial very early in the day—not long after 7:00 a.m. Ceremonies held each year on both dates at the memorial take place significantly later than this, by which time the shadow and solar disk show would have long since passed. Only the very few people who are in possession of the necessary information would be likely to visit the WWII Monument at the requisite times.

There is one final day each year during which the monument and the sun put on their impressive show—it is a date we mentioned in chapter 12 in association with the Constitution day event, which takes place on September 17. It is on this day, in the evening, that the shadow of the monument travels east, up the Mall to the place where it hovers momentarily at the western doors of the Capitol. In reality, this event takes place twice each year and is replicated on March 25. One might assume that this second occurrence is just a natural consequence of the way the shadows work in conjunction with the ever-moving position of the sun at dawn and dusk, but this is far from being the case. In the true genius that inspired such a careful placing of the Washington Monument, together with scrupulous detail regarding its height and the yearly movements of the sun, March 25 turns out to be just as significant as September 17, though in a very different way.

When these alignments were designed, great care seems to have been taken to ensure that if any of them were noticed by accident—or in our case because of acquired knowledge—all the alignments could be put down to perfectly normal civic celebrations or notable dates on the

Christian calendar. For example, although the point of the shadow of the monument subtly penetrates the center bottom of the Ellipse on the day of the winter solstice, December 21, it comes close to doing the same thing a few days later on December 25. On this occasion, however, the point of the shadow stops short of penetrating the Ellipse. If we employ the same symbolism as for the December 21 occurrence, in other words the fertilization of the egg of the Earth Goddess by the sperm of the Sky God, we could easily say that the fact that the sperm does not penetrate the egg on December 25 (which is of course Christmas Day) is representative of the virgin nature of Jesus's birth.

Although from the very start the United States was created as a secular state, in other words not responding directly to any religious creed or denomination, it was in the nineteenth century and still remains a predominantly Christian country. Those creating the solar disk and monument shadow events would presumably not have welcomed the accusation that they were marking celebrations of a pagan nature. If this was their wish they were generally successful. For example, although September 17 was the most significant date in the yearly celebrations of the Mysteries of Demeter in Eleusis, it was also, self-evidently, the day on which the American Constitution was signed. It can therefore be counted as a civil celebration and not a religious one. This is true of all the solar events we have mentioned, except for the one that occurs on March 25.

The best we can say about March 25 in terms of United States history is that it was the date upon which the first horse race was staged in 1668! In any other realistic sense it has been an extremely quiet calendar day in the United States. So, if March 25 is not a civil celebration, and assuming it does not repeat the September 17 event purely by chance, does it have some other significance? Indeed it does.

We have seen how closely associated were the beliefs of those who fought for and founded the United States with ancient myths related to the Earth Goddess and her association with an annually born and dying god of the harvest. This story of the Goddess and her son/consort is to be found in many forms and across countless thousands of years.

The most recent manifestation of this story is of course enshrined in Christianity, because Jesus represents a version of the harvest god. Like many of his counterparts, Jesus was born of a virgin, was ultimately persecuted and killed, but rose again from the dead. Although the date of Jesus's Passion, Crucifixion, and rising from the dead has become a movable festival, which Christians call Easter, computed astronomically from the vernal equinox and the phases of the moon, things were not always this way.

In the earliest days of the new faith, when aspects of other prevalent myths were attaching themselves to the Jesus story, one of the greatest sources from which Christians drew their material was the story of Cybele and Attis. Cybele was yet another name of the Great Goddess, as she was worshipped in Phrygia, which was part of modern-day Turkey. The cap of freedom, so closely tied to the United States and its independence, came from the same region and for this reason is still known as a Phrygian cap. This region seems to have been of significant interest to the Founding Fathers of the United States, especially the Masonic ones.

In the story Cybele falls in love with a beautiful shepherd boy named Attis. As with all the dying and reborn gods of the harvest, Attis meets a terrible death. Cybele mourns his passing and determines to bring him back to life. According to myth, his death took place on March 22, and he was brought back to life three days later on March 25. The cult of Cybele and Attis was massive in its day and could have been a significant threat to the developing beliefs of Christians. Always accommodating when it came to copying the practices of its opposing beliefs, Christianity in many regions of the Roman Empire adopted Attis's date of resurrection, March 25, as being that of Jesus's own resurrection.

Other aspects of Attis, Mithras, Dionysus, Adonis, and other dying and reborn gods were also collected from across the empire and became attached to Christianity. In truth, and despite the fact that many of its adherents would deny the fact with their dying breath, Christianity is merely the most recent and most successful of a wealth of Mystery religions, most of which found an expression somewhere in the Roman Empire. Ultimately, Christianity began to celebrate Easter, the time of

Jesus's death and resurrection, as a movable feast and it lost its connection with March 25. Still, the fact remains that for a great many people, across a very broad span of time, March 25 was considered to be a day of rejoicing and celebration at the rebirth of their patron god on this specific date.

Even if their efforts to mark so many of the important calendar days by means of the solar disk and shadow events had somehow come to be widely known, those responsible would have had some difficulty explaining March 25. It is no longer a specifically Christian time of celebration and clearly betrays its pagan origins.

What all the events highlighted by the Washington Monument and its shadows have in common is that they are all connected in some way with death and rebirth. In the case of September 17 it is the death of colonial rule and the birth of the republic and also of course the ritual death and rebirth of those who took part in the Mysteries of Demeter. July 4th celebrates the birth of a new federal United States of America, while the WWII Memorial events of May and August demonstrate the end of a world war and the birth of a new world in which it is hoped that through cooperation and through control of the globe by the superpower America such a happening will never come about again. At the same time the dates celebrate the hope that all of those who died in the conflict will be raised to a new and eternal life.

December 21 sees the death of the sun's journey south with the attendant hardships that come with the winter. The sun is reborn and begins to move north again, bringing longer days and better weather. June 21 celebrates the true birth of summer with its promise of the harvest. Finally, as we have seen, March 25 is probably the most potent date of all because it represented the resurrection of Attis, one of the most potent of the old harvest gods, and this from a civilization that also gave the United States the Phrygian cap and its overtones of liberty and freedom.

Part Three

New York:
The City of
Osiris

15

ST. PAUL'S CHAPEL

A Miraculous Survivor

As the North and South Towers of the World Trade Center in Manhattan, New York, came crashing down on the morning of September 11, 2001, they also did considerable damage to the psyche of the United States. The terrorist attacks of 9/11 are an important part of our common history, and it is quite understandable that many thousands of people each year make their way to this part of Manhattan to stand and contemplate the horrific incidents of that terrible day. Many of those who do visit the site will also spend at least a little time in the peaceful surroundings of St. Paul's Chapel, which once stood in the shadows of the doomed buildings.

Apart from being a haven of peace in the midst of a busy city, St. Paul's Chapel is loved for other reasons. First, it was a near miraculous survivor of the events of 9/11. The chapel is tiny in comparison with the huge skyscrapers that surround it, and yet despite the carnage and destruction of that fateful day it survived intact—with not even a crack to any of its windows. As a result, it became a symbol of hope, as well as serving many practical functions in the days, weeks, and months after the 9/11 atrocities. It was to the calm of St. Paul's Chapel that exhausted emergency personnel would come to take a few moments to

Fig. 15.1. The old Chapel of St. Paul's and the Freedom Tower, New York
Photo courtesy of Scott F. Wolter

rest and to escape the trauma of that terrible event. Here they and the construction workers that followed them could find coffee and a sandwich, a listening ear, or simply the peace that comes from being in a sacred place.

Demonstrating her usual intuition it was Janet who suggested we might take a closer look at St. Paul's Chapel. This was initially because of the significance of the measurement between this part of New York and the center of Washington, D.C. We had noticed much earlier, during the research for the book *Before the Pyramids,* that St. Paul's Chapel, New York, was exactly 3 Megalithic degrees from the center of the Ellipse in Washington, D.C. This is equivalent to 1,080 × 366 Megalithic Yards. This measurement is not a rough approximation but is as good as exact, across 204 miles (328.3 km). However, as odd as the geographical relationship between St. Paul's Chapel and the National Mall in Washington, D.C., might be, we almost immediately found something else in Manhattan's St. Paul's Chapel that proved to be deeply relevant to the Washington Monument. Almost instantly this seemed to point specifically toward the monument's true functions and the intentions of those who created it.

St. Paul's Chapel first became a place of worship in 1766, back in the days when the United States was still a series of colonies dependent on the British Crown. It was what is known as a chapel at ease of Trinity Church, a much more magnificent building not far away in New York. A chapel at ease is a sort of satellite church and originally came about because it was sometimes inconvenient or even impossible for people to make the journey to their actual parish church. From the start St. Paul's Chapel was less formal and more quiet than Trinity Church, and so was popular with those in the district of Lower Manhattan. St. Paul's now has the distinction of being the oldest place of worship in New York City, because Trinity Church had to be rebuilt after a fire in the nineteenth century.

Anyone familiar with some of the parish churches in the city of London would recognize the style of St. Paul's Chapel in New York, because it was built to resemble the Church of St. Martin-in-the-Fields, one of the many churches rebuilt after the Great Fire of London of 1666 and designed by Sir Christopher Wren. St. Paul's is a simple, elegant building with a classical portico and an uncluttered interior. It may have been its simplicity that made it so attractive to the Revolutionary forces who struggled long and hard to gain America's independence from Great Britain—or, as we shall see presently—they might have known something about the site that drew them to the spot. For whatever reason, St. Paul's Chapel became very important, and the more so between 1785 and 1790 when New York served as the capital of the United States. Members of the first free United States government worshipped regularly in St. Paul's Chapel, and George Washington came there to offer thanks after his first inauguration as president in 1789. President Washington had his own pew at the chapel, which is marked

Fig. 15.2. The Emmett Obelisk at St. Paul's Chapel, New York
Photo courtesy of Scott F. Wolter

Fig. 15.3. The Worth Monument, Manhattan, New York
Photo courtesy of Scott F. Wolter

these days by a painting of the great seal of the United States.

Anyone strolling around the interior of St. Paul's Chapel would be bound to notice that the church contains a number of small obelisks. There is nothing particularly unusual about this fact. From the end of the seventeenth century obelisks became an important part of memorials, especially in the case of those who had been practicing Freemasons during their lifetime.

However, there is one specific obelisk associated with St. Paul's that did attract our attention and which turned out to be deeply significant in terms of our solar disk and shadow research.

Placed partly under and partly covering the large window at the center of the portico of St. Paul's Chapel and outside the body of the main building at the east end is a memorial dedicated to Brigadier General Richard Montgomery. Montgomery was an early leader of the forces of the American Revolution who was killed while the Revolutionary forces were storming Quebec in 1775. The death of any soldier is a tragedy, but in the case of Richard Montgomery it was especially deeply felt by the first leaders of a free United States. Richard Montgomery was well known to those who formed the first administration and was a personal friend of George Washington. He was also an enthusiastic Freemason and therefore a "brother" to many of those who had led the revolution and who were prosecuting the war against Great Britain.

Soon after his death it was decided to commemorate Richard Montgomery in some special way, and Benjamin Franklin, who was at the time American ambassador to France, ordered a memorial to be made that could be shipped to the United States and erected in some suitable location. Franklin himself was a leading Freemason, so it is not surprising that the sculpture he chose would have distinct Masonic overtones.

The monument, which was finally erected over the large window in the wall separating the chapel from its portico, was made of several types of Pyrenees marble. It has two squat pillars enclosing a memorial plaque. Upon these is a pedestal supporting a broken pillar surmounted by flags and flowers. On top of the broken column is an urn, and rising behind this is a flat-topped obelisk. The only slightly unfortunate fact

Fig. 15.4. Memorial to Richard Montgomery on
the exterior of St. Paul's Chapel, New York City
Photo courtesy of Scott F. Wolter

was that the monument had been designed to be fastened not to a window, but to a wall. The rear of the sculpture had therefore been left unfinished, and none other than Pierre Charles L'Enfant, the man who first designed Washington, D.C., pointed out to those who managed the chapel that this was the case. He was charged with creating something that could either encase or go behind the Montgomery monument so that its unfinished rear could not be seen from within the chapel. It would certainly have looked unsightly because it would have been seen through the large window, directly over the altar.

The reason L'Enfant received this commission was probably because he was one of very few people in the colonies at the time who had received a formal training in architecture and art, but it is also likely that he undertook the task because he was a Freemason, as had been Richard Montgomery. What L'Enfant created is extraordinary for a number of reasons. He made a sort of box into which the obelisk on the Montgomery memorial was clearly intended to go. There is only one surviving photograph of the rear of the frame. It is not a particularly good snapshot and appears to have been taken during the 1920s, when the window was changed from stained glass back to clear glass, as it originally had been in the late eighteenth century.

What makes the design of the frame so odd is that it was erected *inside* the chapel—that is, on the other side of the window to the back of the Montgomery memorial. We wondered at first if this was because L'Enfant had made his masterpiece of wood and maybe there was fear that it might deteriorate, yet even if it had been outside the chapel proper it would have been well protected by the portico of the building, so this did not seem to be much of a reason. Nevertheless, one fact appeared clear. If L'Enfant had intended the frame to go on the opposite side of the window of the memorial he would surely have given it a flat back and not one of the exact proportions for the obelisk on the memorial to fit inside it.

In a way, L'Enfant was faced with something of a dilemma. If his frame were indeed mounted outside of the window, whatever he had placed upon its face would only be seen *inside* the chapel through the glass of the window, whereas the ever showy Pierre Charles L'Enfant clearly wanted to make a very definite statement. What he actually created was not simply a cover for the back of the Montgomery memorial but rather a wonderful altarpiece that was filled with Masonic symbolism and yet was appropriate enough to be placed inside a Christian chapel.

The face of the frame was elaborately crafted and beautifully carved and painted. It represented what was known as a Glory, similar to a stylized halo. In 1947 Margaret Henry, writing in the *Trinity Bulletin of 1947,* published by Trinity Church of which St. Paul's was a part, described the finished creation, as seen from inside the chapel, as follows:

Fig. 15.5. The L'Enfant altarpiece (the Glory)
St. Paul's Chapel, New York

The result of L'Enfant's work was the carving of the great Shekinah, or Glory which focuses all eyes on the altar. The design is inspired by Old Testament symbolism, Mount Sinai and the Tables of the Law, Jehovah (in Hebrew), in a Triangle surrounded by rays, representing the Deity, and a background of clouds and lightning, suggesting the power and majesty of God. There are several such "Glories" in French churches. . . . It fulfills the purpose indicated in Didron's *Christian Iconography* emphasizing the supreme holiness of the altar, the Throne of God's Presence in the Great Sacrifice . . .

The Shekinah surrounded two marble tablets, inscribed with biblical texts. These were on a shelf that also included a crucifix that was two feet high.

This description drew our attention for a number of reasons. First, the use of the word *Shekinah* is very interesting. The Shekinah is a strange concept derived from Hebrew. Shekinah is a feminine word that is often meant to describe the presence of God, as for example in the holy of holies in the Temple of Jerusalem. To try to define the meaning of the Shekinah is fraught with problems, not least of all because it represents different things to different people. The Shekinah can be the special relationship that people have with God, or it can be that part of God that is present when people gather and pray, or when Hebrew law is being discussed or handed down.

The Shekinah is also often referred to as representing the Bride of God or the personal, approachable nature of God. In some cases the Shekinah can also represent a cosmological event. Some years ago Alan worked with British authors Christopher Knight and Robert Lomas on their book, *Uriel's Machine.* In this book it was suggested that the Shekinah had actually been a conjunction (coming together) of the planets Mercury and Venus when seen on the eastern horizon from the temple in Jerusalem. It was said that the Shekinah heralded the coming of a new king of the Hebrew people.

Pierre Charles L'Enfant's altarpiece is specifically referred to as being a "Glory." Such creations are to be found in some French

Catholic churches, but as far as we could ascertain the one in St. Paul's Chapel is the only example ever to be placed in a Protestant church. It is interesting to note that the famous All-Seeing Eye that appears so often in a Masonic context and that is also depicted on the great seal of the United States and on U.S. dollar bills is generally shown in a triangle with lines radiating from it (see fig. 15.6). These lines are correctly referred to as a Glory. The triangle is also included in L'Enfant's altarpiece, though the All-Seeing Eye is absent in this case. Even without the eye the Masonic relevance of the Glory L'Enfant used on the altarpiece is not in doubt.

As can be seen from figure 15.4 showing the reverse side of the altarpiece (the side that would surround the Montgomery memorial), L'Enfant did not restrain himself from embellishing both sides of the altarpiece he had created. Though the picture we do have is not a good one, it is possible to make out a sun that once the frame was in place would appear above the obelisk of the memorial. Also present, on the left-hand side, is a cherub or angel. We are told by a description con-

Fig. 15.6. All-Seeing Eye surrounded by a Glory

temporary with the erection of the altarpiece that this angel is in fact a representation of the Greek god Hymen. Following is the description that appeared in the *New York Daily Advertiser* the day after the Glory was raised into place.

> Hymen, extinguishing his torch mourns over his tomb. From behind the pyramid rises a Sun with thirteen rays, which enlightens the quarter of a terrestrial globe, emblematical of America. Above the whole is the American eagle flying from east to west, carrying in his talons a starry curtain in which the globe appears to have been wrapped.

With regard to the eagle flying from east to west we wondered if this was a specific reference to the fact that the Venus Families had come from the east to the west.

Presumably the reporter for the *New York Daily Advertiser* of November 22, 1787, was repeating what had been told by L'Enfant himself, because there is nothing to specifically identify the cherub as Hymen. The fact that it is Hymen seems at first to be distinctly odd. Hymen was a Greek deity who was often called upon at the time of weddings. We cannot find any other single example of this god being invoked in relation to a death or a memorial. A close look at the torch Hymen holds downward shows that it most likely had a deliberate double meaning to L'Enfant. Such is the shape the flames of the torch make on the top of the obelisk that it seems to complete the pyramid with which all true obelisks are topped. The true presence of Hymen on the reverse of the altarpiece would only make absolute sense to us in the fullness of time.

Although Hymen is not a god generally associated with funerals or memorials, he is far from being out of place on L'Enfant's creation because he does have a very strong association with the Mysteries of Demeter, which are mentioned frequently throughout the pages of this book. Stories about Hymen connect him specifically with women attending the Mysteries, and it appears as though his original function was probably somewhat more complex than his later personification as a god auspicious at the time of weddings. A particular form of Greek poem, known as a *hymenaios,* a word related to Hymen's name, was sung during the procession of a bride to the bridegroom's home. The word *hymenaios* is also related to the English word "hymn," which is a religious song or chant sung in a Christian church.

It seemed likely that L'Enfant was employing a deep form of symbolism in his use of Hymen on the reverse of the Glory. Hymen is also the name of a thin piece of tissue that surrounds the vaginal opening of women, and which it was always assumed (wrongly as it happens) is broken when a woman first has sexual intercourse. The linguistic relationship of the two words—that is, the god's name and the vaginal tissue—is not fully understood, but it would seem to be self-evident in terms of the physical conjoining that follows a wedding. Certainly the two are connected in terms of folklore. The presence of the god and the significance of his name in terms of the vagina in association with an object as blatantly phallic as an obelisk clearly represents L'Enfant telling the informed observer *something* of significance.

Above the form of the god Hymen is a representation of the sun that stands on top of the obelisk, as it does during the sun disk and shadow events in Washington, D.C. In front of the sun is what the *New York Daily Advertiser* described as being "a quarter of the terrestrial globe," which is said to represent America. We have our doubts about this interpretation, because much more than a quarter of the globe is shown. Perhaps L'Enfant did intend this other orb to be the Earth, but it has to be said that it actually looks much more like the moon. This would make sense if what we are actually looking at was the shadow of the moon passing away from the sun's disk at the end of a total solar eclipse. L'Enfant could have been alluding to the passing of the shadow of death, giving way to the glory of everlasting life, which, once again, would square very nicely with what we know of the Mysteries of Demeter. In the final stages of initiation those seeking the Mysteries would be taken physically from a place of hellish darkness to a glorious, sunlit region of peace and plenty.

Also present is the bald eagle, a symbol of the free United States, who holds the American flag with is stars in its talons. Those attempting to understand the symbolism of this side of the Glory altarpiece have suggested that it merely means the new sun of freedom—in the form of the Revolution—shining down on the United States. Undoubtedly this would be what L'Enfant would have wished the average viewer of his masterpiece to assume. None of those commenting on the symbolism have had any idea why the god Hymen should be present, and because the cherub or angel present has been referred to as Hymen from the start, this is undoubtedly who L'Enfant intended him to be.

The true significance of L'Enfant's masterpiece and particularly the decoration on its reverse side did not fully come home to us until we measured the orientation of St. Paul's Chapel. It is commonly assumed that in most cases Christian churches are built in such a way that their altars face due east, supposedly toward Jerusalem. In reality this is often not the case. Back in the Middle Ages, when many of Europe's churches were created, compasses were nonexistent. To most people east merely represented that place on the horizon where the sun rose in the morning. Because of the passage of the sun up and down the eastern horizon throughout the year, east could be considered any point between roughly northeast and southeast.

What usually happened when a new church was planned was that it was built in such a way that the altar faced that part of the eastern horizon where the sun rose on the day that was special to the patron saint of the church. For example, if the church was to be the church of St. Stephen, whose feast day is on December 26, its altar, and therefore the whole building, would point toward the place in the east where the sun rises on December 26.

This practice was still broadly in use when St. Paul's Chapel was planned in New York, but it was definitely not adopted in the case of St. Paul's Chapel itself. St. Paul has several feast days. He shares one with St. Peter on June 29, and there is another to celebrate his conversion to Christianity on January 25. In addition, there is a third day on which there is a celebration of the shipwreck that was a major event in the life of St. Paul. This is on February 16. Looking at an astronomical computer program it was easy to see that St. Paul's Chapel had not been orientated to sunrise on any of these dates. Instead it was orientated to 122 degrees, which is the place on the eastern horizon at which the sun rises in New York on December 21, the day of the winter solstice. The winter solstice is the day at which the sun reaches its farthest southern point of the year before it begins to move north again and back toward summer.

It seems almost certain that St. Paul's Chapel was given this orientation deliberately and not as a result of any arbitrary factor, such as the angle of the road on which it was built. The chapel is one of the oldest buildings in this part of New York, and although it is quite hemmed in now by high-rise buildings it once had a sizable churchyard. In other words, its designers and builders could have given it more or less any orientation they wished. For some reason they deliberately decided to have the altar facing the point on the horizon where the sun rises at the latitude of New York on the winter solstice.

Since the Montgomery memorial is mounted at the very center of the east end of St. Paul's Chapel, and because the chapel points toward sunrise on the day of the winter solstice, it follows that the memorial points in that direction too. It occurred to us from the start that to have put the memorial where it now stands was rather odd. It is a sizable piece of sculpture, and it definitely does block at least some light from entering the windows at the east end of the chapel, but suddenly everything dropped into place and we could understand why the memorial was placed where it is and what the symbolism L'Enfant's additions are pointing to.

In order to understand this we have to cast our minds back to the winter solstice behavior of the shadow of the Washington Monument. It is at this time that the point of the shadow penetrates the Ellipse, which is symbolic of the supposed union of the sky and the Earth, which pagans believed took place on this specific day. This has to be the reason why L'Enfant included the Greek god Hymen on the reverse of the altarpiece. At one and the same time, Hymen represents a wedding and also that most significant part of a vagina. There was a time when a wedding and its consummation took place on the same day. What L'Enfant is telling us is that he considered the winter solstice to be the wedding between the Sky God (or perhaps more specifically the Sun God) and the Earth Goddess. He also makes it plain via the symbolism that this is also the day when sexual congress takes place and the Earth Goddess "conceives" the bounty of nature to which she will give birth at the harvest in the following September.

Once the symbolism is understood there can be no ambiguity. L'Enfant took a perfectly normal Masonic memorial and turned it into something much more explosive and informative. By positioning it where he did, and as a result of the ornamentation he placed around it, he showed himself to be no Christian in the generally accepted sense of the word. Bearing in mind what took place later in Washington, D.C., we can be sure that he was not alone in his pagan beliefs. In all probability George Washington and most likely a number of other leading members of the Revolutionary government shared L'Enfant's slant on religion.

This is the best demonstration we have that what took place when Washington, D.C., was designed and built, and later when the Ellipse and the Washington Monument were added, did not start on the borders of Maryland and Virginia. The unusual and ancient beliefs that funded the United States' federal capital had been present for some time. Indeed, the very fact that St. Paul's Chapel was built with its altar facing dawn on the winter solstice shows all too clearly that pagan beliefs were already present among the ruling elite of the colonies even before the Revolution began.

We would suggest that L'Enfant's extraordinary piece of art confirms that there is and always has been a branch of Freemasonry that extends far beyond the normal conventions of the Craft as appreciated by most of its members. We would further postulate that Pierre Charles L'Enfant, in his handling of these symbols, was pointing out that Richard Montgomery was a member of this advanced form of Freemasonry, as he undoubtedly was himself and as was his former commanding officer, the first president of the United States, George Washington. These men were followers of something to which Freemasonry aspires but that extends beyond it into the realms of the Mysteries of ancient times. It is appropriate at this stage to point out to our readers that associations with the Mysteries of Demeter have occurred elsewhere in our search so far—not least in the rituals and practices of the National Grange of the Order of Patrons of Husbandry. In each case there is a close association with the Venus Families who were likely to have been ultimately responsible for the St. Paul's Chapel Glory.

We had to ask ourselves whether the fact that the reverse of the Glory was never seen *directly* surrounding the Montgomery memorial may be because L'Enfant had second thoughts about its presence there. The present glass of the window has a greenish tinge and is meant to replicate handmade glass of the sort that would have been produced when the chapel was built. The result is that although the glass is clear it does not allow a perfect view from one side to the other. The reverse of the Glory, as it surrounds the Montgomery memorial, therefore appears to be slightly ghostly and somewhat indistinct. We wondered whether L'Enfant, or someone such as George Washington, considered that its symbolism was just too obvious to be seen directly. On the other hand, this tableau now remains hidden in plain sight, which is entirely appropriate considering its pedigree and the man who created it.

The appearance of the solar disk on top of an obelisk in the case of St. Paul's Chapel predates the building of the Washington Monument by a significant period of time, but the connection between the two is evident. It seems pertinent to ask where this particular symbolism came from. Janet's persistence in terms of research paid dividends once again when she contacted Alan about a couple of possible leads she had uncovered. However, there was one clue regarding the sun and obelisks about which we both already knew, and it led us across the Atlantic to Paris, France.

16

MORE SUNS AND OBELISKS

Situated not far from the center of the French capital is a very unusual
church known as St. Sulpice. It was built in 1646 but was the second
church of the same name on the site, the earlier structure having dated
back to the thirteenth century. St. Sulpice is a big church, only slightly
smaller than the better-known Notre Dame de Paris. Not that St. Sulpice
has failed to attract a good deal of attention in its own right. Back in the
1960s St. Sulpice figured prominently in a series of documents known
as the Dossiers Secrets, which mysteriously appeared in the Bibliotheque
Nationale, the most famous of the libraries of Paris. Supposedly written
by an organization known as the Priory of Sion, these documents have
recently been largely discredited and pronounced to be a hoax—or at
least that is what we are clearly *supposed* to believe. The documents suggested an association between the seminary of St. Sulpice and a secret
bloodline of Jesus, which, it was suggested, extends forward in time to
the present day.

The story is a complicated one and involves a small village in the South
of France called Rennes-le-Chateau. The story of St. Sulpice, Rennes-le-
Chateau, and the bloodline of Jesus spawned many books and a great deal
of speculation. In particular, it was used by Dan Brown in his 2003 block-
buster novel, *The Da Vinci Code*. In reality, much of the attention focused
on the church of St. Sulpice has been on account of a very strange object

Fig. 16.1. The Gnomon obelisk at St. Sulpice Church, Paris
Photo courtesy of Scott F. Wolter

placed there in 1727. Officially the object, or rather series of objects, is called a gnomon. The device was put in place by Jean-Baptiste Languet de Gergy, who was the priest of St. Sulpice at the time.

The story goes that the priest was trying to figure out the true time for the celebration of Easter. According to the Council of Nicaea, which was held by the Christian Church in 325 CE, Easter Sunday should be the first Sunday to fall on or after the first full moon following the vernal equinox each year. Easter therefore is a movable feast, and it is true that its rightful place in the yearly calendar was a great bone of contention in the early years of Christianity and indeed right up until the seventh century. However, this was certainly not the case by the time Father Jean-Baptiste Languet de Gergy had the gnomon built in St. Sulpice Church. At this time tables were being printed and circulated by the Vatican in Rome that told all of the faithful when Easter and all the related festivals should occur in any given year.

In reality, the whole calendar had been in disarray prior to the sixteenth century. The former calendar of the Roman Empire, known as the Julian calendar, had become hopelessly incorrect and reform was definitely needed. This was brought about by Pope Gregory XIII, who arranged for renowned astronomers to regulate the calendar and to propose a way that it might be brought back to a high degree of accuracy. The problem had come about because the length of the solar year is not divisible by a number of whole days but is 365.2564 days in length. If the correct compensations are not made, the civil or official year, which includes Christian celebrations, will get out of step with the solar calendar. This would eventually result in celebrations such as Easter and Christmas taking place in entirely the wrong part of the year.

The new calendar, known as the Gregorian calendar, was adopted by France in 1582, nearly 150 years prior to the placement of the gnomon in St. Sulpice Church. So whoever suggested that the good Father Jean-Baptiste went to all that trouble in order to understand when the spring equinox and therefore Easter might actually be is deluded. It is likely that this is the reason Father Jean-Baptiste gave for the construction of the gnomon, but it was definitely an excuse and not the genuine reason.

Into the floor of St. Sulpice Church, running across the floor at right angles to the altar, was laid a meridian line made from brass. To the north of the altar a tall obelisk was built (or rather half an obelisk as it is placed against a wall). In a window in the south, opposite the obelisk, is a clear piece of glass that was made into a lens. At the time of the winter solstice, around December 21 at noon, sunlight enters the lens and shines at a particular point high up on the face of the obelisk. On the days of the equinoxes, March 21 and September 21, once again at noon, sunlight penetrates the lens and reaches a brass plaque on the floor of the church, level with the altar. The sun's light also shines directly onto a further plaque that designates the summer solstice. The light that appears is elliptical in shape, as is the equinox plaque.

What makes this ingenious device even more pertinent to our unfolding story is the fact that it is specifically the winter solstice that marks the highest position of the sunlight on the obelisk in St. Sulpice

Fig. 16.2. The plaque on the floor of St. Sulpice Church in Paris marking
the position of the equinoxes
Photo courtesy of Scott F. Wolter

Church. In addition, on top of the marble obelisk is a representation of the sun's disk, just as we find at St. Paul's Chapel in New York. Both appear in connection with the winter solstice, and there is another tangible connection between the two.

Pierre Charles L'Enfant, who created the St. Paul's Chapel altarpiece, was not born in Paris, but he did spend a great deal of time there while studying prior to departing to America to fight in the Revolutionary War. He studied both art and architecture, and he cannot have failed to have visited the Church of St. Sulpice, which had only been completed a few decades before. St. Sulpice represented the leading edge of architectural sophistication at the time. In addition, both Benjamin Franklin and Thomas Jefferson spent a considerable amount of time in Paris. Both were leaders in the Revolutionary government, and each of them had a fascination with architecture.

St. Sulpice is far from being just *any* church. For a long time it was rumored that those trained to the priesthood at the seminary attached to the church were indulging in heretical studies. This is made all the more likely because the seminary of St. Sulpice has an acclaimed library that contains all manner of books associated with distinctly un-Christian subjects. As we have seen, St. Sulpice has been closely associated for decades with the Priory of Sion, the purpose of which was to bolster and support the idea of a bloodline descending from Jesus, who, it is said, had children and descendants of his own. Advocates of the Priory claim that this bloodline was present in the early French kings until the killing of Dagobert II in 679 CE. This murder happened with the tacit approval of Rome, and it caused a split between the supporters of the bloodline and the developing Catholic Church that has never been healed.

St. Sulpice seminary always attracted intellectuals within French society and, at a later date, the American revolutionaries would become inextricably linked with Father Bérenger Saunière (1852–1917). Saunière was a priest from southern France whose name is associated with a schism affecting Catholicism in which Mary Magdalene features strongly. Mary Magdalene was one of Jesus's disciples, and in the opinion of many she was also Jesus's wife and the mother of his children. Her ossuary was present in the Talpiot tomb, along with that of Jesus, his mother, Mary, his son Judah, and other members of his family (see chapter 5).

One of the problems of introducing intellectual thought to an establishment such as the seminary of St. Sulpice is that it sometimes backfires. Trainee priests introduced to schismatic ideas—in order to give them the ammunition they need to counter such possible heresies or deviations—sometimes find themselves in a dilemma. They may come to the conclusion that a particular schism has more sense and greater validity than normal dogma. It has been suggested—though in our opinion never adequately proved—that religious teaching at the seminary of St. Sulpice was of a schismatic nature.

The reputation gained by St. Sulpice and its seminary for being unusual, whether or not justified, has certainly amplified the mystique surrounding both. The existence of the gnomon right by the altar in St. Sulpice Church can only add to this mystique. After all, it is an extremely large obelisk—which is a pagan, phallic structure—and was certainly known to be such when it was erected there in the eighteenth century.

At the time L'Enfant, Franklin, and Jefferson were present in Paris, the Church of St. Sulpice was the favored place of worship for many of the members of the French Academy of Science—itself a hotbed of radical and revolutionary thought. A significant number of members of the academy at that time were also Freemasons. The most famous Paris Masonic lodge for the scientists and free-thinkers was La Loge des Neuf Sœurs (Lodge of the Nine Sisters). It was established in 1776, but the allusion in Masonic circles to the nine sisters, who were the muses of Greek mythology, was already a long one. Benjamin Franklin was not only a member of the Loge des Neuf Sœurs but for a while its Grand Master. There is also significant proof that Thomas Jefferson was a member of the lodge when he was in Paris.*

---

*Scott F. Wolter, *Akhenaten to the Founding Fathers,* 163–64.

Whether or not he was, there is no doubt that he willingly and enthusiastically rubbed shoulders regularly with many of those who met at the lodge. It seems almost certain that the Lodge of the Nine Sisters was also of interest to and probably run by the Venus Families.

There are quite tangible links between New York at the start of the American War of Independence and the French capital—more than enough to suggest that Pierre Charles L'Enfant was very familiar with the St. Sulpice gnomon when he embarked upon his extraordinary altarpiece for St. Paul's Chapel. Many of the ideas and most likely the beliefs that accompanied L'Enfant's creation and the later Washington Monument had undoubtedly come from France.

By their very nature these beliefs were secret, so we hardly expected to find anything that would connect the St. Paul's sculpture directly with the Washington Monument, but in fact we did.

As we have seen, the Washington Monument had originally been the subject of a competition that received several hundred entries. The entrant chosen for the commission was Robert Mills. But was this a foregone conclusion despite the competition? Robert Mills was a Freemason who was born in 1781 in Charleston, South Carolina, where he studied under James Hoban, an Irish-born architect and another Freemason who designed the White House and who also worked extensively on the Capitol. Hoban had been born in 1758 and so was more than twenty years older than Mills, but the two were good friends.

Mills worked with Hoban on the White House and got on especially well with Thomas Jefferson, who was the first president to actually live in the White House. Robert Mills always considered Jefferson to have been an important influence on him. Thomas Jefferson died in 1826, some nine years before the competition was held to find an architect for the Washington Monument, so Jefferson could not have had any influence upon Mills being chosen. Nevertheless, there could be a connection, because both men were very familiar with St. Paul's Chapel in New York. In terms of its solar disk and shadow events, the attributes of the Washington Monument were a natural progression from L'Enfant's sculpture at St. Paul's Chapel, but to function correctly the monument had to be of a very specific height and built in a precise location. We have the distinct feeling that these matters had been under discussion for some time, and the same continuum of thought and belief that had contributed to St. Paul's Chapel and almost certainly the gnomon of St. Sulpice had been prevalent during the intervening period.

There is one piece of information that, if not proving these connections, definitely supports them. Most probably in 1802 Robert Mills completed a detailed drawing of St. Paul's Chapel. This drawing still exists, and because it was once the property of Thomas Jefferson, it is assumed that Mills gave the drawing to President Jefferson in 1803. The inference is that St. Paul's Chapel, as small and relatively insignificant as it was in the grand scheme of the developing United States, did mean something specific to both Mills and Jefferson. Did both men know the chapel's secret? It seems almost certain that they did, because that secret was carried through into Mills's design for the Washington Monument. It may be no coincidence that he got the job!

We now had to ask ourselves whether a depiction of the sun's disk at the top of an obelisk was a brand-new concept when it appeared in St. Sulpice Church in Paris. At this point in our investigation St. Sulpice was as far back in time as we had managed to trace such a representation. Resolute in her search, Janet came up with an even older example that was also French. It comes from the book *Poussin and France: Paintings, Symbolism and the Politics of Style* by Todd Olson.

Paris in 1594: Various triumphal arches had been created for King Henry IV's arrival—together with all sorts of street scenery—but of particular interest and fascination was an obelisk. There is no reference to the obelisk's size, but it was created so cleverly by the artists that it looked exactly as if it were made of bronze. On its sides were painted and sculpted the various tasks of Hercules, with whom the king was being compared. On the point of the obelisk was an unmistakable sun, complete with sunbeams and a smiling face.

But was there more to this tableau than simply a fawning attempt to lift the monarch to the level of superhero? It would appear that this was the case. On top of the sun was a giant version of the letter *H*. This of course stands for both Henry and Hercules. Hercules was a Greek hero and god, but he was also known to the Egyptians. The Hellenistic rulers of Egypt, Cleopatra being the most famous example, equated Hercules with the Egyptian god Horus—in fact they were worshipped as the same deity. Horus of course also begins with an *H*. Horus was the son of Osiris who avenged his father by killing the god Set, who had imprisoned Osiris and then torn his body apart. Because all deities associated with Osiris were also considered to "be" Osiris, as were Egyptian pharaohs, the Paris obelisk of 1594 was equating King Henry with Osiris. As we have seen, Egyptians believed that Osiris resided within obelisks, while at the same time considering the obelisk to be his phallus.

The presence of the sun on top of the Paris obelisk, together with the letter *H,* which ultimately represents Osiris, shows that these matters were well understood more than 150 years before the gnomon in St. Sulpice Church was created.

Is it possible to push back the association of an obelisk with a sun on its point even further than this? Thanks to Professor Bernard Frischer of the Department of Informatics at Indiana University and John Fillwalk, Director of the Institute for Digital Intermedia Arts at Ball State University, it would appear that it is.

Very near the center of Rome, in what is now part of the Vatican, is St. Peter's Square. This stands at the front of the famous St. Peter's Basilica. The square was laid out in the seventeenth and eighteenth centuries, and included in its decoration was a four-thousand-year-old obelisk that had been brought to Rome back in the days of the Emperor Augustus (63 BCE–14 CE). Augustus conquered Egypt, and many obelisks and other treasures found their way from the new province to Rome.

After the conquests early in his reign, Augustus became known for ushering in a period of comparative peace in the Roman Empire, and the senate decided to mark the fact in the creation and dedication of a large, marble altar in the center of Rome known as the Ara Pacis (the "altar of peace"). Another obelisk—now known as the obelisk of

Montecitorio—already existed close to the Ara Pacis, and it was always assumed that the structures had been so designed that the shadow of the obelisk would fall upon the face of the Ara Pacis on the Emperor Augustine's birthday, which was in September.

Frischer and Fillwalk, together with their teams, decided to find out whether this had indeed been the case. Like us, they consulted sophisticated astronomy computer programs that are capable of displaying the sky as it appeared eons ago. Also like us, they allied their astronomical findings to trigonometry to test the idea of the shadow on the Ara Pacis. What they actually found was something far more spectacular. When viewed from the Via Fambia, a road leading away from the Ara Pacis, on one day each year the disk of the sun could be seen standing on the point of the obelisk of Montecitorio. The day in question was October 9. This particular day was highly significant because it marked the day that was the festival of the Palatine Apollo. Apollo was Augustus's patron deity, and he had personally dedicated a new temple to the god in 28 BCE.

In this case the spectacle of the solar disk on top of the obelisk was not set to any of the two equinoxes or solstices but to that of the anniversary of Apollo, who was a major solar deity. All the same, the technique used to create the spectacles involving the Washington Monument definitely applied to the obelisk of Montecitorio two thousand years ago in Rome. Of particular surprise with this regard is the fact that the discoveries about the obelisk of Montecitorio are extremely recent. About fifty years before these discoveries were made it was generally accepted that the shadow of the obelisk had merely fallen on the Ara Pacis on the emperor's birthday. In other words, those who designed and built the Washington Monument appear to have known something that had been forgotten by the world at large for two millennia.

No matter how hard we have searched, it has proved impossible for us to discover a known instance of the ancient Egyptians using an obelisk in this specific way. All the same, bearing in mind the association of the obelisk to sun worship in Egypt, it seems highly likely that the Romans were merely copying something the Egyptians had done before them. We will keep searching among Egyptian records and documents to prove this was the case.

Far from both the shores of the United States and the glory of Rome are the islands of Britain. Some of the structures found in Great Britain and Ireland make even the ancient Egyptian obelisks look young by comparison. Surprisingly or not, the interest shown regarding the winter solstice at St. Paul's Chapel in New York and in association with the Washington Monument had a significant part to play in the little-understood religious beliefs and practices of Late Stone Age Britons. Back to at least 3500 BCE the first farmers in the British Isles were beginning to create some amazing structures of their own. Among these creations were some extremely tall standing stones. Close to Alan's home in East Yorkshire is the village of Rudstone, where Britain's tallest standing stone is to be found. It soars into the air a majestic twenty-five feet now, but experts think it was once significantly taller and a large percentage of it now lies beneath the graveyard of the church, next to which it stands.

It is quite possible that the standing stone at Rudstone—and indeed a number of others across the British Isles—were once used in a similar way to the Washington Monument and that our ancient ancestors knew exactly where to stand to see the solar disk rest on the top of such stones. They are not obelisks in the strict sense of the word, but they may have served a very similar function. Certainly the people who cut them from the earth and hauled them into place were fascinated by the equinoxes and solstices, a fact that is attested to by recovered alignments from a multitude of Megalithic sites.

One particular example is also one of the very oldest. Not far from Dublin in southern Ireland is the valley of the River Boyne, one of the most impressive Late Stone Age, Bronze Age, and Iron Age landscapes to be found anywhere in the world. The Boyne Valley is specifically famous for its passage graves, one of which is absolutely relevant to winter solstice veneration.

As its name implies, a passage grave is one in which a chamber, thought to have been used for burials or partial burials, is accessed down a stone-lined passage. All that can be seen above the ground is a large, fairly circular mound. The oldest of the passage graves in the British Isles dates back to around 3500 BCE, which is a thousand years before the first pyramids were built in Egypt.

The Boyne Valley region of Ireland has at least three major passage graves that have survived, though it is thought there were once more. Around these three giant mounds are numerous smaller mounds that may have contained single graves. The whole area was clearly a very important ritual landscape for maybe three thousand years or more. The most famous of the passage graves of the Boyne Valley, though not the largest, is that of Newgrange; it is around 249 feet (76 meters) across, and the mound rises to around 39 feet (12 meters) in height. The single passage into Newgrange is 60 feet (19 meters) in length and has a cruciform shape.

When the tomb was excavated by archaeologists and the nature of the passage was fully defined, it became obvious that the whole structure had been very carefully created so that the rising sun at the time of the winter solstice would shine down the passage and illuminate the chambers. Considerable skill had gone into the alignment and also into the construction of the passage grave itself. Many thousands of man-hours must have been taken up in its construction, and the quality of the engineering involved is breathtaking. Even when the passage grave was new it was not necessary for the entrance itself to be fully open for the midwinter sun to penetrate the passage. An ingenious light box had been created over the entrance, built in such a way that only at the time of the first rays of the rising sun would the passage and the chambers be illuminated.

With Alan as a consultant, in their book *Uriel's Machine*, Christopher Knight and Robert Lomas had calculated that it was not merely the rising sun that had interested the builders of Newgrange. As with many other Megalithic sites they explored, it became obvious to Knight and Lomas that the planet Venus had played a part in whatever rituals took place at the site. Over the light box is a stone lintel. This carries eight diagonal crosses, carefully carved in relief into the stone. These diagonal crosses

Fig. 16.3. The X pattern carved onto a stone that was found over
the entrance to Newgrange Chambered Tomb, Boyne Valley, Ireland
Photo courtesy of Scott F. Wolter

are very telling because they appear elsewhere in a Megalithic context, for example in another passage tomb, the Gavrinis in France, and also at Fourknocks, not far from Newgrange.

Knight and Lomas became convinced that the reoccurring diagonal cross was a form of shorthand that our Megalithic ancestors used to define the passage of a full year.*

The fact that there are eight such diagonal crosses on the stone lintel over the light box at Newgrange is a significant clue that the builders of the monument were tracking the planet Venus, which is the brightest celestial body in our skies apart from the sun and the moon.

Because its orbit lies inside that of the Earth, Venus appears to keep a very complicated path through the heavens. When seen from the Earth it takes 584 days to get from the start of a full cycle back to its start again. During this period Venus changes from being seen in the morning sky to being an evening star. This behavior of Venus seems to have had particularly fascinated our ancient ancestors, because many cultures showed the same regard for and virtual obsession with Venus. Doubtless they were also intrigued by the apparent relationship

---

*A full explanation of how they came to this conclusion is to be found in *Uriel's Machine.*

between the orbit of Venus as seen from the Earth and the length of an Earth year. This is because five Venus cycles (synodic periods) are almost equal to eight Earth years.

As we saw earlier, Venus held a fascination for the Megalithic people of the British Isles and France because it was used to set the pendulum that made it possible to define the absolute length of a Megalithic Yard (see chapter 10). There are also significant reasons for believing that Venus was seen as being representative of the female Godhead (and of course the planet still carries the name of a significant Roman goddess) and that it may have had an important part to play in the idea of death and rebirth.

The eight diagonal crosses on the light box lintel at Newgrange seem to point to the fact that on one occasion during every eight years Venus casts her own light down the passage and into the chambers. A re-creation of the events in the sky in 3500 BCE proves conclusively that this did in fact happen. It occurred at a time when Venus was a morning star, rising ahead of the sun, when its orbit attained the same position as the sun on the horizon. These crosses would become extremely important to our research in conjunction with the work of Scott Wolter and especially his findings relating to pre–Columbian/European presence in North America. The obsession shown for Venus in these remote times never diminished. This is why we consider the continuum of thought and action that appears throughout these pages so regularly to be a result of the Venus Families, the name that was first used by Scott Wolter. Venus and her orbital patterns were also significant factors in the layout and ultimate decoration of Washington, D.C.

While undertaking the research related to the Boyne Valley, we were pleased to be able to answer an outstanding question regarding one of the other three passage graves in the area. This one is called Knowth, and it is even larger than Newgrange. Knowth has been badly damaged over the centuries, but it originally had two passages that led to chambers. One of these had its entrance toward the east and the other to the west. Trying to find significant solar alignments at Knowth has been problematic. Logic might assert that if Newgrange was aligned to the midwinter sun, Knowth might have been positioned to catch the first rays of the rising sun at the time of the vernal and autumnal equinoxes, and then to replicate this happening in the west at the time of the sun's equinoctial setting later on the same days. Unless the designers of the Knowth mound made a significant mistake, this cannot be the case. The eastern passage at Knowth is aligned to around 83 degrees, whereas if accurate it should be 90 degrees. The western passage is also out of line with the equinox sunsets by a similar amount.

This realization gave Alan a hunch based on his long study of ancient astronomy. What appears to have been the case at Knowth is that its builders were not specifically interested in the rising or setting of the sun at the equinox but rather that of the planet Venus. Models created for the period and the location demonstrate that on one autumn equinox in every eight years Venus would have risen at exactly 83 degrees on the horizon, ahead of the sun. It would therefore have cast its light down the eastern passage at Knowth. A similar situation took place once every eight years when Venus was an evening star. Following the sun down to the western horizon it would have cast its light down the western passage of Knowth to illuminate the chambers. This might seem unlikely for something as small and apparently insignificant as a planet, but in fact, particularly on a moonless night, Venus can be extremely bright and is easily able to cast a significant shadow.

This situation did not particularly surprise Alan. Some years ago, when he was assisting Christopher Knight and Robert Lomas, he had made several visits with them to a passage grave in Wales named Bryn-celli-Ddu. Although a much smaller mound than Knowth, Bryn-celli-Ddu also seems to have been a deliberately created "Venus Chamber." Alan had the privilege on two occasions to see the extraordinary effect that takes place at Bryn-celli-Ddu when the light of Venus enters the chamber and is reflected from a deliberately created dish-shaped rock that illuminates a large central stone pillar. We have not been party to such observations at Knowth, but the astronomy and mathematics of the situation hold good for a fine display at both passages, once every eight years.

One of the most intriguing facts regarding the Boyne Valley is the name of its most famous passage tomb: Newgrange. This name immediately started bells ringing in our minds. The reader will recall our investigations earlier in the book relating to the Cistercian order. From the very outset the Cistercian order was important to the writing of this book, because it was their association with the Grange movement in the United States that started our investigations.

The reason we were alerted to a possible Cistercian association with Newgrange was because of the *grange* component of the word. It did not take us long to discover that the whole region in which the three major passage tombs are located in the Boyne Valley was once land owned and farmed by the Cistercians. The very first Cistercian abbey in Ireland was nearby at Mellifont. This was an abbey specifically created at the request of St. Bernard of Clairvaux and with the influence of his close Irish friend St. Malachy.

A little more investigation led us to discover that the Cistercians had built significant structures right on the top of Knowth passage tomb and also very close to Newgrange. Newgrange was literally the "New Grange" or "New Farm" belonging to Mellifont Abbey. The Cistercians controlled this land exclusively for a couple of centuries at least before the circumstances of the order changed, and the land was rented out to tenants. In other words, they had plenty of time to do any research they wished regarding all of the Boyne Valley tombs. The entrance to Newgrange was reopened in relatively modern times in 1699. But had the Cistercians entered the tomb more than five hundred years earlier? The same could also be true for Knowth and also for the third large passage tomb, Dowth.

What interest could medieval monks have had for such ancient sacred structures? Absolutely none, one might at first think. But we knew already that there was far more to the Cistercians and their fighting sister order, the Knights Templar, than at first meets the eye. We were aware that the Cistercians had shown a very definite interest in the feminine aspect of religion, and we also knew that they had been created as part of a very definite effort on the part of *someone* who wanted to radically change Christianity and to work toward destroying the repressive feudal system upon which all of Europe depended. We had also been party to Scott's research that demonstrated that the Cistercians and also the Knights Templar had visited North America before the days of Christopher Columbus and that they had enjoyed good relations with the indigenous population.

At this stage some of the connections between the different strands of our research were tangled and difficult to comb out. Nevertheless, Alan had already indicated in his book *City of the Goddess* how important both solar alignments and Venus alignments had been in the design of Washington, D.C., and our more recent research was showing that these factors had also been considered in other parts of the United States, for example, in New York. We could also see that the solar and shadow achievements of the designers and builders of the Washington Monument showed they had been interested in exactly the same astronomical happenings as people who lived five thousand years ago. In addition, the people who had created the passage tombs in Ireland were the same Megalithic culture that first used the Megalithic Yard and Megalithic geometry that was also used in the creation of Washington, D.C.

Previously it had been extremely difficult for Alan and Christopher Knight to explain how a system of geometry and measurement that seemed to have disappeared around 2000 BCE could have resurfaced in eighteenth-century America. Chris and Alan more than suspected that the Cistercians, the Knights Templar, and Freemasonry had been involved in this continued knowledge, but any connection had been tenuous at best. Our discoveries in the Boyne Valley of Ireland and the presence of the Cistercians there had at last offered what could be the missing conduit.

17

THE FRENCH CONNECTION

L'Enfant Terrible

Our investigations into the strange monument of Richard Montgomery and therefore into St. Paul's Chapel in New York coincided with an opportunity to meet in Paris when Janet accompanied Scott on a shoot for his television program at St. Sulpice Church.

We were both understandably excited at the prospect, because it would give us the chance to look in greater detail at this fascinating structure. Alan had been there on several occasions previously, but it would be Janet's first visit to this most remarkable church. We were able to spend a whole day exploring every nook and cranny of the massive church—and we had good reason for wanting to do so.

As suggested in chapter 16, on the other side of the Atlantic we were seeing very strong connections between Pierre Charles L'Enfant, who had first drawn out the plans for Washington, D.C., and his work at the little chapel of St. Paul's in New York. We had suspected that he may have been motivated in his design for the surround of the Montgomery monument by the extraordinary gnomon of St. Sulpice, but we never could have guessed just how influenced L'Enfant had been by St. Sulpice and all he had seen there.

L'Enfant was the son of a painter in the service of the French king, so he would have grown up surrounded by art. We already knew that he had been schooled at the Royal Academy of Painting and Sculpture in Paris. This was an elite and extremely important institution that had strong connections with similar institutions in Italy, which was the wellspring of many of the artistic traditions of the eighteenth century.

We also arrived at St. Sulpice seeking to find out more about Jean-Baptiste Languet de Gergy, the priest of St. Sulpice who had been responsible for the installation of the remarkable gnomon that tracked the progress of the sun at noon each day across the floor of the church and up the flat marble obelisk at the north side of the building, not far from the altar.

To make the situation plain again, just to the west of the main altar is a brass line set into the floor of the church, which goes from north to south across most of the building. At the south end, and once again set into the floor at the end of the brass line, is a plaque explaining the use of the gnomon for purposes of working out the angle of the sun. The stone plaque marks the place where the sun shines at noon on the day of the summer solstice. At the center of the church and within the semicircular confines of the high altar is an elliptical, brass plate. This is where the sun shines at noon on the day of the vernal and autumnal equinoxes.

At the northern end of the brass line is the representation in marble of an obelisk. This is almost 11 meters in height (just over 35 feet). The brass line on the floor continues up the center of the obelisk on top of which is a golden globe representing the sun. At the time of the winter solstice the sun shines at the very top of the brass line on the obelisk, close to the golden globe.

The sunlight is provided via a lens fixed into a window on the south side of the church and the arrangement works because at noon each day the sun is always due south and at its highest point of the day in the sky. Since this height varies throughout the year, so does the angle of the sun relative to the lens in the window. This in turn causes the spot of sunlight at noon to move along the brass meridian line throughout the year.

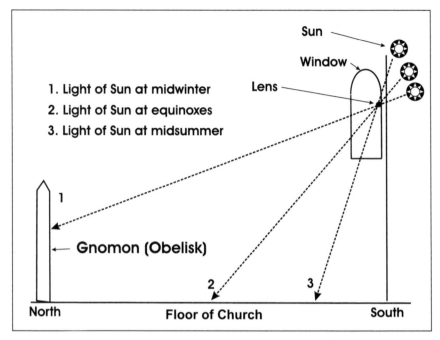

Fig. 17.1. Explanation of how the sun behaves through the lens at St. Sulpice Church across a full year. At midday on the equinoxes the oval light shines onto an equally oval brass plaque in the floor, at the summer solstice it shines on a marble plaque in the floor, and at midwinter it shines high up the gnomon (obelisk).

Although responsible for having the gnomon installed circa 1728, Jean-Baptiste Languet de Gergy did not design or create the device himself. It was originally conceived by an English clockmaker by the name of Henry Sully. Sully was born in 1680, and although he learned his craft in England he spent many of his adult years in Paris. A leading exponent of the clockmaker's art, Henry Sully also spent much of his adult life chasing what was, at the time, something of a Holy Grail: the creation of a timepiece that could be used to accurately ascertain the longitude of a ship at sea. Sully built many examples, some of which worked extremely well in calm weather, but they were all pendulum clocks that were subject to major fluctuations when storms arose. It was left until the next generation for another Englishman, John Harrison, to iron out the problems and to create the first genuinely useful marine chronometer.

Henry Sully lived for years in Paris and must have rubbed shoulders with members of the famous Academy of Science there. This fact, together with his great skill in the art of keeping time, undoubtedly led to him being chosen by Jean-Baptiste Languet de Gergy to create the famous gnomon for St. Sulpice. As it happened, Sully died before the project was completed. He had undertaken most of the calculations, and the brass meridian line had been set into the floor of the church, but for the construction of the obelisk and for the final calculations Languet de Gergy had to call upon the assistance of the Observatory of Paris.

We questioned some of the staff at St. Sulpice concerning the true reason for the gnomon having been installed in the church. Some sources suggest that Languet de Gergy was seeking to establish the true time of the equinoxes in order to set Easter at exactly the right time. More local traditions suggest that Languet de Gergy wished to establish the exact and correct time of day for the ringing of the church bells. Neither of these explanations seemed to fit the results, because we knew the gnomon system of St. Sulpice to be incredibly accurate. As an example, it had been used by a leading French astronomer, Pierre Charles Le Monnier (1715–1799), to assess variations in the Earth's angle of inclination, a very demanding subject of study at the time for which the gnomon seemed ideally suited. It would be incorrect to compare the gnomon of St. Sulpice with, say, a simple sundial, because it represents a far more sophisticated scientific instrument. Despite our best efforts we are still not convinced that we have gotten to the bottom of the reason for Languet de Gergy having it made.

We did find one significant clue in St. Sulpice itself that also strengthened the link between the church and St. Paul's Chapel. Jean-Baptiste Languet de Gergy died in 1750, and he was laid to rest in St. Sulpice itself. Judging by the memorial that was created for him, he must have been a man of means. Opposite the obelisk, on the south side of the church, are a series of side chapels. One of these is occupied with

Fig. 17.2. The funerary monument of Priest Jean-Baptiste
Languet de Gergy (1674–1750), St. Sulpice Church, Paris
Photo courtesy of Scott F. Wolter

a statue of St. John the Baptist but also contains an extremely elaborate sculpture beneath which Languet de Gergy is interred.

The whole edifice appears to have been created in various types of marble. The lower part is an extraordinarily beautiful sarcophagus on top of which an elaborate scene was created. To the left is a stunning sculpture of Death, depicted as a skeleton holding a long-handled scythe. Immediately to the right of this is a more-or-less life-size effigy of Languet de Gergy himself, in an attitude of supplication, with his hands outstretched. To the right of Languet de Gergy is a wonderful sculptured angel who is holding back an elaborate and exquisitely carved cloth that extends behind the whole scene. At the back of all of this is the form of the bottom part of an obelisk in speckled red marble that extends from the bottom of the monument to its top.

Such are the angle of the faces of both Languet de Gergy and the angel that they appear to be looking across the body of the church toward the white marble obelisk on the opposite wall. The allegory of the scene is supposed to be obvious. The Christian angel is drawing back the veil of death, allowing Languet de Gergy to view the eternal paradise that awaits him, thanks to his strong faith.

There were several aspects of the monument that puzzled us. First there is not a single Christian symbol involved in the structure—no image of Christ or the Virgin—and no representation of the cross. A close look at the angel shows the figure to be most definitely female, which itself is slightly unusual. Angels are often depicted as being somewhat androgynous in form or else they are quite pointedly male. The presence of an obviously beautiful young woman in this context is not common. It cannot be denied that the features of the angel bear a striking resemblance to those on ancient sculptures of the goddess Demeter. In the context of all our other discoveries relating to obelisks this appears to make great sense.

In other words, this may indeed be intended to represent a wholly Christian memorial, but the presence of a representation of an obelisk in the scene could equally well indicate to the initiated that this is far from being a Christian scene. If the sculpture of Languet de Gergy and that of the angel are indeed both looking across at the top of the white marble obelisk opposite, they are effectively looking at the winter solstice. At the same time, opposite this tableau is one representing St. John the Baptist, and we were only too aware that in a symbolic sense John the Baptist has always been taken to represent the summer solstice. There seemed to be something more than coincidence at work in this quiet corner of the church.

The addition of the gnomon to St. Sulpice turned what was a normal east-to-west-orientated church into something quite different. With the addition of the gnomon the church effectively became something more akin to an ancient Greek temple. The presence of the gnomon meant that those in the know could fully recognize and probably also revere the date of the winter solstice, and in conjunction with an obelisk. No such conversion was necessary in the case of St. Paul's Chapel in far-off New York, because the whole building was orientated toward the winter solstice sunrise. In addition, St. Paul's Chapel was furnished with a circular tower from which astronomical observations of all parts of the sky could be undertaken.

This interest (or indeed more properly, obsession) with astronomy is not unique to these two churches. Alan's two books with Scottish writer and researcher John Ritchie, *Rosslyn Chapel Decoded* and *Rosslyn Revealed,* demonstrate that the extraordinary Rosslyn Chapel in Scotland was also specifically built to be as much an astronomical observatory as a place of worship.

Notwithstanding the extraordinary nature of the St. Sulpice gnomon or the remarkable tomb of Languet de Gergy, we found everything we needed within St. Sulpice itself to identify the source of Pierre Charles L'Enfant's inspiration for his creation at the east end of New York's St. Paul's Chapel.

Both the Languet de Gergy monument and the reverse of L'Enfant's altar surround for St. Paul's Chapel had angels (which may in fact both actually be deities). Both also contain a large cloth or cover. An integral part of each is the presence of an obelisk. The top of the obelisk on the Languet de Gergy monument is not shown, but there is a sun placed on top of the marble obelisk, which is part of the gnomon, and L'Enfant also included a sun to surmount the top of the Montgomery memorial in St. Paul's Chapel.

As far as the face of L'Enfant's creation is concerned (the part that faces into the body of the church), it is usually referred to as being a Glory. At the extreme east end of St. Sulpice Church, set into the apse, is a statue of the Virgin and Child standing on what is probably meant to be the Earth and surrounded by a golden Glory. There are other representations of Glories in St. Sulpice, any or all of which may have provided L'Enfant with the inspiration he needed for his creation in St. Paul's Chapel.

Copying is one thing, but *understanding* is something quite different. So can we say with any certainty that Pierre Charles L'Enfant truly comprehended what the St. Sulpice gnomon and the Languet de Gergy monument were telling him? The answer has to be an unequivocal "yes." L'Enfant could not have failed to appreciate that St. Paul's Chapel is orientated directly to sunrise at the time of the winter solstice. The Montgomery monument is placed in the center of the east end of the chapel, looking directly at the dawn sun during the winter solstice. L'Enfant topped the obelisk on the Montgomery memorial with a sun and also added the connection with the Greek god Hymen. He also included what looks very much like the end of a solar eclipse, which allegorically means moving from darkness to light. L'Enfant even went so far as to make Hymen's downturned torch look like a pyramid top for the obelisk on the Montgomery memorial.

We returned from France utterly convinced that Pierre Charles L'Enfant had received the inspiration for the St. Paul altarpiece from St. Sulpice Church. We could also say with some certainty that he knew very well what it actually meant. It represented his recognition of the orientation of the chapel and of the significance, to some people at least, of the winter solstice.

Nor did things stop at this point, because although by that time L'Enfant himself was dead, the whole theme would be taken up again in Washington, D.C., this time in a stunning three-dimensional form the like of which had never been seen before. In other words, the Washington Monument was part of a natural progression from the obelisk of St. Sulpice via L'Enfant altarpiece, to the Rising Sun Chair in which George Washington sat for several months, to the Washington Monument itself.

18

ORION'S BELT
IN NEW YORK CITY

Sometimes, in the midst of research, the most remarkable facts turn up almost by chance. One morning Alan received an e-mail from a member of the research team at Committee Films. Like us, Scott and the devisers of the *America Unearthed* series were fascinated by obelisks and were planning an episode dealing with American examples. One of their researchers had come across an article that pointed out that there were a number of obelisks across New York City (see "Mystery of the Obelisks" by Martin Langfield). In particular, there are three very large obelisks that stand in a line (more or less) running north to south from Central Park to Lower Manhattan. What the researcher wanted to know from Alan was whether he thought such an alignment could have come about by accident.

A similar e-mail had been sent to Janet, and before Alan could respond to the initial inquiry he received a communication from Janet that proved to be of the utmost importance. She had noticed that the distances between the three obelisks in question were proportionately similar to the distance between three stars that form a pattern in the winter sky known as Orion's Belt. Janet included an image that showed all three obelisks in their relative positions within New

Fig. 18.1. The obelisk in Central Park, New York
Photo courtesy of Scott F. Wolter

York. As it turned out, this inspiration on Janet's part could not have found a better target than Alan—he just happens to be something of an expert on examples from the remote past when our ancient ancestors have re-created a version of Orion's Belt on the ground. In more than one instance this appears to have been a reflection of the heavens brought down to ground level.

For Alan the Orion's Belt story began in 1984 with the publication of a book by the researchers Robert Bauval and Adrian Gilbert titled *The Orion Mystery*. Bauval was born and raised in Egypt and has a background in engineering. However, he was also interested in both history and astronomy. While viewing an aerial photograph of the Giza Plateau near Cairo, Bauval had noticed that the three major pyramids on the plateau form a pattern that is very similar to that of the three stars of Orion's Belt.

Orion's Belt is just a part of a much larger constellation of stars that is known as Orion the Hunter. Our ancient ancestors were very keen on creating imaginary patterns in the sky, and Orion had gone down in mythology as being a great warrior and hunter. His shape was conceived in the mind of the stargazers across a large section of the sky, and the three stars Alnitak, Alnilam, and Mintaka appear to form the belt from which Orion's sword is suspended. Of course the stars that make up the constellation of Orion—or indeed any of the constellations—are not directly related at all. Some are at vastly greater distances from Earth than others, and the pictures our ancestors painted in the sky are the result of nothing more than their active imaginations.

What is quite peculiar about the three stars of Orion's Belt is that they appear to be almost equidistant from each other (though not quite), and they also seem to form a straight line, (though again, this is not exactly true). They are, nevertheless, a very memorable group of stars and have been noticed and commented upon by practically every developing civilization from ancient times onward.

Robert Bauval was not so naive as to believe that there might be some deliberate connection between just *any* three structures on the ground and the stars of Orion's Belt. What made him sit up and take

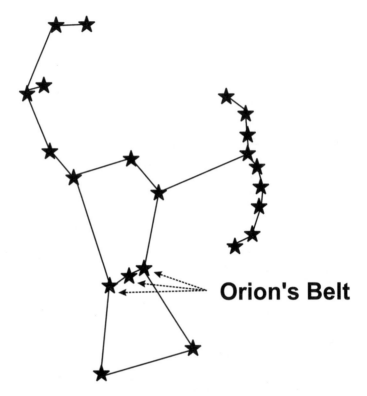

Fig. 18.2. The constellation of Orion the Hunter

Mintaka   **Alnilam**   **Alnitak**

Fig. 18.3. The three stars that form Orion's Belt as they appear
in the sky when parallel with the horizon

notice in terms of the three pyramids on the Giza Plateau were the relative distances between the pyramids, together with the fact that they are not *exactly* in a straight line. A slight dogleg is present, which is identical with the dogleg that appears in the case of Orion's Belt. He also noticed that the relative brightness of the stars in question might be reflected in the relative sizes of the three pyramids.

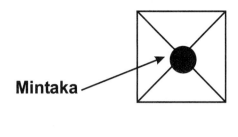

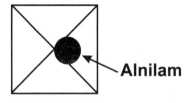

Fig. 18.4. The stars of Orion's Belt superimposed
onto the Giza pyramids

Not content with what might be simply an unlikely but nevertheless possible coincidence, Robert Bauval started to trawl through what was known about ancient Egyptian religion and mythology to try to ascertain whether a deliberately created model of part of the sky created at Giza might have made any sense to the ancient peoples of the Nile. In the end he found a wealth of evidence that pointed to an early series of beliefs on the part of the Egyptians that could easily confirm the Giza–Orion's Belt hypothesis. Much of the evidence came from carvings found inside a series of very early pyramids from the Egyptian Old Kingdom that are situated in the region of Saqqara. It is generally accepted that the texts carved into the Saqqara pyramids represent the oldest religious texts ever created by humanity. Whether this is actually true or not, it is certain that the Pyramid Texts survived because of the medium used to record them. The pyramids themselves were very robust, while the texts written on their walls were protected from both the hand of man and from the elements for many centuries.

The reason Alan was so familiar with the material contained within the Pyramid Texts, and indeed the knowledge of the Giza pyramids and their connection to Orion's Belt, was because of his research with Christopher Knight for their book *Before the Pyramids*.

Robert Bauval and Adrian Gilbert had demonstrated that the Pyramid Texts talked repeatedly about the sky and about the ancient Egyptian belief that the gods lived among the stars. Furthermore, they also considered that when human beings died they too were translated to the heavens to dwell in specific regions with particular gods. The most important of the gods in question was Osiris, who was always associated with death and rebirth.

Egyptian beliefs were complex and often strange to our sensibilities. For example, although Osiris dwelled among the stars—specifically in the region close to Orion's Belt—he was also always represented on Earth. This was because during their lifetimes the kings of Egypt, known as pharaohs, were considered to actually *be* Osiris. According to the Pyramid Texts, when a pharaoh died he was expected to take a journey to the stars to be with Osiris for eternity, or more likely to *become* a part of the god.

Together, with the work of Bauval and Gilbert, Alan and Chris were able to demonstrate that the ancient Egyptians had believed that following death and mummification a given pharaoh would embark on a sacred boat in order to make the necessary journey. This trip would commence down the Nile, which is the life-giving river to which Egypt owes its very existence. However, the journey did not end on the earthbound Nile. As we still can today, every night the Egyptians could see that vast band of phosphorescence in the night sky that we call the Milky Way. It sweeps away across the sky and is actually part of our own galaxy composed of billions of stars, though many are at such a vast distance they cannot be seen by the naked eye as individual points of light. The Egyptians called the Milky Way the Nile in the Sky. It appears they considered that the pharaoh's journey after death was not simply down the watery Nile, but then on up the Milky Way until the sacred boat arrived at Orion's Belt, which was the home of Osiris and also the virtuous dead.

Anyone standing on the raised Giza Plateau at night, as Alan and Chris did, can easily see how this belief might have come about. Looking south into the blackness of the desert, stars and the Milky Way are reflected into the water of the Nile as it winds its otherwise unseen way into the distance. Beyond a certain point the only recognition that the Nile exists is because of the reflections of the sky. It is virtually impossible to ascertain with the naked eye where the earthly river ends at the horizon and where the heavenly one begins. Alan and Chris found the nighttime observations on the Giza Plateau to be a truly strange and quite remarkable experience. The spectacle is at its very best at certain parts of those nights when the base of the Milky Way coincides with the disappearance of the Nile on the southern horizon.

Specifically created boats have been found associated with tombs in Egypt, in particular buried in pits alongside the largest of the three great pyramids on the Giza Plateau. Ancient Egyptians believed in a human soul or essence that they referred to as a person's ka. Perhaps they also originally accepted that inanimate objects, such as a boat, could also possess a ka. So, although the actual boat provided for the pharaoh's last journey remained in its burial pit, its ka was the spirit boat in which the ka of the pharaoh made his last journey. Similarly, it is possible that re-creating certain stars in the heavens as structures on the ground represented bringing the holy essence of the stars down to humanity: a sort of heaven made on Earth.

All of this made a great deal of sense, but it had not been the starting point of Alan and Chris Knight's research. Their journey to Egypt had been a long one, all the way from the north of England.

Not far from the ancient and beautiful little city of Ripon in the county of Yorkshire is something that should genuinely be considered one of the surviving wonders of the ancient world, and yet hardly anyone knows of its existence. The British Isles are justifiably famous for all the structures left by the ancient peoples who inhabited these islands. The most famous of these are the stone circles, such as Avebury and Stonehenge, together with elaborate chambered tombs, hill forts, and impressive trackways. Less well known but much earlier than any of the stone monuments of the British Isles are the henges.

A "henge" is the name given to a circular earthwork created by digging a deep ditch and then by throwing up the earth to create a bank. A true henge has the bank on the outside of the ditch. Because of this fact it is quite obvious these were never intended to be defensive structures or indeed corrals for livestock. They could only have served some ritual purpose. There are still many hundreds if not thousands of henges to be found across the British Isles, though many have been plowed out over the centuries and are now little more than parch marks in the grass, which can be seen from high above.

Henges range from the very small to the extremely large, but few match the scale of the three that are to be found at Thornborough, near Ripon. The total distance covered by the Thornborough Henges is around 1.08 miles (1.74 km), and each of the three henges, which all have the same dimensions, is so large it would be possible to fit an entire medieval cathedral within it and still have room to spare.

To qualify as henges such structures have to possess at least one entrance. In the case of the Thornborough Henges each example has two entrances, and it is believed that the three henges were also connected by ritual avenues. Limited archaeological surveys have demonstrated that the henges were even larger in diameter than originally estimated, and dating evidence from the site pushes their commencement back to at least 3500 BCE, which is long before any of the stone circles of the British Isles appeared, and well over a thousand years before the first pyramids were built in Egypt.

It was the offhand remark of an archaeologist that first alerted Alan and Chris to the true significance of the Thornborough Henges, which they had first started to study because of the ancient measuring system upon which they were based. A tongue-in-cheek suggestion had been

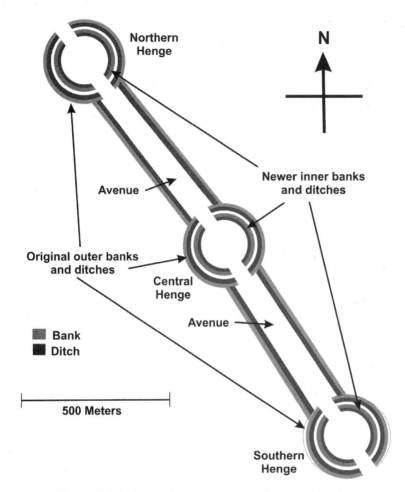

Fig. 18.5. The Thornborough Henges from 3500 BCE

made that the Thornborough Henges, like the Giza pyramids, closely resembled the stars of Orion's Belt, though archaeology steers clear of such ideas. It was left to Alan and Chris to determine just how similar Orion's Belt and the Thornborough Henges are. It is worth mentioning at this point the scandalous situation regarding these truly remarkable structures. The Thornborough Henges, which stand on privately owned land, are barely protected by law and under most circumstances are closed to the public. Only by committing the offense of trespassing is it possible for most researchers to access the site.

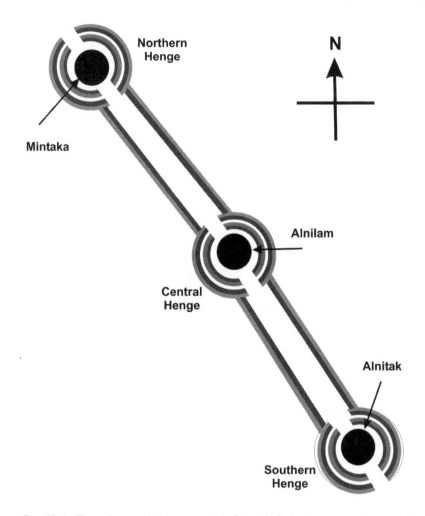

Fig. 18.6. Thornborough Henges with Orion's Belt stars superimposed

One of Alan's specialties is the study of ancient astronomy and the way it relates to ancient structures (usually known these days as *archaeoastronomy*).* His first task regarding the Thornborough Henges was to take a snapshot of what Orion's Belt looked like when seen from

---

*This is a subject that has been made much easier in recent years because of sophisticated astronomical computer programs that can reproduce the position of planets and stars as seen from any part of the Earth back into ancient times.

the north of England in 3500 BCE and to superimpose it onto the Thornborough Henges. The result was utterly stunning.

As can be seen from the diagram, the fit of the stars onto the henges is incredibly accurate. To understand just how remarkable this is we have to take into account that when seen with the naked eye the three stars of Orion's Belt span a part of the sky no bigger than a man's thumbnail with one's arm fully stretched in front of the eyes. To ascertain the relative distance between the stars together with the subtle dogleg in the arrangement and to translate this into something as huge as the Thornborough Henge array was little short of miraculous. This exercise alone surely demonstrates that there can be no doubt that the Thornborough Henges were a deliberately created copy of the stars of Orion's Belt.

As with the situation in Egypt, a river runs close to the south of the henges and winds its way off into the distance. In this very flat landscape and with a river that historically would have been much wider than it is today, it would have been possible to view the stars of the heavens and the Milky Way reflected in the river. At specific times in winter one leg of the Milky Way would have coincided with the river, giving the same impression as that in Egypt of a river of stars that continued up into the heavens, leading ultimately to the constellation of Orion and to Orion's Belt.

The conclusion must surely be that there was a similarity of belief between these truly ancient Britons and the people of Egypt. Unfortunately this cannot be proved because we have no knowledge of the religious beliefs and practices of the New Stone Age inhabitants of the British Isles.*

With Janet's observation regarding the three obelisks running down through New York City and their possible association with Orion's Belt in mind, we took note of the topographical circumstances of the area. It was first necessary to look closely at the distance between the

---

*Readers who wish to know more about these findings and to understand the true connections between the Thornborough Henges and the pyramids of the Giza Plateau should read *Before the Pyramids*.

obelisks and the alignment they share. The oldest of the three obelisks, at least in terms of the period in which they were erected in New York, is known as the Emmet obelisk, and it stands in the churchyard of St. Paul's Chapel in Manhattan. This obelisk was built to commemorate the life of Thomas Addis Emmet, an Irish-born American who was one of the first independent legal advocates in the free United States. Emmet does not lie below the obelisk, which was erected in his memory around 1830.

The next of the three obelisks to be erected was placed much higher up in the city, at the point where Broadway and Fifth Avenue cross. It is known as the Worth obelisk and was constructed in 1857 as a memorial to General William Jenkins Worth, an American army officer who gained great fame for his victories in the Mexican wars. In this case Worth actually does lie beneath the obelisk.

Finally comes the most famous of New York's obelisks. Although not erected until 1881, it is by far the oldest of the three obelisks, because it was brought to the United States from Egypt. It dates back three thousand years and was one of a pair that had been brought by the Romans to Alexandria in Egypt from Heliopolis. The sister of the obelisk that now graces Central Park is to be found on the Thames Embankment in London, England. It is worth noting at this point that all three obelisks have strong Masonic connections. Thomas Addis Emmet was a practicing Freemason, as was General William Jenkins Worth. As far as the Central Park obelisk is concerned, it was from donations by wealthy Freemasons that allowed it to be brought to the United States, and it was erected amid great Masonic ceremony.

The distance between the Central Park obelisk and the Worth obelisk is 14,945 feet (4,555 meters), and the gap between the Worth obelisk and the Emmet obelisk is 12,804 feet (3,902 meters). In terms of alignment there is a dogleg in the line joining the three obelisks that conforms very closely to the one observable in Orion's Belt. In the case of Orion's Belt, the gap between the first star, Alnitak, and the second star, Alnilam, is slightly larger than the gap between Alnilam and the third star, Mintaka. This is also true of the three New York obelisks, because the gap between the Central Park obelisk and the Worth obelisk is greater than that between the Worth obelisk and the Emmet obelisk. The proportional nature of the gaps between the obelisks does not conform precisely to those of the stars (as is the case at Thornborough), but there is a very good reason for this state of affairs.

When the Egyptian monument was placed in Central Park it had to be placed somewhere where the ground had sufficient strength to support its mighty bulk. The best location available was Grey Whacky Knoll, very close to the Metropolitan museum (the proximity of the museum may have been an additional incentive for the choice of this location). If the Egyptian obelisk had been placed in a position with its companions that would have created a pattern identical to Orion's Belt, it would have had to be placed two hundred feet south of its present location. Not only would this have meant it was farther from the museum, it would also have had to be placed in boggy ground near what is today known as Conservatory Water. Nevertheless, it cannot be denied that the three obelisks do form a very close approximation to the stars of Orion's Belt, including the dogleg that truly distinguishes the relationship of these three stars. The total distance from the Central Park obelisk in the north to the Emmet obelisk at St. Paul's Chapel in the south is 5.25 miles (8.45 km).

As we are always willing and in fact even eager to point out, coincidences do happen, and it is quite conceivable that the apparent alignment of these three obelisks in New York is nothing more than a random-chance event. However, there are a number of circumstances involved that make such a coincidence virtually impossible, and the most significant of these has to be the very location of the Emmet obelisk, right at the bottom of Manhattan, very close to the North Bay and in the churchyard of that most extraordinary of structures, St. Paul's Chapel.

The central part of what is today New York City (Manhattan) is comprised of a long spit of land bounded on two sides by water. It comes to a point at the southern end and looks out over the North Bay where New York first developed. St. Paul's Chapel and therefore the

Emmet obelisk is situated very close to water on three sides and is less than a mile from the North Bay.

The chapel is presently utterly dwarfed by the many large skyscrapers that surround it, but at the time it was built it stood quite alone in a wheat field. As we have already noted, there were significant complaints at the time that the church authorities should want to build the chapel in such a remote location. It is only the passing of time and the unbelievable development of New York that led to its present state, dwarfed by its huge neighbors.

St. Paul's Chapel also possesses a round tower, which, up until the advent of high-rise buildings, would have offered an unparalleled view of the water surrounding this part of New York on three sides.

Taken as a single example of what could be seen from this location, if anyone had stood in the tower of the chapel around 4:00 a.m. on the winter solstice looking west of south, they would have seen the Milky Way reflected in and also rising from the dark waters of the North Bay. This would have swept up to the right, leading to the constellation of Orion and to Orion's Belt. In the dark days before the massive light pollution of a city the size of New York, the view would have been breathtaking—at least as good as that once enjoyed from either Thornborough Henges or the Giza Plateau.

If we take the alignment of the New York obelisks together with the strange placement of St. Paul's Chapel and the physical location of the whole, it seems self-evident that there was something far more than random chance at work in the planning and placement of the obelisks. What makes the matter even stranger is that these obelisks are all traditional examples with pyramid tops. All were of course inspired by ancient Egypt, and one of them actually comes from Heliopolis, once one of ancient Egypt's most sacred cities. Heliopolis occupied part of what is today the city of Cairo, which, in turn, is so close to the three pyramids on the Giza Plateau that it would be possible to throw a stone between them.

All of this raises a great mystery regarding the knowledge of those who brought the obelisks together in this way and also those who planned and built St. Paul's Chapel. The chapel was completed in 1766, and the last of the obelisks to be put in place—the genuinely Egyptian example—was raised in 1881; well over a century separated the beginning of the quest and its completion. This does not unduly surprise us. We have well learned that the Venus Families are incredibly patient and have often been willing to allow long periods of time to achieve their objectives. What is more puzzling is how they came by the knowledge of Egyptian religion and mythology that makes sense of the creation of Orion's Belt on the ground.

As far as we are aware, until Robert Bauval and Adrian Gilbert made the connection, nobody had drawn the conclusion that the Giza pyramids were a copy of Orion's Belt. To prove the connection it was necessary to look closely at very early Egyptian religion, and this has only been possible thanks to the translation of the carvings in the Pyramid Texts. Much of what we know about these texts, most of which represent charms and words used during the burial of a pharaoh, we owe to French Egyptologist Gaston Maspero. Maspero was born in Paris in 1846 and showed an early interest in history. His interest in Egyptian hieroglyphics also began early, and by the time he was twenty-one he had managed to interpret a very complex series of hieroglyphics in under two weeks.

In 1880, Maspero traveled to Egypt and there began to undertake the arduous task of copying and translating many of the Pyramid Texts. Although for the moment we cannot prove the fact, it seems fairly evident that Maspero was a practicing Freemason, and he was undertaking his work on hieroglyphics at a time when all things Egyptian were becoming extremely popular, especially among Freemasons. Had Maspero been in Egypt a few years earlier it might have been possible to explain the Orion's Belt of New York in terms of his work and translations of the Pyramid Texts. However, the last obelisk to be put in place rose over Central Park in 1881, at a time when Maspero had only just commenced his epic work on the texts.

We can assume that the plan to create the copy of Orion's Belt in New York must have dated back to the positioning of at least the second obelisk, that of General Worth, which took place in 1857. This was more than two decades before Maspero went to Egypt and well before any of the Pyramid Texts had been translated. There are only two possible explanations for this state of affairs. Either the Pyramid Texts had actually been translated significantly earlier than history suggests, or the knowledge necessary to create the Orion's Belt in New York came from another source.

The alignment of the obelisks across Manhattan closely parallels the alignment of the three stars in Orion's Belt. The middle obelisk, working from north to south, is slightly to the right of a line joining the first and third obelisks. If we reproduce a drawing of the way Orion's Belt looks as it rises in a winter sky above New York it can be observed that the star Alnilam is indeed slightly to the right of the other two stars.

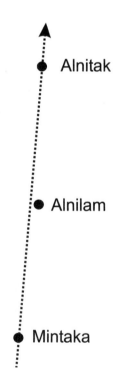

Fig. 18.7. Orion's Belt as it looks rising over New York on winter nights. The middle star is to the right of a line connecting Alnitak and Mintaka.

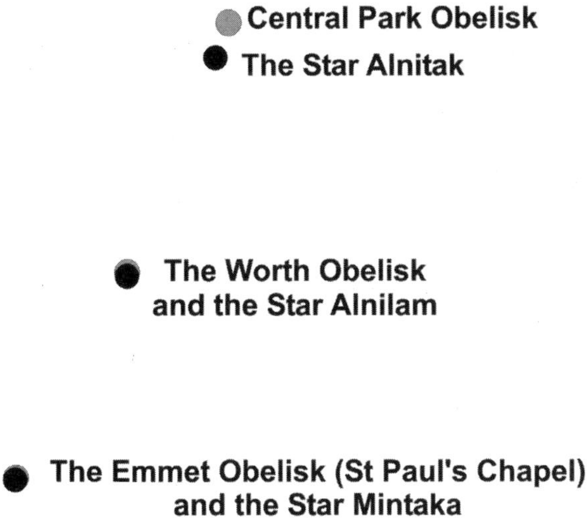

● **Central Park Obelisk**
● **The Star Alnitak**

● **The Worth Obelisk**
   and the Star Alnilam

● **The Emmet Obelisk (St Paul's Chapel)**
   and the Star Mintaka

Fig. 18.8. Orion's Belt and the New York obelisks

If we now look at a drawing with both Orion's Belt and the New York obelisks included we can see that the stars and the obelisks form the same pattern (with the Central Park obelisk just a little farther north, as mentioned earlier).

This arrangement is in contrast to both the Orion's Belt represented by the Giza Pyramids and the Orion's Belt represented by the Thornborough Henges in Northern England. In both these examples the stars appear as a mirror image of the sky. Of the three representations of Orion's Belt only the New York example appears on the ground precisely the same as it appears in the sky overhead on winter nights. This conforms more to the way humanity comprehends the stars in more recent times.

The Central Park obelisk, which was the last one to be put in place, was brought to America thanks to the generosity of William H. Vanderbilt, whose Venus Family connections seem certain.

At the same time the Egyptian obelisk was being raised into its final position in Central Park, completing the New York Orion's Belt, the Washington Monument was almost finished in Washington, D.C.

In both cases there is clear evidence of knowledge being present that according to conventional sources should not have been available. Once again this infers that Freemasonry was at least one of the conduits through which this knowledge had traveled. As the nineteenth century drew toward its close, a subtle yet powerful group of very special people were flexing their muscles in the United States. The Nation of the Goddess was definitely taking shape.

FREEMASONIC SYMBOLISM IN BASEBALL

Obelisks have a very masculine overtone, though—as in the case of the Washington Monument, with the Vesica Piscis geometry at its base—wherever we find the God, the Goddess is almost always present. However, there are significant instances across the whole of the United States in which the symbolism of the Goddess reigns supreme.

Baseball is one of the most popular games played in the United States. Its actual origins are lost in the mists of time, and it almost certainly represents a synthesis of other bat-and-ball games that immigrants brought with them from the Old World. It most resembles a game called rounders that is still played in Great Britain, mostly by girls. All the same there are subtle differences, and it is clear that as the game is played now, baseball is a uniquely American invention. Constantly flying high above the United States on research trips and while en route for television shoots, Janet and Scott Wolter regularly pick out baseball diamonds on the ground far below and often discuss the seeming similarities between the pitches that are specific to baseball and Masonic iconography.

This is probably not as surprising as it might sound. Although there has been a great deal of controversy over the years regarding who it was who created baseball as it is played today, the chief contender seems to have been a man by the name of Alexander Cartwright (1820–1892), and for most of his adult life he was also a passionate and committed Freemason. Alexander Cartwright was born in New York, the son of a merchant sea captain, but it appears that a life on the rolling waves was not favored by the young Alexander, who instead first worked for the New York stock market and later became a bank employee.

As a young man there was nothing Alexander liked better than to go to play bat-and-ball games with his friends in the local streets and later in any one of New York's developing parks and open spaces. Alexander Cartwright was also a volunteer fireman, and it was through the fire stations of New York that these early games with bat and ball gradually turned into something more organized. The first time we actually hear of a formalized game of baseball it was played between the Knickerbockers, which was Alexander Cartwright's fire station team, and another team known as the New York Nine. This took place in June of 1846 and was played (as it turns out very appropriately) at Elysian Fields in New Jersey.

Cartwright seems to have had the biggest input into the game becoming what it is today. He was the person who turned the game field around somewhat; rounders had originally been played on a square field, whereas baseball is played on a diamond-shaped field (although in fact it is not a true diamond but rather a square). Cartwright also fixed the sides of the square as being ninety feet, as well as settling on the use of foul territories, three strikes per batter, and nine players allowed on the field. In addition Cartwright seems to have suggested flat bases and got rid of the rule in rounders that said a hitter was out if he was struck by a ball thrown by a fielder.

Many Americans still hold to the idea that a man named Abner Doubleday was ultimately responsible for developing the rules and procedures of baseball in Cooperstown, New York. Previously, this claim was upheld by the Baseball Hall of Fame, located in Cooperstown, but today the Hall of Fame has changed its position, as will anyone researching the situation. Researchers will discover, as we did, that modern baseball relies much more on Cartwright's influence.

Alexander Cartwright went on to have an interesting life. At one time he joined the gold rush to California but eventually settled in Hawaii, where he became the fire chief in Honolulu and also a trusted adviser to the Hawaiian king. Of course Alexander introduced the game of baseball to Hawaii and was also an important member of the Hawaiian Masonic fraternity. Scott and Janet were certainly not the first people to recognize a relationship between baseball and Freemasonry. This is something that has been discussed for a very long time. The initial reason for this is that the field (or diamond, more correctly) on which baseball is played has so many similarities with what is the most iconic of all Masonic symbols—the Square and Compass.

American author Randy Lavello points out these similarities in his online article "Occult Symbolism: As American as Baseball."

> Baseball was obviously created by Freemasons, as it bears the unmistakable marks of Freemasonry. The field, from home plate to the left and right field wall forms a compass; the entire outfield wall is the semicircle which this compass draws. Upside-down, overlapping this compass, the bases form the square. Thus, the baseball field is the emblem of Freemasonry.
>
> Three strikes per batter and three outs per inning were assigned because three is the principle sacred number of Freemasonry. Four is a number of significance because it represents a square (the shape) and deals with the four directions, thus: four balls, four bases. Nine is sacred because it is three squared . . . there are nine fielding positions and nine innings. This brings us to a total of twenty-seven outs per team a game . . . and guess what?

We are indeed indebted to Randy Lavello for such a concise introduction to the primarily numerological associations of baseball and Freemasonry, but the relationship also clearly exists on a symbolic level—the very design of the baseball diamond, or field, introduces the

Fig. 19.1. Masonic Square and Compass

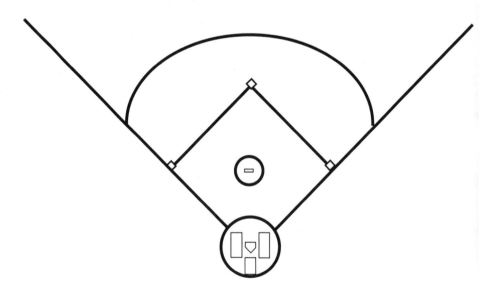

Fig. 19.2. A typical baseball diamond with outfield and foul lines

knowing observer to aspects of Masonic belief that are not even necessarily understood by a great many Freemasons themselves. The most
potent of the messages linking baseball with Freemasonry relate to what
we personally refer to as the Goddess at the heart of Freemasonry. A
writer who has similar ideas to our own regarding the Goddess aspects
of Freemasonry is William Bond. In his book *Freemasonry and the
Hidden Goddess* he makes a convincing case that the Goddess is evident
in nearly every aspect of Freemasonry, if one knows where to look. In
chapter 1 of his book he says:

> The Compass and Square image is probably the most popular sym-
> bol in Freemasonry. The fundamentalist Pastor Ron Carlson, who
> has spoken about Freemasonry in evangelical churches in many
> parts of America, claims that the square represents the earth, the
> compasses represent the sky, and the square and compasses when
> united, represent the sky impregnating the earth with its showers.
> He goes on to state that this is a symbol of sexual intercourse. The
> official Freemason line is they are just tools of the Masonry Trade.

In fact as William Bond quite clearly knows, the symbolism goes
much deeper than this. Freemasonic iconography is awash with triangles, which is part of the fascination, for geometry generally abounds
in the Craft. The diamond shape that is created on the famed Masonic
symbol by the compass and the square is actually not two triangles
but two *V* shapes. This *V* is a symbol that has been of supreme importance since ancient times, and it is a vagina symbol. When two appear
together, as in a diamond, they represent the sacred sexual union that
was significant in all ancient religions. The more streamlined version of
the diamond is something we have come across earlier in our research
and one that is evident around the base of the Washington Monument.
This is the Vesica Piscis, a symbol that in its own right also occurs in
Freemasonic symbolism. There is no more potent symbol for either
the Goddess or the sacred feminine generally than the diamond and
the Vesica Piscis. These symbols go back many thousands of years, and

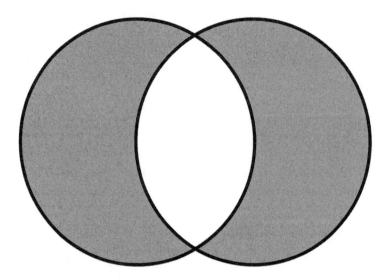

Fig. 19.3. The Vesica Piscis, formed by the interlocking of two circles, is synonymous in sacred sexual symbolism with the diamond and represents the vagina of the Goddess.

the Vesica Piscis is held as being sacred by the Christian Church even though few Christians know what it means.

As we have seen before it is possible to create two equilateral triangles within the Vesica Piscis, and of course a triangle is simply a *V* with a line across the top. It is said that a single *V* is taken as representative of the feminine and the Goddess because it has the same basic shape as the area covered by a woman's pubic hair. The pubic triangle therefore is symbolic of where life comes from.

With regard to the Masonic article above by William Bond, it is also worth bearing in mind that $3 \times 3 = 9$ may relate to human gestation. Three months per trimester, so again $3 \times 3 = 9$ months. Also the intersecting circles of the Vesica Piscis could allegorically represent the reproductive cells of a man and a woman. Janet reflects that the Vesica Piscis itself is ultimately the shape the vagina takes when seen by a midwife or doctor as a woman is giving birth and the baby's head begins to crown.

These are symbols that underpin baseball, simply because the shape of a baseball diamond or field is utterly Masonic in shape. Whether Alexander Cartwright had any ideas about the relationship between Freemasonry and the sacred feminine when he abandoned the square of rounders for the diamond of baseball is a matter of conjecture, but it cannot be denied that baseball is a game built on and dependent on geometry. Initially it was also a fraternal game, and it was probably many years before competitive teams of women baseball players became common. Baseball is, in every respect, a perfect game for Freemasons to play. These factors could not have been lost on such a committed Freemason as Alexander Cartwright.

The point we wish to make here is that hardly anyone denies a relationship between baseball and Freemasonry, but few people are aware that it uses the very symbols within Freemasonry that point to something that Freemasonry itself ultimately derived from the Venus Families. We have no doubt that the *G* that so frequently appears in the center of the Masonic Square and Compass stands for Gaea, the name of the Earth itself and also the Goddess it represents in ancient Greek. The *G,* as used in Freemasonry, could hardly stand for God because it appears in many different countries, and the local word for God does not start with a *G* in all languages. In France, for example, where much that was to become American Freemasonry developed, the name for God is "Dieu." On the other hand, because it is a Greek word and is universally used, the name Gaea would always be understood, and its placement within the sacred diamond would make sense.

What convinces us that either Alexander Cartwright or someone from whom he derived his original rules for baseball *did* know about the Goddess symbolism in Freemasonry is the size of the diamond ultimately used.

Self-evidently this would be measurable in feet because that was the linear unit used in the United States at the time, but there are a couple of reasons why the baseball diamond ended up with sides of ninety feet.

First, 90 is the number of degrees in a right angle, and right angles are very important in Freemasonry because they are the measure of a "true square." But there is a deeper and much more hidden reason for the 90 feet of the baseball diamond. If we turn the 90 feet into Megalithic Yards, it comes out to 33 Megalithic Yards, to an accuracy of 99.8 percent. For all intents and purposes, 90 feet is the same as 33 Megalithic Yards. (The difference is just over 1 inch, or one part in over 1,000.) We have seen time and again how important the Megalithic Yard is to Washington, D.C.: the Megalithic Yard being a geodetic measurement that splits the Earth rationally and equally.

The significance of this to any Freemason would be self-evident. In Scottish Rite Freemasonry the 33rd degree is the highest numerical degree of Freemasonry that can be achieved. It is actually held by very few Freemasons, and only those having achieved the 33rd degree can serve on the governing body of Scottish Rite Freemasonry.

If any or all of this is viewed by our readers as little more than a series of chance events, we can go even further. During our research for this book we looked at many aerial photographs of significant structures, but no structure was more important to our research than the Ellipse, which, as we mentioned earlier, is situated at the very center of the District of Columbia and just south of the White House in Washington, D.C.

The symbolism of this giant park runs deep, and we are convinced that it represents the most significant location in the United States to those who are members of the Venus Families. At one and the same time it is a representation of the All-Seeing Eye and also the sacred "egg" of the Great Goddess. At its center lies the chamber, dug in 1881. We believe this chamber contains a plethora of treasures and documents held sacred by the Venus Families, together with the recovered bones of Jesus and Mary Magdalene.

Readers will recall that there is an elaborate and giant arrow pointing at the center of the Ellipse, constructed from a series of lines of specifically Megalithic length that run from the center of the Ellipse to the various grand intersections that were present on the original map of Washington, D.C. At one time these were not the only arrows of a Megalithic nature that were pointing at this sacred spot. An aerial photograph dating back to 1949 shows that Ellipse Park was once used

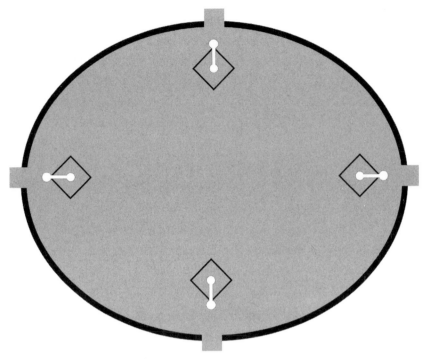

Fig. 19.4. Ellipse Park in Washington, D.C. This is a drawing taken from a 1949 aerial photograph of the Ellipse. The position of the four baseball diamonds that were placed in the park are clearly marked, forming four arrows that point inward toward the sacred center of the Ellipse.

for baseball—though the arrangement of the diamonds placed onto it was very specific. The photograph in question is indistinct and not ideally suited to reproduction in our book, so we have made a drawing of the situation as it was to better highlight what the planners of Washington, D.C., had done.

There were four baseball diamonds placed on Ellipse Park. Each of these was arranged so that the batter's box is close to one of the entrances of the Ellipse, at north, south, east, and west. The pitcher's mound in each case was therefore closer to the center of the Ellipse, and each diamond takes on the appearance of an arrow, all of which point inward toward the center of the Ellipse.

⟨⟩

In addition to being a square with sides of the very significant 33 Megalithic Yards, each baseball diamond is also a tiny representation of the shape of the District of Columbia, at the center of which is the Ellipse itself. The District of Columbia is also a diamond based on a square, although it is of course massively bigger than a baseball diamond. The sides of the square that forms the District of Columbia are 10 miles in length, but they are also 53 × 366 Megalithic Yards. This is one of the few comparisons to the mile and the unit of 366 Megalithic Yards (996.25 feet) where both units come together in integer numbers. (The comparison is well over 99.99 percent accurate, and the difference is just 1 part in nearly 53,000.)

The position of the pitcher's mound in baseball is right in the center of the diamond, in exactly the same place as the location of the secret chamber at the center of the District of Columbia was estimated to be by the original surveyors of the district. They were slightly off in their surveying, but there is no doubt about their intention. They were in fact only wrong by a matter of yards.

In a sense, every baseball diamond in the United States is a miniature Megalithic representation of the federal District of Columbia, and because of the symbols upon which it is based, it is also a *sacred* area dedicated to the Great Goddess, and of course each has Masonic overtones. This proves that to the "knowing eye" truth can easily be hidden in plain sight. There is, in effect, at least one and usually many "temples" ultimately dedicated to the Goddess in every village, town, and city of United States, and also attached to most schools and colleges.

Could this state of affairs have come about at least partly because it was and is the Venus Families' way of sending a message to the Goddess that they are *in* the United States, the New Jerusalem?

In the words of a much-used American phrase and one often associated with baseball commentators, "Who'd a thunk it?"

20

THRESHING FLOORS
AND HENGES

Potent Places for Magic

Much of our research for this book has led us into the world of Freemasonry, which associates many of its rituals and its supposed origins with parts of the Hebrew scriptures—in particular the story of the building of the first temple in Jerusalem by King Solomon. Freemasonry puts its own slant on the story of Solomon and his temple, and it was while we were comparing the Masonic version with the story as related by the Bible that we discovered something that turned out to be of great significance to our own research.

Although Solomon was the king who built the Jerusalem temple, it was his father, King David, who had chosen its site. The events in question most likely took place around the tenth century BCE. The Hebrews had conquered much of the area around Jerusalem in the previous decades, but it was during the reign of King David that the Hebrew scriptures tell us that the Hebrews had sinned against their all-powerful God and that as a result he had visited a terrible plague upon them. It was immediately after this plague that an angel of God approached Gad, who was the leader of one of the Hebrew tribes. The angel told

Gad to instruct David to build an altar on the site that eventually became that of the famed Temple of Jerusalem. As stated in 2 Samuel 24:18–21:

> And Gad came that day to David and said to him, "Go up, erect an altar to the LORD on the threshing floor of Araunah the Jebusite." So David, according to the word of Gad, went up as the LORD commanded. Now Araunah looked, and saw the king and his servants coming toward him. So Araunah went out and bowed before the king with his face to the ground. Then Araunah said, "Why has my lord the king come to his servant?" And David said, "To buy the threshing floor from you, to build an altar to the LORD, that the plague may be withdrawn from the people."

In 2 Samuel 24:22–24, it goes on to suggest that Araunah wished to make a present of the place to David:

> Now Araunah said to David, "Let my lord the king take and offer up whatever seems good to him. Look, here are oxen for burnt sacrifice, and threshing implements and the yokes of the oxen for wood. All these, O king, Araunah has given to the king." And Araunah said to the king, "May the LORD your God accept you." Then the king said to Araunah, "No, but I will surely buy it from you for a price; nor will I offer burnt offerings to the LORD my God with that which costs me nothing." So David bought the threshing floor and the oxen for fifty shekels of silver.

The inference is clear. The site of the threshing floor was to be sacred to God. As a result David would not accept it as a gift, most likely because then it would be seen as having been acquired by conquest. Rather David wanted such a potentially sacred site to be acquired appropriately, as a purchase.

The fact that the site of the temple in Jerusalem had been a threshing floor was of great interest to us. There is a strong inference in the

Book of Samuel and elsewhere in the Hebrew scriptures that the place in question was already considered sacred *before* David chose to acquire it for his own altar to God, and we set out on a quest to discover what might have been special about this threshing floor or indeed threshing floors in general.

As the name implies, a threshing floor is a place where cereal crops such as wheat and barley are brought once they have been cut from the fields and allowed to stand and dry in the sun for a while. The stalks are then spread out on a previously prepared site, and the grain is separated from the stalks, originally by stamping on it and later with the use of flails and other mechanical techniques. From the medieval period a threshing floor was often inside a barn, but we know from archaeological sites across the Mediterranean and in the Middle East that in biblical times that grain was threshed at deliberately chosen locations outdoors.

Sometimes a wooden sledge was constructed that had flint or metal blades on its underside. This was dragged around the circular threshing floor by oxen. The stamping of the animals, together with the cutting action of the blades, chopped the straw and separated the seeds. The resulting mixture was then thrown into the air with the aid of winnowing forks or fans so that the wind blew away the chaff and the grains fell at the winnowers' feet where they could be collected for use or storage.

Before beasts of burden were regularly used it is certain that the separation of the grain from the chaff was brought about entirely by the constant stamping of people as they walked around and around the threshing floor. The word *threshing* originally meant to "stamp noisily."

Threshing floors are mentioned regularly in the Bible. Often there is a strong implication that threshing floors were considered to be "places apart," and perhaps even considered sacred in some way. One gets the impression that they were also places of gatherings, which would not be at all surprising. Threshing floors were carefully made and either paved or composed of solidly beaten earth. Where farming communities lived in close proximity it is likely that a number of farms would have shared the same central threshing floor, which would also have been a natural place to thrash out community disputes or to hold communal celebrations. Indeed, at the temple itself the Sanhedrin—a powerful body dedicated to preserving and handing out Hebrew law—had originally met at a threshing floor. Once the temple was built a part of the outer courtyard was set aside for the Sanhedrin, whose members would sit in a circle as they had done on the ancient threshing floor.

The Hebrew scriptures also seem to infer that the threshing floor was a place of sexual congress. We find an explicit reference to this in the Book of Hosea 9:1, which says:

> Do not rejoice, O Israel, with joy like other peoples, for you have played the harlot against your God. You have made love for hire on every threshing floor.

There is also a fascinating story in the Book of Ruth 3:7, in which Ruth is instructed by her mother to go to the threshing floor and there to lay with a man named Boaz. In this instance it appears that sexual congress did not take place, but the sexual symbolism is unavoidable. Ruth uncovered Boaz's "feet," a euphemism employed elsewhere in the Hebrew scriptures to represent genitalia.

The connection between threshing grain and procreation is not at all surprising. As we have seen time and again the cycles of nature and the cycles of human beings were inextricably tied together in ancient religion. Just as surely as the stalks of grain bring forth fruitfulness, so it was that human fertility could also be assured by a direct association with the harvest. In a more direct sense the threshing floor was a "place apart," away from the prying eyes of others and therefore somewhere that a degree of privacy could be found.

Nor is it remotely surprising that the threshing floor should have religious or spiritual overtones. The act of separating grain from seed heads was an expression of the sacrifice of the grain god, a story that is highlighted in all the ancient Mystery religions. If the Goddess was to be found anywhere it would be in the place that represented both her sorrow and her joy, sorrow at the fact that her son was being torn apart, joy in the knowledge that her people would have food to eat across the coming year. These conflicting emotions are an important part of the mystery itself: death follows life, but life follows death. Greek mythology tells us that when the Mysteries of Demeter commenced, the goddess herself called her followers to the threshing floor at Eleusis where eventually her massive temple would be built.

Threshing floors also seem to have been places where significant power could be demonstrated by the gods and goddesses. In chapter 5 we mentioned the Ark of the Covenant, which was carried for decades through the desert by the Hebrews before finding a home in the holy of holies in King Solomon's Temple. On one occasion during its travels, the oxen bearing the ark stumbled, and it appeared that the sacred box would fall to the ground. With the best of intentions a man by the name of Uzzah reached out and steadied the ark. Unfortunately only very specific people were allowed to make any contact with the ark, and as a result Uzzah was struck dead on the spot.

The story in question appears in 2 Samuel 6, starting at verse 6, and the narrator makes it plain that the incident took place at Nachon's threshing floor. It appears that these were powerful places and ones where the pleasure or displeasure of the deity could be felt strongly.

It seemed unlikely to us that we would ever be able to see an ancient threshing floor, but how wrong we were. All across the islands of the Mediterranean they still survive. None of them are now used, but it could be on account of their mystical and spiritual overtones that they have been left intact. There are good examples on both Cyprus and Crete. The threshing floor is defined by a circle of large stones that would have prevented excessive water from heavy storms running onto the carefully prepared threshing floor and ruining its surface. However, the stones also doubtless speak in their own way of the circle's existence as a place apart. Some of these circular threshing floors were paved with stone while others were comprised of beaten earth; no doubt it depended on the local topography. The age of some of these surviving examples is difficult to judge, but because the basic Mediterranean threshing floor does not seem to have changed substantially until recent times it probably does not matter whether they can be absolutely tied down to a specific era. Where it does exist, dating evidence pushes them back well into prehistory.

Upon looking at a number of the surviving examples of threshing floors our thoughts immediately turned to henges, structures in the British Isles that have puzzled archaeologists for decades (see chapter 10).

Henges are to be found all over the British Isles though they do not exist on the mainland of Europe or its islands. A henge is an enclosure, circular in shape, and is defined by a ditch and a bank and has one or more entrances. What sets henges apart from other enclosures is that in almost all cases the ditch is inside the mound. This would make such an enclosure useless for defensive purposes. In the case of other structures, such as hill forts, ditches are always outside of banks, thus offering those inside the structure the best possible opportunity

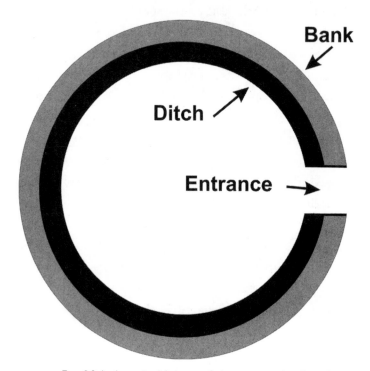

Fig. 20.1. A typical henge of the sort to be found
all across the British Isles

to harass enemies that were trying to gain entry. Attackers would be vulnerable as they attempted to cross the ditches, because the defenders could stand on the bank tops and hurl missiles down on them. In the case of henges the reverse would be true and the attackers would be at a distinct advantage.

This arrangement of ditches and banks in the case of henges has always puzzled archaeologists. As a result they have speculated on the possible intended use of henges, many of which were constructed as long ago as 3500 BCE to 4000 BCE. Because henges would also have been as good as useless for protecting livestock because the animals would have regularly tumbled into the ditches, routine suggestions as to their use have been along the lines of ritual spaces and perhaps meeting sites for clans and tribes.

As sometimes happens by chance during historical research, we found ourselves arriving at a conclusion regarding henges that as far as we are aware has never been put forward before. Our suggestion might not only answer the puzzle regarding henges themselves but also might tell us a great deal about the way life was lived in the British Isles during the Neolithic or New Stone Age period.

It is interesting to note that henges almost never occur on hilltops but commonly in valley-bottom settings adjacent to fertile land. It seems to us that henges were originally a more elaborate and better functioning version of the threshing floors still to be seen on the Mediterranean islands. Great Britain tends to be very wet, which is why it is so green and fertile. No matter how good stones might be in keeping out much of the storm water in the hotter and sunnier Mediterranean, they would probably be virtually ineffectual when it came to doing the same job in the British Isles. On the other hand an earthen bank would do the job admirably. The only associated problem would be that if the banks were good at keeping water out of the henge, they would be equally effective at keeping it in. Such a problem is negated by the inclusion of the ditch inside the bank, which would ensure that water falling inside the henge quickly drained away into the ditch.

Finding a context for henges and establishing precisely what they may have been has been difficult, not least of all because very little is understood about what society was like in the New Stone Age of the British Isles. All the same we can draw some conclusions from archaeological finds. For example, there is no indication that this period in the British Isles was one obsessed with warfare or conquest. On the contrary, the British Neolithic seems to have been a time of comparative peace and must certainly have been one of widespread cooperation.

Many of the later henges of the British Isles were extremely large, so big that they could only have been completed with significant cooperation across clans and tribes. When henges were eventually added to or superseded by stone circles the cooperative nature of the society at that time becomes even more emphasized. If the wider society had constantly been preparing itself for war, sites such as Avebury and Stonehenge could never have been created.

The concept of ownership, though doubtless already existing in the Neolithic British Isles, was much less emphasized than it became in the later Bronze Age. Neolithic burials were communal, and warrior or individual graves are unknown. This apparent disinterest in individuality seems to have extended to the land itself. Although both animal husbandry and the growing of cereals were present in the Neolithic British Isles, the landscape is devoid of individual field boundaries of the sort that become very evident by the Bronze Age. It seems highly likely that land was held in common by clans, the members of which participated in the farming that took place. We might envisage small villages, or more likely series of extended family habitations, that cooperated with other extended families in the same clan to provide what the community needed in terms of food. In such a situation the henge—as not just a threshing floor but also a place of worship and of social gatherings— seems highly appropriate. It is possible that threshing floors elsewhere in Europe occupied a similar community role.

One possible legacy of the henge as both a threshing floor and a center of ritual and social gatherings remains in the form of folk dancing, which has a rich tradition across the British Isles. Although many of these dances may have disappeared forever, work around the beginning of the twentieth century by a group of determined historians saved and preserved many. Most of the British dances are circular in nature and involve a complex interweaving of the participants. The result is that every part of the circle in which the dances take place is stamped on time and time again. What better way could there be of threshing the crop while at the same time participating in an exercise that was doubtless both spiritually motivated and enjoyable? It is amazing to reflect on traditions such as Maypole dancing, Morris dancing, hip-hop dancing, and many other examples that could be the descendants of grain threshing dances that go back several thousand years.

The henges were doubtlessly important not simply at harvesttime but throughout the whole year. They are likely to have been the location of meetings to decide on local farming strategy and a place to settle disputes and to seek judgments and decisions meted out by community elders. We can envisage henges as being considered beyond the constraints of ownership and belonging to everyone in a particular community. With the passage of time it is entirely possible that the original threshing function of henges was either forgotten or marginalized, while the henge's religious and social functions were retained. What makes this extremely likely is an observation made by archaeologists about the nature of prehistoric farming in the British Isles.

The most recent and perhaps persuasive study of cereal growing in the prehistoric British Isles comes from Chris J. Stevens, Dorian Fuller, and Martin Carver, who carried out an intensive assessment of archaeological data relating to the cultivation of cereal plants in the British Isles during the Neolithic period. This study was titled "Did Neolithic Farming Fail?" Using a wealth of collected data the compilers of the report came to the conclusion that although the cultivation of wheat and barley had come to the British Isles as early as around 4000 BCE, cereal growth underwent a severe decline after 3000 BCE, from which it did not recover until a new cereal crop revolution began after 1500 BCE. It seems that during this lull in cereal production most of the inhabitants of the British Isles led a pastoralist style of life, which included the breeding of animals and a good deal of gathering of natural food resources. The authors of the report suggest that this decline in cereal growing also highlighted a fall in population and may have been connected to climatic changes.

If henges had evolved as long ago as 4000 BCE (and it is a fact that most henges are extremely ancient), they already may have been an important and even a fundamental part of early agricultural life in the British Isles. So by the time cereal production declined, the importance of the henge as a place of communal gathering and religious practice had become so significant that the henge itself continued to be created in ever larger and more elaborate forms.

The largest of the henges still to be seen in the British Isles are colossal. Many of these giant henges are now nothing more than parch marks on cropland that can be observed at certain times of year on aerial photographs. Their banks have been leveled and their ditches filled in centuries ago. A few do survive more or less intact, such as the three at Thornborough in Yorkshire mentioned in chapter 18. Each of the henges at Thornborough is so large it would be quite possible to place a large cathedral inside its banks with plenty of room to spare.

Many if not all of the larger henges were built with a deliberate reference to the sky and to the passage of time. Most have entrances purposely created to face specific points on the horizon, such as the rising of the sun at the winter or summer solstice or the equinoxes. Chris Knight and Alan discussed such alignments fully in their book *Before the Pyramids,* and even often-skeptical archaeologists are now willing to admit that these larger henges were used as naked-eye observatories. Since at such an early date there would have been no differentiation between the movement of heavenly bodies, the passage of time, and religion it appears that from humble origins henges became deeply significant structures. One can only imagine the effort that went into creating the Thornborough Henge array, which is 1.1 miles in length (1.78 km) and the construction of which involved moving many thousands of tons of earth.

While we are on the topic of henges created to make astronomical observations it is worth mentioning one of the most important facts relating to the Thornborough Henges. The southern entrance of the center henge at Thornborough points in the direction of midwinter sunrise at the time the henge was created. This is significant, but a further observation is also worth making: At the time Thornborough was created the star Sirius was rising in the southern entrance of the middle henge when seen from the henge center. Sirius is a star that in ancient Egypt was most probably called Sothis, and Sothis was sacred to the goddess Isis. It is possible that the watchers at Thornborough believed that at each winter solstice the presence of Sirius was preventing the sun from traveling even farther south on the horizon. We know ancient peoples saw this time as being the triumph of the sun, and perhaps they thought it was the presence of Sirius that caused the sun to start its northern journey toward spring again. In other words, the Goddess was rescuing the God, as is reflected in nearly all the Mystery religions.

These giant henges never would have been used as threshing floors, but they retain exactly the same shape and characteristics of earlier and smaller henges. When the people of the British Isles first began to move massive stones around the landscape it was to preexisting henges such as Stonehenge and Avebury that the stones were brought and erected. It seems to have been a later development for stone circles to be created that were not based within the sacred space of a henge.

Between the references we have regarding the area inhabited by the ancient Hebrews, the threshing floors that still exist across the Mediterranean islands, and the many hundreds of henges in the British Isles, it becomes obvious that threshing floors were potent places of magic. We know of several instances within living memory in which Maypoles were erected at the center of henges in Britain, for example at Glastonbury and at Cern Abbas in Southern England. Maypoles are tall wooden poles often painted in bright colors that were once a common sight in many towns and villages in the British Isles. Both men and woman danced around the Maypoles not only in May but also at other times of the year. Nobody doubts that the Maypole is a phallic structure, and incorporating it into the feminine threshing floor would have created the same sort of symbolism to be seen to this day in Washington, D.C., with regard to the Washington Monument and the Vesica Pisces created at its base.

Doubtless village communities in the Neolithic period met at their local henge/threshing floor at significant points of the year. Village clans may have traveled to tribal henge/threshing floors, and the largest of all the henges, such as those at Thornborough, were probably erected at the intersections of different tribal territories. In religious terms the difference between the smallest henge/threshing floor and the largest is no different from a simple preaching cross that, structure by structure, eventually gave way to a huge cathedral on the same site.

The survival of concepts or ideas in language is a constant source of wonder, and this is certainly true with regard to the threshing floor and words associated with it. One of these words is *threshold,* which literally means "the entrance to a threshing floor." It is likely that the word evolved as a result of small wooden lintels placed across the floor at the doors of the threshing floors when they had been brought indoors, usually to barns. This piece of wood prevented the valuable grain from blowing out of the barn when doors at either end of the building were open to allow the passage of breeze that was necessary to separate the grain from the chaff.

We talk about being on the threshold of a new opportunity or even the threshold of a new age. However we use this word it tends to indicate something significant or even amazing, and we wonder if this is another one of those instances in which a truly ancient concept has come down to us in common speech without us necessarily realizing where it originated.

To Janet's mind came the age-old tradition of a bridegroom carrying his new wife across the threshold. There is more than one interpretation of what lies behind this ritual. Some sources suggest that it would have been extremely bad luck for a new bride to trip as she entered her new home, and another explanation is that the act of the bridegroom carrying his bride for this ritual is a stylized version of a kidnapping. Perhaps at one time marriage ties were made within the threshing floor and the prospective husband carrying the wife to the sacred spot was to emphasize their future as one unit?

This book is primarily about the survival of incredibly ancient concepts and beliefs into the modern era, and this certainly seems to have been the case with regard to the henge/threshing floor. The unit of measurement employed when planning and building the largest examples of British henges was the Megalithic Yard, and in particular the larger geodetic unit of 366 Megalithic Yards. This same measurement was used extensively in the planning of Washington, D.C. It is also the longer diameter of Ellipse Park, which itself seems to be a modern, stylized version of the threshing floors and henges that formed such an important part of Goddess worship at a very remote date.

It is not hard to see that Ellipse Park has been and still is being used for many of the social gatherings that the henges and threshing floors witnessed. What is also quite telling is that on many occasions a ritual burial has been found at the center of British henges. Presumably to be buried in such a location would have been a supreme honor and probably one reserved for people who had been of great significance to their communities. At this juncture it seems appropriate to remind our readers that there is ample evidence to show that the bones of some particularly important people are almost certainly contained in a chamber at the center of the Ellipse.

The almost total reliance on the unit of 366 Megalithic Yards in the creation of Washington, D.C., appears to suggest that the whole of the center of the city was built to be a sacred space of the same kind represented by ancient threshing floors, and right at the center of that sacred space is the Ellipse.

There is one more aspect of threshing floors that rightly deserves a mention here. We know for a fact that the very first theaters that were ever written about were in Greece and especially in Athens. We also know that these early theaters were the legatees of threshing floors. The first theatrical performances mentioned by the ancient Greek writers were songs and dances performed in the name of Dionysus, god of wine and one of the representatives of the dying and reborn god of nature. These performances were originally carried out on communal, outdoor threshing floors. It took a long time before theaters adopted the form of a proscenium arch with a stage divorced from the audience. Even now, the popularity of theaters in the round is returning, bringing with it a memory of the threshing floors of old. Theaters in the round are becoming so popular because as far as the audience is concerned it makes the performances more inclusive.

All Greek theaters were circular, even when they were custom built and had not been threshing floors. Seats rose in tiers around the periphery of the central area, which itself leads back to a contemplation of henges. It occurs to us that the banks surrounding henges may have served more than one purpose. In addition to keeping floodwater away from the threshing floor, the banks would have made an excellent place for members of an audience to sit while community rituals were taking place upon the threshing floor.

In essence this is little different from what took place in Grange halls all over the United States. The nature of the climate across much of the United States precludes an outdoor setting for the rituals performed at Grange meetings. In any case, by this period outdoor threshing floors had been superseded by barns, which is exactly what many Grange halls resemble. (It is more than likely that until local Granges had their own custom-built halls, convenient barns or indoor threshing floors were used for the purpose.)

Were those who organized the Grange aware of the similarity? It is impossible to say, but the element of theater attending Grange meetings cannot be denied nor can the fact that those present, especially the young women, were always dressed in classical costumes. Bearing in mind the constant reference to farming practices and the presence of so many grain goddesses it seems unlikely that those who thought up the Grange and its attendant rituals were ignorant of these associations. In fact the only character missing from the Grange rituals is Dionysus, but because he was first and foremost the god of wine, there was no place for him in the strictly temperance setting of the Grange.

21

VENUS FAMILIES
AT WORK

When a Bavarian by the name of Adam Weishaupt persuaded a group of intellectuals in 1776 to join him in a brand-new organization called the Illuminati he could never have dreamed just how successful the word itself would become, even if hardly anyone these days knows what *Illuminati* means or what the organization stood for.

At the time of writing this chapter our research showed that there are presently 102,000,000 Internet sites that make reference to the word *Illuminati*. This is staggering considering that the original Illuminati lasted only nine years and was, to say the least, singularly unsuccessful in its objectives. The word *Illuminati* is a plural version of the Latin word *illuminatus,* which means "enlightened." The original Illuminati were a product of the Enlightenment, a term that describes a period from the late seventeenth century when *reason* and *individualism* became the buzz words among many thinkers in Europe. During the Enlightenment, which is also known as the Age of Reason, tradition and superstition were abandoned in favor of logic and the rise of scientific experimentation.

Adam Weishaupt was a great fan of the Age of Reason. A very specific influence on his life was a man by the name of Johann Adam

Freiherr von Ickstaff, who was Weishaupt's godfather and a professor at the University of Ingolstadt, which Weishaupt attended. Von Ickstaff was a famous rationalist and had in his own turn been influenced by earlier voices in the Age of Reason. Adam Weishaupt grew to be a radical from a radical family who took the ideas of rationalism and reason and molded them into something so contentious and so frightening to those in power it could never have hoped to survive.

Weishaupt's Illuminati was a secret society, somewhat along the lines of Freemasonry but significantly more sinister. Many of the aims of the Illuminati do not sound especially radical these days. Weishaupt wanted to oppose superstition and prejudice and to advance the cause of equality for women. Slightly unfortunate, considering the political and religious climate of Central Europe at the time, he also wanted to destroy the power of religion (especially that of the Roman Catholic Church) and also to curb state power.

Weishaupt became a Freemason in 1777, just a year after declaring the existence of the Illuminati, and had every intention of turning the Craft into a tool that could be used to spread Illuminati influence. This never happened, but Weishaupt organized the Illuminati along roughly Masonic lines. The movement was comprised of cells in different regions. Secrecy was paramount to the extent that many operatives within the Illuminati did not even know the name of their immediate superior in the organization: all members used false names. Everyone in the Illuminati swore a binding oath to follow any instruction handed down to them from above, and despite the lofty intentions of the group regarding personal freedom there was nothing remotely democratic about the institution itself.

At its most popular Weishaupt claimed that the Illuminati had two thousand members represented in most European countries, which itself may have been a gross exaggeration. Membership of the Illuminati did briefly include some fairly important people, but not for long. Neither church nor state was going to relinquish its hold on society to a bunch of intellectual upstarts, though both were deeply worried about the existence of the Illuminati for a while. By 1785, Karl Theodor, duke of Bavaria, clearly thought things had gone far enough. He outlawed all secret societies, but it probably did not matter. The Illuminati was already tearing itself to pieces in arguments about who should be the head of the organization. The whole extremely shaky edifice fell to pieces, and the Illuminati as Weishaupt had envisioned it ceased to exist.

Although the organization had gone away, the paranoia it had inspired did not. Church officials, kings, and princes remained alert to the possibility of the Illuminati—or something like it—resurfacing. For years supposed members of the Illuminati were arrested and interrogated, even though the institution itself no longer existed. The public—then as now, keen to read anything of a controversial nature—lapped this up, and books such as *Memoirs Illustrating the History of Jacobinism* by Augustin Barruel and *Proofs of a Conspiracy* by John Robinson fed the fascination. When something as earth-shattering as the French Revolution came along in 1789, those who lost the most—the French monarchy, the aristocracy, and the Roman Catholic Church—were eager to find a scapegoat. As a result the revolution was blamed on the Illuminati, despite the fact that the true causes of the French Revolution had been simmering below the surface of French society for generations. This reaction is not surprising. After all the church, the monarchy, and the aristocracy were hardly likely to blame themselves for what had happened.

For more than two centuries the very name of the Illuminati has been synonymous with secret societies that have supposedly sought the destruction of personal liberty and the imposition of authoritarian rule. This is quite amusing when one considers what Weishaupt and his original followers had wanted for society. Nevertheless it is obvious from the Internet that at least 102,000,000 people in the world today, and probably many more, are willing to believe that we are all being hoodwinked and that below the surface of society worldwide there is a secret organization that has hidden agendas and that is working on a daily basis to ensnare and enslave us.

An offshoot of the belief in the Illuminati is the concept of a "One-World Government," often also referred to as the "New World Order." This is a concept that emerged among those from the Far Right of

American politics and also among certain groups of fundamentalist Christians but is actually not a new tactic at all. It was something similar that allowed the Nazis to gain power in the Germany of the 1930s, on the back of a supposed Jewish conspiracy to control humanity. The only real difference these days is that there is no real consensus as to who is planning and stage-managing the New World Order.

There can be no doubt that certain groups in the world that have considerable power and commonality of interests do sometimes form secret cartels to further their objectives. This happens at both a political and an economic level. Most of us hate massive international banking corporations, which we blame for many of the ills of the world, and few of us trust politicians who we suspect of being self-seeking and corrupt. Aside from this natural distrust, conspiracy theories are fascinating in their own right, and in any case it seems to be the nature of humanity to constantly blame *them* for anything that appears to be going wrong, even when we have no real idea who "they" might actually be.

Paradoxically, although the comprehension of conspiracies is growing exponentially, the ability of really significant conspiracies to be sustained is becoming more and more difficult. Information has never been as available as it is today. Even the most fundamental secrets of the most powerful nations in the world regularly appear on the Internet, where anyone can view them. *Everyone* in public life is wide open to the most intense scrutiny, and getting away with anything underhanded is virtually impossible.

In view of all this it seems strange that we have written a book dealing specifically with what must be the greatest conspiracy the world has ever known. What is more, the suggestions we make and the evidence we put forward prove conclusively that this particular conspiracy *must* be real. In addition, no matter how coincidental or how remote it may be, a relationship between the events we have outlined and the Illuminati as well as the New World Order are hard to avoid. It cannot be denied that what must be a fairly small group of very influential and powerful people genuinely are doing their best to mold the world into the shape they want it to have. What is more, they are doing all of this in secrecy and have been following more or less the same agenda for at least nine hundred years and probably much longer.

Whether or not the aims and objectives of those we have called the Venus Families are in the best interests of humanity really depends on the personal beliefs of those observing what has taken place. Anyone committed to authoritarian rule—either in religion or by the state—would probably be appalled by the evidence of this book. Those across the globe who already dislike and distrust the United States and its policies are hardly going to be happier in the knowledge that the world's remaining superpower is a deliberately planned, potential utopia, ultimately controlled by a secret faction with its own agendas and ways of functioning.

If we look at just a couple of examples we can see just how much power the Venus Families actually have. The whole of the capital of the United States is a Venus Family creation. Even very recent structures, such as the United States World War II Memorial, were clearly influenced by the Venus Families so that the result would suit their own intentions. This surely means that the Venus Families must be represented at all levels of local and national government, as well as possessing the influence to sway the decisions of dozens of committees and planning authorities.

Fig. 21.1. The World War II Memorial, the Mall, Washington, D.C.
Photo courtesy Scott F. Wolter

The same is true in New York where since the eighteenth century the Venus Families must have been extremely influential in terms of decisions made regarding the development of the city. It took significant clout to gradually create the Orion's Belt constellation of obelisks that runs down the spine of New York and even before this to influence the shape, style, and orientation of St. Paul's Chapel.

These are essentially local issues and though impressive enough they are small fry compared with the realization that the involvement of the United States in something as significant as the Second World War was also stage-managed by the Venus Families.* Of course this was far from being the first time that the Venus Families had involved themselves in international events. Right back in the eleventh century they had instigated the First Crusade and in a sequence of moves planned in Champagne had taken a series of steps that would ensure the destruction of feudalism and the gradual rise of democracy (see chapter 4).

It is not beyond the realms of possibility that some of the religious and secular leaders who responded so swiftly to the supposed threat of the Illuminati actually did know *something* about the Venus Families. Going further back in time it cannot be proved but seems likely that as the early fourteenth century secular and religious leaders also understood, there was a powerful group manipulating events behind the scenes. This may have been an extra motivation for the attempted destruction of the Knights Templar.

If we look at the broad span of history we might also see the hatred of Freemasonry by the Catholic Church as the recognition of something powerful within society that did not support the church's interests. It is still a sin punishable by excommunication for a practicing Catholic to become a Freemason, which in this day and age when practically everything regarding Freemasonry is available to study seems a gross overreaction. Does the Catholic Church actually know about the existence of the Venus Families? It certainly does

---

*As Alan demonstrated in his book *City of the Goddess: Freemasons, the Sacred Feminine, and the Secret Beneath the Seat of Power in Washington, D.C.*

assume that Freemasonry and similar organizations have been guilty of attacking the church and has said so in a number of edicts from Rome.

Even if this was the case it seems obvious to us that the Venus Families were always one step ahead of the church and often used it as a springboard to achieve their own objectives. In response—a little like the United States in the McCarthy era, when paranoia grew about the possibility of a red under every bed—the Catholic Church has sometimes probably invented evidence that pointed to a deliberate and international plot to undermine its influence.

One such example was a document titled the *Alta Vendita,* which appeared in the nineteenth century. It was supposedly a message circulated among the lodges of a proto-Masonic group in Italy called the Carbonari. The Carbonari definitely did exist. The word means "charcoal burners," and although organized along the lines of Freemasonry, the Carbonari was infinitely more political and subversive.

There is now great doubt as to whether the *Alta Vendita* ever originated within the Carbonari itself, even though the Carbonari did actively hate the church. It seems more likely that it was created within the establishment of the Catholic Church as a means by which Catholics could be alerted to a potential threat, though most likely one the church itself did not really understand. Certainly the source of the *Alta Vendita* in its published form did not originate with the Carbonari but at the insistence of two different popes: Pope Pius IX and Pope Leo XIII.

The *Alta Vendita* suggests that the Carbonari and other similar groups were aware that it could never defeat or destroy the church by way of a direct attack. It is a lengthy and wordy document though well written and utterly fascinating. The writer of the document ultimately suggests that the way to achieve its objectives would be to infiltrate Catholic groups dedicated to young people. This was a technique used by the Catholics themselves when evangelizing, especially by the Jesuits. The *Alta Vendita* makes it plain that with enough influence on the young and with its own advocates gradually rising through the church

Catholicism can eventually be subverted and ultimately destroyed *from the inside out*. What it would need to achieve this objective would be a significant number of cardinals and ultimately a pope.

It stands to reason that the Catholic Church itself would have had a great deal to gain by publishing a document such as this. It would alert the laity to an implied threat and heightened awareness when it came to the manipulation of young and impressionable minds. But even if the *Alta Vendita* genuinely did arise from outside of Rome, in our opinion it is very unlikely to have originated from sources within the Venus Families. Although the Venus Families periodically chose to infiltrate the church—and did so very successfully—it was not something that appears to have been a sustained policy. If we look at the late eleventh century we can certainly see that Pope Urban II (real name Odo of Lagery) was a Venus Families "plant." He was followed by several other popes who seem to have had Venus Family connections. These may have included Paschall II, Gelasius II, and Callixtus II, but quite definitely Honorius II, Innocent II, and Celestine II, the last two of whom were literally *made* pope thanks to the intervention and influence of St. Bernard of Clairvaux.

What we can see from this is how the Venus Families only went to the trouble of maneuvering the situation in Rome when it most suited its own objectives at the time. Urban II was necessary to start the first Crusade, while Honorius II was the man who made the Knights Templar into a full-fledged monastic order. Innocent II was incredibly well supported by St. Bernard of Clairvaux and was needed to offer support for the rapidly expanding Cistercian order and that of the Knights Templar. It is clear that the Venus Families could not get their own way in the case of every pope, but they gained another useful pontiff in 1145 with the election of Pope Eugene III. This man had formerly been a Cistercian novice under the direct tutelage of St. Bernard of Clairvaux. It was during the reign of this pope that the Second Crusade was called, which was necessary because the Venus Families had not until that time achieved all their objectives in the Holy Land.

After Pope Eugene III it appears that the Venus Families no longer craved or needed the support of specific popes. With the success of both the Cistercians and the Templars and with Champagne growing rapidly in economic strength and general influence, Rome was no longer of any significant interest.

The truth is that as far as we can establish the Venus Families never sought to destroy Roman Catholicism. It might even be considered strange if they had ever attempted to do so. It is possible to see the intentions and beliefs of the Venus Families reflected through Freemasonry and in the actions of the Founding Fathers of the United States. What people wish to believe is their own business. The only provision is that no religious belief or affiliation should be allowed to influence civil government or the education of children.

As far as the New World Order or the concept of a one-world government is concerned, because the whole thrust of the Venus Families' agenda is toward genuine democracy it follows that the ultimate destination of humanity in a political and economic sense will be decided *by* humanity.

It is clear that the Venus Families have their own religious agenda (though perhaps the word *spiritual* would be more appropriate). If it were possible to talk to a Venus Family representative it is likely that she or he would admit to a reverence for the Mystery religions of old with their gender-balanced approach to spirituality. It appears from our evidence that such a person may also have a deep regard for a form of Christianity, although in all probability a version that would look very different from the mainstream examples of the religion. To the Venus Families Jesus is a representative of the annually dying and reborn god of nature and the sky. Meanwhile Mary Magdalene specifically and probably also the Virgin Mary are representative of the Goddess herself. Our representative might also own up to beliefs that when balanced against Christianity as it is practiced today could be referred to as "pagan."

Cosmology features significantly in the beliefs of the Venus Families. There is an appreciation of the Earth and its place in the universe and a recognition that our planet can and perhaps should be seen as a "mother" to all of us. However, as influential and important as the

Venus Families have been, there is not the slightest evidence that any-one was ever coerced into sharing either its philosophy or its spiritual motivations. Indeed the very reverse is true, because it appears that anyone who ultimately shared the beliefs of the Venus Families would, of necessity, have gone through a long accumulation of knowledge to arrive at such a destination.

Many questions remain. For example, are the Venus Families a cohesive body? Do its members get together on a regular basis to assess how things are going and to make plans for future strategies? Are these most influential people genuinely part of a genetic family or are new individuals accepted into the fold?

The answers to these questions are not easy to discover. The Venus Families choose to be secretive. This almost certainly stems from a time when they had no choice unless they wanted to suffer the same sort of persecution that Christianity meted out to a huge number of people with beliefs that differed from its own. It is only comparatively recently that the luckiest among us have lived in societies in which one's opin-ions and beliefs do not lead to falling foul of either the civil or religious authorities. Even then, caution would be necessary. History shows that democracies can fall and that prejudice and tyranny can soon replace tolerance and justice. We must remain ever vigilant.

This is a quiet and almost unbelievably patient revolution. It is likely that every person involved has undergone something akin to a Masonic journey or one closely associated with the Mysteries of Demeter. Freemasonry itself has some implacable enemies, but when it comes to assessing the Craft, people ultimately have to judge for themselves. Although neither of us is involved in the Craft personally, we both have high-ranking Masonic friends. It has been our experience that such people set high moral standards for themselves, do not judge others, are loyal, trustworthy, and tolerant. They invariably fail to demonstrate the slightest trace of prejudice and are egalitarian by instinct.

In our individual and our common research we have both almost certainly met people who are members of the Venus Families. We have been fortunate to be introduced to some amazing individuals. Alan in particular often receives extremely strange e-mails with origins that simply cannot be traced but which point to them having been sent by members of the Venus Families. It is only fair to admit to our readers that even if we did know the real identity of such people, it would be unlikely that we would name them in this book.

At the end of our quest we find ourselves drawn back to its start, with that most incredible of institutions: the Grange. It appears that this organization is presently receiving a new transfusion of energy, because in great measure it is being adopted by people who have a new and revolutionary approach to farming. The Green Grange is made up of those who seek to work *with* nature and not manipulate their land or subject it to genetically manipulated crops or saturate it with chemicals. Throughout our research and the writing of this book our minds have regularly and almost inevitably turned back to that day when we first entered a Grange hall—a now venerable and historic building in Minnesota. Neither of us can forget the almost overwhelming sense of peace and inclusivity that seems to emanate from the very walls of that wooden hall.

This Minnesota Grange hall came into being at a time when all farming was "green" because there was no other way to behave. If the farmers of the United States wished to prosper and gain influence they had no choice but to embrace new ideas, but it was almost certain that it was never their intention that massive, corporate farming enterprises should one day *own* the industry. Perhaps it isn't surprising that a rising number of Grange members are now trying to redress the balance in favor of working *with* nature, rather than *against* it.

What is not surprising is that despite the tremendous influence they have exerted over centuries, the Venus Families seem to remain committed to protecting the Earth. In this regard it is coming of age, because humanity is now beginning to realize that this planet upon which we all live is *all* we have. We might be able to buy a new computer or a new car, but the Earth is a one-off, never-to-be-repeated experiment in cooperation. In the developed world rivers and lakes that were once toxic and sterile with chemicals are being made into living ecosystems again. Species of animals and fish that were forced to the brink of extinction are returning. Huge national parks offer sanctuary to indigenous species that could so easily have disappeared altogether, and we are encouraging the natural diversification that our immediate ancestors never appreciated.

It cannot be denied that in many respects our world is a deeply troubled place, where wars are still being fought and ordinary people are ignored and sidelined, often in an attempt by the larger nations to monopolize natural resources. But at the same time we are also learning to harness the very fuel that can be supplied by the planet, in the form of solar, wind, and wave power. As imperceptible as the change seems to be when seen from the perspective of our relatively short lives, things are improving. Human beings are now living longer than they ever have and are much less likely to die as a result of war, crime, or injustice. This trend may not be universal but it is irrepressible, and the concept of protecting what we have as a species is spreading.

Across the broad span of history the Venus Families have endured like a golden thread—through the sometimes faded and often far from beautiful tapestry of time. There is still much to be done, and it may be decades or centuries before the genuine New Jerusalem envisaged is a reality in the United States, let alone across the entire planet.

The evidence of such a great conspiracy as is proved by our findings will not find favor everywhere, and it is certain that it will be used by pressure groups as supposed proof of the devil worship and subversion of humanity that suits their purposes to propose. But the form of the Goddess is irrepressible. She was the first resort of humanity's reverence, and despite the hiccup that has occurred—during which the gender-balanced view of spirituality has been skewed in favor of an often vengeful and intolerant father figure—she is once more coming into full focus in the minds of humanity.

This is how Janet explained what we both think has taken place within Christianity, the form of belief in which we were both raised—at least culturally—but it also reflects our combined thoughts regarding all the male-dominated faiths that have arisen across the past two millennia.

The whole scenario very much reminds me of how things are in a bad marriage where the man is physically abusive to his wife. If we use this analogy the husband represents the church, the wife the Goddess, and their children the Venus Families and Knights Templar. The husband is insecure and somehow subconsciously fears his wife's power to bring life forth. He also hates the fact that she knows what he really is: a bully. In truth she can see right through him and will one day leave him taking her children with her—leaving him alone, cold, and vulnerable. Cognizant of this he tries with all his might to control her and their children and in desperation tries to destroy them all. But some of the children get away, and make a new home, and keep their mother hidden in plain sight.

The children leave reminders to the bully in symbols and architecture all over the planet to make him aware they are alive and well and doing just fine without him. And everything they do brings reverence to their mother.

This is surely as it should be. The vast majority of us do all we can to protect and cherish our mother, each one of whom is a representative of the whole amazing circle of life. Why should we do any less for the very planet that gives us life and sustains us?

Empires may rise and fall; power brokers will come and go. The selfish will always try to twist the truth to suit their own ends, but still the Goddess is returning. Actually, those who look at the broad sweep of history without prejudice will soon become aware that she never really went away.

POSTSCRIPT

THE SIGNIFICANCE OF THE TWO PILLARS

It is amazing how often the completion of a book coincides with a flurry of activity in terms of research. Such was the case for us, partly because the end of our quest coincided with two visits to New York by Janet and Scott Wolter. They were there for a long weekend, and a couple of weeks later Scott was in the city to film an episode of *America Unearthed*. In the weeks leading up to these trips we had cooperated heavily with Scott regarding our own findings related to New York in particular the three obelisks that form the Orion's Belt pattern across Manhattan (see chapter 18). At the same time Scott had kept us informed of his own discoveries. As a result of these trips to New York our final considerations regarding the city came too late to appear in the body of our book, but they did enable us to add this postscript, which we are certain will represent a fine ending to our quest—at least for now.

High above the main concourse in the splendid building that is Grand Central Terminal in New York, the designers of the building decided to place something quite unusual, especially bearing in mind the purpose of the building. Grand Central Terminal, also more commonly called Grand Central Station, was created by the rich Vanderbilt family and was heavily influenced by architects Whitney Warren and Charles D. Wetmore. The building was completed in

Fig. P.1. The zodiac painted onto the ceiling of Grand Central Station,
New York
Photo courtesy of Scott F. Wolter

Fig. P.2. Part of the zodiac ceiling of Grand Central Station, New York,
depicting the constellation of Orion
Photo courtesy of Scott F. Wolter

1913, and Whitney Warren, who was related to the Vanderbilt family, had a great deal of input regarding the details of this magnificent temple to transport.

Depicted across the ceiling of the main concourse of the station is a representation of part of the night sky as it would have been seen from a location in the Mediterranean in ancient times. Not all the stars in the heavens were reproduced on the ceiling, because the design deals specifically with a section of the plane of the ecliptic. The plane of the ecliptic is a band of the sky through which the sun, moon, and planets appear to travel when seen from Earth. Historically this band was divided into twelve roughly equal units, and these were named for the patterns or constellations of stars that appeared within them. These constellations, in which our ancient ancestors saw representations of fantastic creatures, gods and goddesses, heroes, and even domestic utensils have always been known as the signs of the zodiac. The part of the zodiac depicted on the ceiling of Grand Central Station is what would have been seen at night, around midwinter from the Mediterranean region, probably around 1000 BCE or earlier. In addition to the zodiac constellations there are a couple of other constellations depicted that do not actually fall on the plane of the ecliptic. By far the largest of these is Orion.

There is something very strange about the way the zodiac has been depicted on the Grand Central Terminal ceiling. It was created by the post-impressionist French artist Paul César Helleu from drawings made for him at Columbia University. The odd thing is that all the zodiac constellations on view have been reversed. In the real sky the zodiac constellations rise in the east, and after crossing the sky they set, one by one, in the west. In the case of the paintings on the ceiling they are shown as if they were rising in the west and traveling to the east. This may not be quite as odd as it sounds. We know this is meant to represent a view of the heavens from ancient times. It was sometimes the habit of those depicting the sky in the classical period to show it as it might be seen from outside looking in. In reality this would be quite impossible, because the patterns of stars we see from the Earth are entirely coincidental. What we observe is a line of sight effect, and some stars forming a particular part of a given constellation are much farther away than others.

The ancients were not aware of this and assumed that the view that God would get of the constellations from heaven would be the same as our view from Earth, but reversed. The ceiling would therefore make sense artistically and historically, if not astronomically. However, there is a significant exception to the reversed sky on the Central Station ceiling, and that is the constellation of Orion. Although the artistic representation of Orion the Hunter has been reversed like all the other constellations, the stars comprising the constellation have not been reversed. In other words, on the whole ceiling only the stars of Orion are the way we would see them from Earth! This is odd in the extreme, because everything else depicted, though reversed, is quite accurate. It is inconceivable that such a state of affairs could have come about by

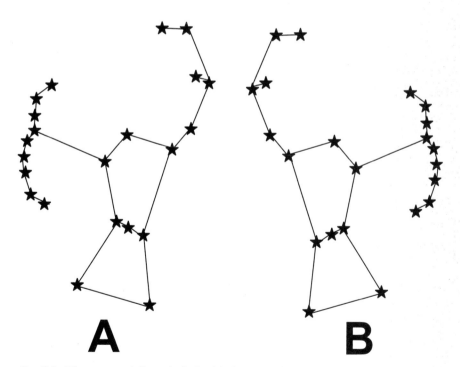

A   **B**

Fig. P.3. The stars of Orion's Belt. (a) As they *should* look to match all other stars on the ceiling of Grand Central Terminal. (b) As they actually look on the ceiling of the station (as they look in the sky).

accident, and although it remains a puzzle to almost everyone, it makes eminent sense to us.

We have already seen how part of the constellation of Orion—Orion's Belt—was re-created across Manhattan by the position of the three obelisks (see chapter 18), and we can only assume that the strange handling of Orion on the ceiling of Grand Central Station is a deliberately created clue that this is the case. We have to remember that Grand Central Station was built by the Vanderbilt family and also bear in mind that it was Vanderbilt money that paid for the Egyptian obelisk, originally from Heliopolis, to be brought to New York and erected in Central Park. It is this obelisk that forms the first star (Alnitak) of the Orion's Belt that crosses Manhattan.

To us this state of affairs is typical of both Freemasonry and what we know of the Venus Families. It is an obvious clue, hidden in plain sight. It did not take long for eagle-eyed, astronomically inclined travelers passing through the station to notice that this apparent error had been made, and it was reported on numerous occasions. Nevertheless it was never rectified through several cleanings and repaintings over the years, and no explanation as to how things came to be this way has ever been forthcoming.

We also found ourselves in possession of more information relating to St. Paul's Chapel, which we discussed extensively in chapter 15. The site of this chapel was of interest to Alan long before we began researching our present book. This was primarily because the chapel stood right by the Twin Towers of the World Trade Center, and Alan had noticed that the distance between the towers and the center of the Ellipse in Washington, D.C., was exactly 3 Megalithic degrees of arc. Because this finding was accurate to within a few feet across over 200 miles (328 km) it seemed to be no coincidence. All the same, there was no tangible reason for this fact, until we began to realize just how significant St. Paul's Chapel was. It eventually became apparent to us that the significant distance Alan had discovered was not between the Ellipse in Washington, D.C., and the Twin Towers but rather between the Ellipse in Washington, D.C., and St. Paul's Chapel. It was not until the last page of this book had been completed that it suddenly dawned on us how significant that fact was.

The existence of two pillars is of supreme significance to Freemasonry. Representations of these two pillars can be seen at the entrance of nearly all custom-built Masonic temples. The importance of the two pillars takes us back to Solomon's Temple in Jerusalem. The Hebrew scriptures specifically say that the temple had two pillars at its entrance. To Freemasons these pillars are known as Jachin and Boaz. Masonic ritual also tells of two pillars created by the patriarch Enoch and erected on the same site that would eventually be chosen by King David for the temple. One of these pillars was of brass and the other of stone. Upon them was written all the scientific information given to Enoch by the mysterious Watchers who had taken him all over the planet and shown him many wonders.

Two pillars flanking the entrance to a temple is not only associated with the temple of Solomon. It was a common practice in ancient Egypt where the two pillars in question were obelisks. Almost no significant temple was created in ancient Egypt that did not have two obelisks standing outside of its entrance. It was while bearing all of this in mind and then thinking about the Twin Towers of the World Trade Center that we suddenly began to realize why the towers had been built adjacent to St. Paul's Chapel and what they actually represented.

The placement of the three obelisks that imitate Orion's Belt across Manhattan effectively made Manhattan a giant temple to Osiris, just as surely as Washington, D.C., in its entirety is a temple dedicated to Isis, the wife and sister of Osiris. The Twin Towers of the World Trade Center represented the twin pillars at the southern entrance to the Manhattan temple of Osiris. They were constructed immediately adjacent to St. Paul's Chapel, with the Emmet obelisk in its churchyard that represented the third star of Orion's Belt (Mintaka). That these particular structures were so deliberately and dramatically attacked and destroyed on September 11, 2001, is very telling. It might be seen as not merely an attack upon the United States but also the Venus Families, with their "one-world" agenda. If this is indeed the case, it becomes obvious that the

Venus Families have their own implacable enemies. This view of events becomes more likely when it is realized that the Pentagon in Washington, D.C., was also attacked on 9/11 and that the intended target of the plane that crashed in Pennsylvania on the same day was undoubtedly the Capitol. These buildings each have a quite distinct and obvious ancient pedigree that associates them with structures built in Europe more than five thousand years ago. In addition, both the Capitol and the Pentagon were planned and built thanks to Venus Family influence.

Fortunately, despite the carnage that took place all around it, the little Chapel of St. Paul escaped the 9/11 atrocity without so much as a cracked window, which is truly extraordinary bearing in mind how close the chapel was to the Twin Towers. The eagle eyes of Scott Wolter picked out a host of details within the chapel that confirm our suspicions that this is indeed an extraordinary structure and definitely no run-of-the-mill church. In addition to our description of the chapel in chapter 15, our attention has now been drawn to several other significant features of the building. The first of these is an extremely pronounced keystone in the middle of the arch that divides the body of the chapel from the altar. This may be seen as nothing more than an architectural detail, but it is one of the most significant of Freemasonic symbols. Keystones such as this have astronomical overtones, and in terms of what Freemasons call the Royal Arch, the keystone represents the period around the summer solstice.

On a matching arch that is situated at the eastern end of the building and immediately over the altar, the place of the keystone carries a Glory, or a winged sun. This is very reminiscent of the decoration on the Glory that Pierre Charles L'Enfant built for the altar and is undoubtedly meant to represent the presence of the Shekinah—that mystical, feminine aspect of the Godhead—that was so important to the ancient Hebrews. At its center are letters in Hebrew that spell out the name of God as the Hebrews conceived it. This is known as a tetragrammaton, and in Latin letters it would be *yhwh*. This is surely the Shekinah, that mystical personification of the feminine quality of the Hebrew God mentioned frequently throughout this book.

Fig. P.4. The winged Glory above the altar in St. Paul's
Chapel, Manhattan
Photo courtesy of Scott F. Wolter

There are many other architectural and decorative details within the chapel that seem to bear out our conviction that this is very much more than a standard, local Christian church, and indeed the very style of the building confirms this. We know that those who built St. Paul's Chapel were unwilling to allow it to be called a church and settled on the term *chapel* instead, but in reality the eastern end of the building with its columns and portico show it to be a temple in the Greek style. There may seem to be nothing innocuous about the classical nature of the chapel, which was a style of architecture that was in vogue at the time of the chapel's construction, but still its templelike looks cannot be denied. In addition there are other compulsive clues as to the intentions of those who placed this structure in the midst of a wheat field—so far from habitation at the time that would-be worshippers complained bitterly about its isolation.

As an aside, it is also interesting to note that long before the Twin Towers of the World Trade Center existed in this part of New York, St. Paul's Chapel already had two structures in its own churchyard that could have been intended to represent the two pillars of the Hebrew scriptures and of Masonic significance. These are both obelisks: one relating to Emmet, and another to a famed doctor who was laid to rest by the chapel.

Janet happened across a charming little story about a program director at St. Paul's Chapel who had always wondered what was contained within its high tower. Joanna Malloy of the *New York Daily News* reports that the director, Omayra Rivera, was eventually able to gain entry and found herself in a wonderland of false entrances, precipitous staircases, and needless rooms. She reported that the tower was comprised of nine chambers, one on top of the other, and just reading this observation caused us both to take a sharp intake of breath. But before we take a trip up the winding staircase of the tower of St. Paul's Chapel, we need to look again at something so important within the chapel itself that we are amazed we did not recognize its significance from the outset.

In the Masonic story of the patriarch Enoch, who had been instructed by the Watchers to ensure that ancient knowledge survived whatever may befall the Earth in the centuries after his death, he did more than simply create the two pillars, one of brass and the other of stone. Enoch dug nine chambers, one below the other. In the deepest chamber he placed a device that Freemasons call the Delta of Enoch. The authors Christopher Knight and Robert Lomas did a great deal to bring together various pieces of esoteric Masonic ritual and information that might otherwise have been lost for good. Many of these can be found in *The Book of Hiram*. Here we find a reference to the

Delta of Enoch on pages 22 and 348. It concerns a vision: "In this vision Enoch saw a mountain and a golden triangle showing the rays of the sun. From that time this device became known as the 'Delta of Enoch.'"

In the ninth chamber below what would one day be the threshing floor of the Jebusites and eventually Solomon's Temple, Enoch placed a golden representation of his vision. Within the golden triangle was a piece of semiprecious stone onto which was written the name of God, as it is portrayed on the winged sun above the altar of St. Paul's Chapel. This very triangle, the Delta of Enoch, was reproduced by Pierre Charles L'Enfant on the Glory altarpiece that stands at the eastern end of the chapel, which was mentioned in detail in chapter 15. On the Glory altarpiece and within what was described when it was created by the *New York Daily Adviser* as "a schematized image of the sun" is an equilateral triangle. Inside the triangle are the letters *yhwh*, which, as we have seen, is a Hebrew name for God. The linguistic origin of this name is related to the Book of Exodus in the Hebrew scriptures, and the name most probably means something like "I am what I am," or perhaps "who gives life."

The concept of the Delta of Enoch appears to be ultimately Freemasonic in origin; it does not appear in the Hebrew scriptures. Its existence at the most reverential part of St. Paul's Chapel—right on the sacred altar—marks the chapel apart and confirms its status as being that of temple rather than church. However, the presence of the Delta of Enoch in the chapel also relates to the chapel's tower, which, in light of the delta's presence, becomes highly significant.

The tower contains nine chambers, the bottom chamber of which forms part of the chapel. From a symbolic point of view it appears that those who planned the chapel intended the highest chamber of the tower to represent the first chamber of Enoch below ground level. This means that anything above the highest chamber of the tower would represent something standing above ground level.

The uppermost structure of the tower has always intrigued us. It is a copy of a symbolic stone lantern that still exists in Athens, Greece.

Fig. P.5. The part of the tower of St. Paul's Chapel, New York, that is a copy of the Choragic Monument of Lysicrates
Photo courtesy of Scott F. Wolter

Fig. P.6. The tower of St. Paul's Chapel, New York, in its entirety
Photo courtesy of Scott F. Wolter

This ornamented stone pillar is known as the Choragic Monument of Lysicrates. The monument dates back to 335 BCE and was created to hold an award given to participants at the Theater of Dionysus.

We saw in chapter 20 how, with the passage of time, threshing floors became theaters, and there was no better example of this than the Theater of Dionysus. Dionysus was a god closely associated with the goddess Demeter. He was also a perfect example of a dying and reborn god of nature. In legend the body of Dionysus was torn apart, boiled, and eaten by the Titans, only to be reborn from his heart, which was recovered by the goddess Demeter.

As the god of wine, Dionysus represented a perfect male counterpart to Demeter, whose primary responsibility was as goddess of cereal crops. Dionysus was celebrated along with Demeter in the Mysteries at Eleusis, but he also had Mysteries of his own, which most commentators see as being virtually identical to the Mysteries of the Egyptian god Osiris.

The first theatrical performances staged in Greece were ritual dances and songs in praise of Dionysus, and these took place on the outdoor threshing floors of Greek villages. It was these threshing floors that ultimately became the famous Greek theaters of which the theater of Dionysus in Athens was the first and best known. With the relationship of Dionysus to threshing floors it seems self-evident to us that the copy of the Choragic Monument of Lysicrates that adorns the top of St. Paul's Chapel tower was put there to represent the threshing floor that marked the site of Solomon's Temple in Jerusalem. Nine chambers below this we find a representation of the Delta of Enoch, placed at the most sacred part of the chapel.

At the same time as the chapel is meant to represent the ninth chamber of Enoch, it is also a deliberately created copy of Solomon's Temple. At the east end of Solomon's Temple was a curtained-off section known as the holy of holies. This is where the Ark of the Covenant was kept. The ark contained the tablets of stone brought down from a mountaintop by Moses. Carved onto the stones in God's own hand were what are known these days as the Ten Commandments. There is no curtain in St. Paul's Chapel to define the holy of holies. This is understandable. In so far as St. Paul's Chapel is a Protestant church it follows nonconformist Protestant tradition, in which there is no separation of the congregation from the altar. However, the Glory altarpiece created by Pierre Charles L'Enfant does contain a representation of the Ten Commandments and so takes the place of the Ark of the Covenant in the original Temple of Solomon.

It took almost a century for the three obelisks that represent Orion's Belt in Manhattan to be put in place. Orion's Belt marks the place in the sky where the Egyptian god Osiris, god of the dead, has his domain. It is to this region of the sky that Egyptians expected to go after death. As we have seen, across a fantastic time scale Orion's Belt has been re-created on the Earth a number of times, making a symbolic connection between the Earth, home of the Goddess, and the sky, which represents the domain of the God.

The destruction of the Twin Towers of the World Trade Center on September 11, 2001, could be seen as an attempt to destroy the Manhattan temple of Osiris, but the spirit of New Yorkers remained unbowed. Almost as soon as the rubble could be cleared, a brand-new World Trade Center began to rise from the ashes of its former self. In what is nothing less than a replay of the sacrificed and risen god of nature, the vast Freedom Tower began to take shape. Neither we nor Scott could avoid observing that the Freedom Tower, which is by far the largest building on the World Trade Center site, looks uncannily like a modern version of an obelisk.

This new guardian of the New York temple of Osiris has been named the Freedom Tower. This is entirely appropriate because another word that means the same as freedom is *liberty*. In turn, Liberty is the name of a goddess who on the shores of America came to be called Columbia. We were eventually forced to the conclusion that New York was symbolically meant to represent Osiris (at least by Freemasons) and that Washington, D.C., was his counterpart, Isis.

New York is a place of driving, thrusting enterprise, and as such it has rightfully been dedicated to the God of America, it is also replete

Fig. P.7. The Freedom Tower in New York, on
the site of the former World Trade Towers
Photo courtesy of Scott F. Wolter

Fig. P.8. Statue of Liberty, New York
Photo courtesy of Scott F. Wolter

with Goddess symbolism. The presence of the Great Goddess has been a part of human consciousness from the moment we began to lift our eyes from the savannas from which we evolved. She funded the first religious stirrings inside us and endured in our hearts for hundreds of thousands of years. For a brief moment in the vast span of time it appears that we lost sight of her, but even then the Goddess remained secure in the consciousness of a few deeply important individuals. When the time came for men and women to decide their own fate, whether or not the majority knew it, it was to the Great Goddess they turned for their continuing inspiration. Out of the great experiment that was the European adventure in the Americas something truly amazing was born. The Goddess once more took center stage, as she had done on those ancient threshing floors that were her first temples. From sea to shining sea the United States of America is replete with images, symbols, and enduring aspirations that when fully understood make it quite plain that this great country truly is the Nation of the Goddess.

BIBLIOGRAPHY

Andrea, Johan Valentin. *Chymical Wedding of Christian Rosenkreuz*. Grand Rapids, Mich.: Phanes Press, 1994.

Bacon, Sir Francis. *The History of the Reign of King Henry VII and Selected Works (Cambridge Texts in the History of Political Thought)*. Cambridge: Cambridge University Press, 1998.

———. *The New Atlantis*. N.p.: CreateSpace Independent Publishing Platform, 2010.

Bond, William. *Freemasonry and the Hidden Goddess*. N.p.: Lulu.com Publishing, 2012. Available as an electronic book at http://masongoddess .blogspot.co.uk (accessed May 4, 2015).

Bauval, Robert, and Adrian Gilbert. *The Orion Mystery*. London: Mandarin, 1995.

Berg, Scott W. *Grand Avenues: The Story of Pierre Charles L'Enfant, the French Visionary Who Designed Washington D.C.* New York: Vintage Books, 2008.

Butler, Alan. *The Bronze Age Computer Disc*. Berkshire, U.K.: W. Foulsham and Co., 1997.

———. *The Goddess, the Grail & the Lodge*. London: O Books, 2003.

———. *City of the Goddess: Freemasons, the Sacred Feminine, and the Secret Beneath the Seat of Power in Washington, DC*. London: Watkins, 2011.

———. *How to Read Prehistoric Monuments*. London: Watkins, 2011.

———. *Dawn of Genius*. London: Watkins, 2014.

Butler, Alan, and Stephen Dafoe. *The Warriors and the Bankers*. Hersham, U.K.: Lewis Masonic, 2006.

Butler, Alan, and John Ritchie. *Rosslyn Revealed*. London: The History Press, 2009.

——. *Rosslyn Chapel Decoded.* London: Watkins Books, 2013.

Chernow, Ron. *Washington: A Life.* New York: Penguin, 2011.

Feuerverger, Andrey. "Statistical Analysis of an Archaeological Find." *Annals of Applied Statistics* 2, no. 1 (2008): 3–54.

Gilman, Rhoda, and Patricia Smith. "Oliver Hudson Kelley, Minnesota Pioneer, 1849–1868." Minnesota Historical Society, Minnesota History Magazine, December 1967. http://collections.mnhs.org/MNHistoryMagazine/articles/40/v40i07p330-338.pdf.

Haagensen, Erling, and Henry Lincoln. *The Templars' Secret Island: The Knights, the Priest and the Treasure.* London: Weidenfeld and Nicholson, 2002.

Henry, Margaret. *Trinity Bulletin of 1947.* New York: Trinity Church, 1947.

Jacobovici, Simcha, and Charles R. Pellegrino. *The Jesus Family Tomb.* London: Harper Element, 2008.

King, Karen L. "'Jesus said to them, 'My wife . . .': A New Coptic Papyrus Fragment." *Harvard Theological Review* 107, no. 2 (April 2014): 131–59.

Knight, Christopher, and Alan Butler. *Civilization One.* London: Watkins, 2010.

——. *The Hiram Key Revisited.* London: Watkins, 2010.

——. *Before the Pyramids.* London: Watkins, 2011.

Knight, Christopher, and Robert Lomas. *Uriel's Machine.* London: Arrow Books, 2000.

——. *The Book of Hiram.* London: Arrow Books, 2004.

Kuhn, Alvin Boyd. *The Lost Light.* Whitefish, Mont.: Kessinger Publishing Co., 1992.

Langfield, Martin. "Mystery of the Obelisks." Forgotten New York. http://forgotten-ny.com/2007/09/mystery-of-the-obelisks-guest-page-by-martin-langfield-author-of-the-malice-box (accessed May 4, 2015).

Lavello, Randy. "Occult Symbolism: As American as Baseball." Alex Jones' Prison Planet. www.prisonplanet.com/analysis_lavello_051403_occult.html (accessed May 4, 2015).

Malloy, Joanna. "St. Paul's Chapel Holds Buckets of Drama after Discovery Is Made in Famed Church's Steeple." *New York Daily News,* September 10, 2010. www.nydailynews.com/new-york/st-paul-chapel-holds-buckets-drama-discovery-made-famed-church-steeple-article-1.439208 (accessed May 4, 2015).

Mann, William F. *The Knights Templar in the New World: How Henry Sinclair*

Brought the Grail to Acadia. Rochester, Vt.: Destiny Books, 2004.

———. *The Templar Meridians: The Secret Mapping of the New World.* Rochester, Vt.: Destiny Books, 2006.

———. *The 13th Pillar.* Saint Cloud, Minn.: North Star Press of St. Cloud, 2012.

Meacham, John. *Thomas Jefferson: The Art of Power.* London: Random House, 2013.

National Grange. *Manual of Subordinate Granges of the Patrons of Husbandry.* Whitefish, Mont.: Kessinger Publishing, 2003.

Olson, Todd. *Poussin and France: Paintings, Symbolism and the Politics of Style.* New Haven, Conn.: Yale University Press, 2002.

Patrons of Husbandry, Indiana State Grange. *Constitution, By-laws, and Rules of Order of the Indiana State Grange of Patrons of Husbandry.* Charleston, S.C.: Nabu Press, 2011.

Rivera, David Allen. *Archaeological Conspiracy at Williamsburg: The Mystery of Bruton Vault.* N.p.: Rivera Enterprises, 2007. http://freescienceengineering .library.elibgen.org/view.php?id=432055 (accessed May 4, 2015).

———. *Mystery at Colonial Williamsburg: The Truth of the Bruton Vault.* N.p.: Rivera Enterprises, 2014. www.scribd.com/doc/237718316/MYSTERY-AT-COLONIAL-WILLIAMSBURG-The-Truth-of-Bruton-Vault#scribd (accessed June 30, 2015).

Stevens, Chris J., Dorian Q. Fuller, and Martin Carver. "Did Neolithic Farming Fail? The Case for a Bronze Age Agricultural Revolution in the British Isles." *Antiquity* 86, no. 333 (September 2012): 707.

Venari, John. *The Permanent Instruction of the Alta Vendita.* Charlotte, N.C.: TAN Books and Publishers, 1999.

Wolter, Scott F. *The Hooked X : Key to the Secret History of North America.* Saint Cloud, Minn.: North Star Press of Saint Cloud, 2009.

———. *Akhenaten to the Founding Fathers: The Mysteries of the Hooked X.* Saint Cloud, Minn.: North Star Press of Saint Cloud, 2013.

Wolter, Scott F., and Richard Nielsen. *The Kensington Rune Stone: Compelling New Evidence,* Chanhassen, Minn.: Lake Superior Agate Publishing, 2006.

Acknowledgments

First and foremost we want to offer our profound thanks to Janet's husband, Scott Wolter, and Alan's wife, Kate Butler, who have both given freely of their time, patience, advice, and their own expertise in order to make our book a reality. And a special thanks to Scott for all the photographs he contributed to this book, for as he knows well, we are both hopeless as photographers. We must also thank Grant and Amanda Wolter for their undoubted patience and help during the process of research and writing, especially as related to technology. Thanks are also due to Inner Traditions, our publishers, and especially to Jon Graham, who saw something new and (we hope) inspirational in our work.

We owe a great debt to Andy and Maria Awes, owners of Committee Films and makers of the series *America Unearthed,* who remained patient when we often distracted Scott during filming. We also offer thanks to the researchers and writers at Committee Films for sharing research with us, especially regarding the discoveries in Manhattan, New York.

Very heartfelt thanks go to our great friend, the ever genial and incredibly knowledgeable John Freeburg, whose resources and contacts in Minnesota helped us tremendously in our research, particularly with regard to the Grange, Freemasonry, and Washington, D.C. John also gave us very useful feedback regarding our theories and the manuscript. His very sensible advice has been a godsend. The advice and feedback provided by our dear friend Bill Mann was also full of tremendous insight, which we greatly appreciated.

It takes many people to make a book happen and most of their names never appear on the cover. How could we forget Andy Perry, who gave so much in terms of practical advice, or the recently deceased and most sadly missed John Ritchie, who knew more about Rosslyn Chapel and all matters Scottish than anyone else we have met. In addition we owe a debt of thanks to Jack Roberts (Alamo Jack), Todd Jovonovich, and Steve St. Clair, who not only offered extraordinary genealogical information but also drove a germ-laden car through unbelievable rain in France when Alan was ill. This was friendship above and beyond the call of duty.

If you helped us in any way and we have neglected to mention your name, we are truly grateful.

INDEX

BOOKS OF RELATED INTEREST

The Ancient Giants Who Ruled America
The Missing Skeletons and the Great Smithsonian Cover-Up
by Richard J. Dewhurst

Secrets of Ancient America
Archaeoastronomy and the Legacy of the
Phoenicians, Celts, and Other Forgotten Explorers
by Carl Lehrburger

The Vatican Heresy
Bernini and the Building of the Hermetic Temple of the Sun
*by Robert Bauval and Chiara Hohenzollern
With Sandro Zicari, Ph.D.*

The Secrets of Masonic Washington
A Guidebook to Signs, Symbols, and Ceremonies at
the Origin of America's Capital
by James Wasserman

The Templars and the Assassins
The Militia of Heaven
by James Wasserman

Founding Fathers, Secret Societies
Freemasons, Illuminati, Rosicrucians, and
the Decoding of the Great Seal
*by Robert Hieronimus, Ph.D.,
with Laura Cortner*

The Suppressed History of America
The Murder of Meriwether Lewis and the
Mysterious Discoveries of the Lewis and Clark Expedition
by Paul Schrag and Xaviant Haze

The Lost Treasure of the Knights Templar
Solving the Oak Island Mystery
by Steven Sora

INNER TRADITIONS • BEAR & COMPANY
P.O. Box 388
Rochester, VT 05767
1-800-246-8648
www.InnerTraditions.com

Or contact your local bookseller